Ariel Feldman
The Rewritten Joshua Scrolls from Qumran

Beihefte zur Zeitschrift für die alttestamentliche Wissenschaft

Herausgegeben von
John Barton · F. W. Dobb-Allsopp
Reinhard G. Kratz · Markus Witte

Band 438

De Gruyter

Ariel Feldman

The Rewritten Joshua Scrolls
from Qumran

Texts, Translations, and Commentary

De Gruyter

G

MIX
Papier aus verantwor-
tungsvollen Quellen
FSC
www.fsc.org
FSC® C016439

ISBN 978-3-11-028980-0
e-ISBN 978-3-11-029005-9
ISSN 0934-2575

Library of Congress Cataloging-in-Publication Data

A CIP catalog record for this book has been applied for at the Library of Congress.

Bibliographic information published by the Deutsche Nationalbibliothek

The Deutsche Nationalbibliothek lists this publication in the Deutsche Nationalbibliografie; detailed bibliographic data are available in the Internet at http://dnb.dnb.de.

© 2014 Walter de Gruyter GmbH, Berlin/Boston
Printing: Hubert & Co. GmbH & Co. KG, Göttingen
∞ Printed on acid-free paper
Printed in Germany
www.degruyter.com

Table of Contents

Abbreviations

Periodicals and Serials

AB	The Anchor Bible
AGJU	Arbeiten zur Geschichte des antiken Judentums und des Urchristentums
AUSS	Andrews University Seminary Studies
BA	Biblical Archaeologist
BETL	Bibliotheca ephemeridum theologicarum lovaniensium
BZAW	Beihefte zur Zeitschrift für die alttestamentliche Wissenschaft
CBQ	Catholic Biblical Quarterly
DJD	Discoveries in the Judaean Desert
DSD	Dead Sea Discoveries
ETL	Ephemerides Theologicae Lovanienses
HTR	Harvard Theological Review
HTS	Harvard Theological Studies
HUCA	Hebrew Union College Annual
JAJ	Journal of Ancient Judaism
JBL	Journal of Biblical Literature
JJS	Journal of Jewish Studies
JQR	Jewish Quarterly Review
JSNT	Journal for the Study of the New Testament
JSP	Journal for the Study of the Pseudepigrapha
JSPSS	Journal for the Study of the Pseudepigrapha Supplement Series
LCL	Loeb Classical Library
MHUC	Monographs of the Hebrew Union College
OLP	Orientalia lovaniensia periodica
PTSDSSP	Princeton Theological Seminary Dead Sea Scrolls Project
RB	Revue biblique
REJ	Revue des études juives
RevQ	Revue de Qumrân
SJJS	Supplements to the Journal of Jewish Studies
SJLA	Studies in Judaism in Late Antiquity
SJOT	Scandinavian Journal of the Old Testament
SJSJ	Journal for the Study of Judaism Supplement Series
STDJ	Studies on the Texts of the Desert of Judah
SVT	Supplements to Vetus Testamentum
SVTP	Studia in Veteris Testamenti Pseudepigraphica
TSAJ	Texte und Studien zum Antiken Judentum
WUNT	Wissenschaftliche Untersuchungen zum Neuen Testament

Reference Works

ABD   D.N. Freedman, ed. *Anchor Bible Dictionary.* New York: Doubleday, 1992.

EDSS   L.H. Schiffman & J.C. VanderKam, eds. *The Encyclopedia of the Dead Sea Scrolls.* New York: Oxford University Press, 2000.

EDEJ   J.J. Collins & D.C. Harlow, eds. *The Eerdmans Dictionary of Early Judaism.* Grand Rapids, Michigan, Cambridge, UK: Eerdmans, 2010.

BDB   F. Brown, S.R. Driver, & C.A. Briggs, *The Brown-Driver-Briggs Hebrew and English Lexicon.* Peabody, MA: Hendrickson Publishers, 1996.

HALOT   L. Koehler & W. Baumgartner, *The Hebrew and Aramaic Lexicon of the Old Testament.* Transl. and ed. by M.E.J. Richardson et al. Leiden, New York, Köln: Brill, 1994-2000.

Preface

The oft-quoted words of John Donne, "No man is an island", describe well the three years spent researching and writing this monograph. This task would have never been accomplished without the support from my teachers, colleagues, friends, and family members. My thanks to Prof. Devorah Dimant, who not only introduced me to the Dead Sea Scrolls and trained me as a Qumran scholar, but also engaged me in her project for re-editing the Qumran texts rewriting the Pentateuch. The present study of the rewritten Joshua scrolls is a part of her vision of a new edition of all the Rewritten Bible texts from Qumran. A generous grant provided by the Newton International Fellowships, UK, allowed me to work on these scrolls under the guidance of Prof. George J. Brooke. I was most fortunate to have him as my mentor. Prof. Brooke's expertise in the Dead Sea Scrolls is well-known. Yet, just as well known are his kindness and generosity. I have benefitted immensely from all of these. Many thanks also to Prof. Elisha Qimron who kindly agreed to review my editions of 4Q378, 4Q379, and 4Q522 and shared with me his forthcoming editions of these scrolls. Dr. Noam Mizrahi answered my numerous questions on linguistic matters. Prof. Yoel Elitzur offered several valuable suggestions on the list of toponyms in 4Q522. Prof. Annette Steudel examined some aspects of 4Q378's reconsruction at my request. Prof. Warren Carter guided me through the final stages of the manuscript preparation. Dr. Nevada DeLapp and Ms. Annelies Moeser proofread it and made countless helpful suggestions. My friends, Eric and Brenda Miller, read the manuscript critically. Prof. Reinhard Kratz supported this research in many ways from its very inception and encouraged me to submit it to the BZAW series. Finally, my deepest thanks to my wife, Faina, and to our two sons, Tal and Jonathan, who have sacrificed a lot to allow me to pursue my academic work. This book is dedicated to the memory of my father-in-law, Mark Altshuler, and my nephew, Almog Dubovi. They are greatly missed.

Brite Divinity School
Fort Worth, December 2012

Introduction

The Book of Joshua fascinated its ancient readers.[1] Over the centuries, Jews and Samaritans, Christians and Muslims produced a vast exegetical literature on the sixth book of the Hebrew Bible.[2] Some of these writings have been subjected to a thorough study. Others are still awaiting their turn.[3] Among the latter are the recently published Qumran scrolls rewriting the Book of Joshua. Dated to the last two centuries BCE, these texts are among the earliest extant witnesses of the transmission and interpretation of the Book of Joshua in antiquity. As such, they are of primary importance for reconstructing the reception history of this book.

While the story of the discovery and publication of the Dead Sea scrolls is well known and does not need to be restated here, a brief overview of the scholarship on the Rewritten Joshua scrolls (henceforth: RJ) is appropriate.[4] The earliest printed reference to a text from Qumran rewriting the Book of Joshua seems to be found in John Strugnell's report on his editorial work on the scrolls from Cave

---

1 The complex textual and literary history of the Book of Joshua lies outside the scope of this study. For the history of the scholarship on these issues see A.H.W. Curtis, *Joshua* (Old Testament Guides; Sheffield: Sheffield Academic Press, 1998); E. Noort, *Das Buch Josua: Forschungsgeschichte und Problemfelder* (Erträge der Forschung 292; Darmstadt: Wissenschaftliche Buchgesellschaft, 1998).
2 For an overview of the Jewish and Christian exegesis of the Book of Joshua see L. Ginzberg, *Legends of the Jews* (Philadelphia: The Jewish Publication Society, 2003), vol. 2, pp. 841-853; J.R. Franke (ed.), *Ancient Christian Commentary on Scripture: Old Testament IV: Joshua, Judges, Ruth, 1-2 Samuel* (Downers Grove, Illinois: InterVarsity Press, 2005), pp. 1-98; T.R. Elssner, *Josue und seine Kriege in jüdischer und christlicher Rezeptionsgeschichte* (Stuttgart: Kohlhammer, 2008). On the Samaritan sources containing traditions on Joshua see P. Stenhouse, "Samaritan Chronicles", in A.D. Crown (ed.), *The Samaritans* (Tübingen: J.C.B. Mohr, 1989), pp. 219-264 (with the pertinent bibliography); A.D. Crown, "Was There a Samaritan Book of Joshua?", in T.W. Hillard et al. (eds.), *Ancient History in a Modern University* (Grand Rapids, Michigan, Cambridge, UK: Eerdmans,1998), pp. 15-22; J. Zsengellér, *Gerizim as Israel: Northern Tradition of the Old Testament and the Early History of the Samaritans* (Utrecht: Universiteit Utrecht 1998), pp. 15-33; I.R.M.M. Bóid, "The Transmission of the Samaritan Joshua-Judges", *Dutch Studies* 6 (2004), pp. 1-30; M. Kartveit, *The Origins of the Samaritans* (Leiden, Boston: Brill, 2009), pp. 34-43. For a brief summary of the Islamic traditions on Joshua see B. Heller & A. Rippin, "Yusha'", in P.J. Bearman et al. (eds.), *The Encyclopedia of Islam* (Leiden: Brill, 2002), vol. 11, p. 351.
3 This is the case with the Samaritan traditions on Joshua. On the need for a more detailed study of the Samaritan Joshua lore see E. Nodet, *A Search for the Origins of Judaism*. Transl. E. Crowley (JSOTSS 248; Sheffield: Sheffield Academic Press, 1997), pp. 195-201; I. Hjelm, "What Do Samaritans and Jews Have in Common? Recent Trends in Samaritan Studies", *Currents in Biblical Research* 3 (2004), pp. 42-44.
4 See, for instance, the recent account by W.W. Fields, *The Dead Sea Scrolls: A Full History* (Leiden: Brill, 2009).

4 published in 1956, some four years after its discovery. In his brief remarks he mentioned a "poorly preserved pseudepigraph, the *Psalms of Joshua*". Strugnell further noted that this pseudepigraph is "cited in the Messianic *Testimonia* of Mr. Allegro's work", known today as 4Q175 (4QTestimonia).[5] In his overview of the Qumran findings published a year later, Joseph Milik also mentioned an unpublished scroll containing an interpretation of Joshua's curse from Josh 6:26, which could have been the source of the fourth quotation in 4Q175.[6] His statement suggested that the provisional title of this scroll, "Psalms of Joshua", follows the opening phrase of the 4QTestimonia's fourth passage: "When Joshua had finished praising and giving thanks with his psalms..." (4Q175 21). In the 1962 edition of the scroll 5Q9, mentioning the names of several geographical localities along with the name of Joshua, Milik again noted the existence of numerous fragments of the "Psalms of Joshua".[7] Yet, this time he added that these fragments apparently belong to two manuscripts. The preliminary ("manual") concordance, prepared between 1957 and 1960, indicates that these two scrolls, known today as 4Q378 and 4Q379, were initially given the sigla SL 14 and SL 15.[8] Their titles, Psalms of Joshua[a] and Psalms of Joshua[b], suggest that already at the early stage of their research Strugnell perceived them to be copies of the same work.[9] In the same edition of 5Q9, Milik also reported another Hebrew scroll edited by Jean Starcky. Listing names of geographical localities, this scroll mentions Joshua, Eleazar, David, and relates the history of the Jerusalem Temple. This appears to be the earliest printed reference to the scroll 4Q522.[10]

For some sixteen years the scroll 5Q9 remained the only published RJ text. In 1978 Émile Puech made available several fragments of 4Q522 containing the

---

5 P. Benoit et al., "Le travail d'édition des fragments manuscrits de Qumrân", *RB* 63 (1956), p. 65 (="Editing the Manuscript Fragments from Qumran", *BA* 19 [1956], p. 93).

6 J.T. Milik, *Dix ans de découvertes dans le désert de Juda* (Paris: Editions du Cerf, 1957), p. 104(=*Ten Years of Discovery in the Wilderness of Judaea*. Transl. by J. Strugnell [Studies in Biblical Theology 26; London: SCM Press, 1959], p. 63).

7 J.T. Milik, "5Q9. Ouvrage avec Toponymes", in M. Baillet et al. (eds.), *Les 'Petites Grottes' de Qumran* (DJD 3; Oxford: Clarendon Press, 1962), pp. 179-180.

8 R.E. Brown et al., *Preliminary Concordance to the Hebrew and Aramaic Fragments from Qumran II-X* (Published privately, Göttingen, 1988). Strugnell's preliminary transcription of 4Q378 and 4Q379 embedded in this concordance was utilized in B.Z. Wacholder & M.G. Abegg, *A Preliminary Edition of the Unpublished Dead Sea Scrolls* (Washington, D.C.: Biblical Archaeology Society, 1995), vol. 3, p. 167ff.

9 See E. Tov & S.J. Pfann, "List of the Texts from the Judaean Desert", in E. Tov et al. (eds.), *The Texts from the Judaean Desert: Indices and Introduction to the Discoveries in the Judaean Desert* (DJD 39; Oxford: Clarendon Press, 2002), p. 63.

10 Milik, "5Q9", p. 179.

remains of Psalm 122 (frgs. 22-25).[11] In this preliminary edition he remarked that this psalm is integrated into a non-biblical work featuring Jerusalem. However, this section of 4Q522 would be published only fourteen years later.

Meanwhile, sometime in the mid-nineties, Strugnell invited Carol Newsom to assist him in editing the scrolls 4Q378 and 4Q379. Relying on his transcription and notes, Newsom published in 1988 a preliminary edition of the selected fragments of 4Q378-379. She described these two non-overlapping scrolls as copies of the same literary work. Already in this publication Newsom noted that the provisional title of 4Q378-379, "Psalms of Joshua", may not be appropriate for the entire work.[12] Later on, in her comprehensive 1996 preliminary edition of these scrolls, she rejected this title, observing that "the content of the text is largely narrative and hortatory rather than poetic", and suggested a new one, Apocryphon of Joshua.[13] In the final edition that she published in the same year the scrolls 4Q378 and 4Q379 appear as Apocryphon of Joshua[a-b].[14]

Soon after Newsom's initial publication of 4Q378-379,[15] Shemaryahu Talmon edited two fragments of a scroll from Masada, Mas 1039-211. He perceived this scroll to be an apocryphal work based on the Book of Joshua and suggested that it is closely related to the Qumran scrolls 4Q378-379.[16] In 1992, Eugene Ulrich and Judith Sanderson published a paleo-Hebrew scroll 4Q123. Belonging to the lot assigned to Patrick Skehan, this badly damaged scroll paraphrases Josh 21.[17]

In the same year, Puech made available a preliminary edition of another section of 4Q522, frg. 9 ii. In this study he suggested that frg. 9 ii is concerned with

11 É. Puech, "Fragment du Psaume 122 dans un manuscript hébreu de la grotte IV", *RevQ* 19 (1978), pp. 547-554. Another fragment of 4Q522 containing Ps 122 was later identified and published by Puech in his "Un autre fragment du Psaume 122", *RevQ* 20 (2001), pp. 129–32.
12 C.A. Newsom, "'The Psalms of Joshua' from Qumran Cave 4", *JJS* 39 (1988), pp. 56, 58.
13 C.A. Newsom, "4Q378 and 4Q379: An Apocryphon of Joshua", in H.-J. Fabry & A. Lange (eds.), *Qumranstudien* (SIJD 4; Göttingen: Vandenhoeck & Ruprecht, 1996), p. 35.
14 C.A. Newsom, "4Q378-379. Apocryphon of Joshua[a-b]", in G. Brooke et al. (eds.), *Qumran Cave 4.XVII: Parabiblical Texts, Part 3* (DJD 22; Oxford: Clarendon Press, 1996), pp. 237-288.
15 Newsom, "Psalms of Joshua", pp. 56-73.
16 Sh. Talmon, "A Fragment of the Apocryphal Joshua Scroll from Masada", in M. Goshen-Gottstein et al. (eds.), *Shai Le-Hayyim Rabin* (Jerusalem: Academon, 1991), pp. 147-157 (Hebrew); idem, "Fragments of a Joshua Apocryphon—Masada 1039-211 (final photo 5254)", *JJS* 47 (1996), pp. 128-139; idem, "Hebrew Fragments from Masada: (b) Mas 1039-211", in idem et al. (eds.), *Masada VI: Yigael Yadin Excavations 1963-65 Final Reports* (Jerusalem: Israel Exploration Society, The Hebrew University of Jerusalem, 1999), pp. 105-116.
17 P. Skehan, E. Ulrich, and J.E. Sanderson, *Qumran Cave 4.IV: Paleo-Hebrew and Greek Manuscripts* (DJD 9; Oxford: Clarendon Press, 1992), pp. 201-203.

David, Solomon, and the building of the First Jerusalem Temple.[18] Concurrently, Robert Eisenman and Michael Wise released an edition of both columns found in this fragment. Since it mentions the High Priest Eleazar (col. ii) and localities referred to in the Book of Joshua (col. i), they entitled this scroll as "Joshua Apocryphon".[19] Soon after, Elisha Qimron re-edited 4Q522 9 ii and demonstrated that it contains a discourse by Joshua. He also suggested that 4Q522 is related to 4Q175 (4QTestimonia), 4Q378, 4Q379, and 5Q9.[20] In his final edition of this scroll in 1998, Puech accepted the interpretation of 4Q522 as pertaining to the days of Joshua, but, as the title, 4QProphétie de Josué (4QapocrJosué^c?), indicates, he questioned its affinity to 4Q378 and 4Q379.[21]

Although the similarities between some of these texts (particularly, 4Q378, 4Q379, and 4Q522) were noted soon after their discovery, it was Emanuel Tov who proposed in a 1998 article that the scrolls 4Q123, 4Q378, 4Q379, 4Q522, 5Q9, and Mas 1039-211 are copies of the same composition, Apocryphon of Joshua.[22] Criticized by some, this proposal is now widely accepted.[23]

The next fifteen years saw a number of studies on the RJ scrolls. In a series of articles Devorah Dimant offered improved editions and in-depth discussions of several key passages from 4Q378, 4Q379, and 4Q522.[24] Her study of the reworking of the crossing of the Jordan in 4Q379 12, its actualizing interpretation of Joshua's curse (frg. 22 ii), and of the prophetic discourse by Joshua in 4Q522 9 ii led her to conclude that the Apocryphon of Joshua, along with the Book of Jubilees,

---

18 É. Puech, "La Pierre de Sion et l'autel des holocaustes d'après un manuscript hébreu de la grotte 4 (4Q522)", *RB* 99 (1992), pp. 676-696.

19 R.H. Eisenman & M. Wise, *The Dead Sea Scrolls Uncovered* (Shaftesbury, Dorset, Rockport, Massachusetts: Element, 1992), pp. 89-92.

20 E. Qimron, "Concerning 'Joshua Cycles' from Qumran", *Tarbiz* 63 (1993-94), pp. 503-508 (Hebrew).

21 É. Puech, "4Q522. 4QProphétie de Josué (4QapocrJosuéc?)", in idem, *Qumrân Grotte 4.XVIII: Textes Hébreux (4Q521-4Q528, 4Q576-4Q579)* (DJD 25; Oxford: Clarendon Press, 1998), pp. 39-74.

22 E. Tov, "The Rewritten Book of Joshua as Found at Qumran and Masada", in M.E. Stone & E.G. Chazon (eds.), *Biblical Perspectives: Early Use and Interpretation of the Bible in Light of the Dead Sea Scrolls* (STDJ 28; Leiden: Brill, 1998), pp. 233-256(=*Hebrew Bible, Greek Bible and Qumran: Collected Essays* [TSAJ 121; Tübingen: Mohr Siebeck, 2008], pp. 72-91).

23 See, for instance, E. Tigchelaar, "The Dead Sea Scrolls", *EDEJ*, pp. 169-170; C. Evans, "Joshua, Apocryphon of", ibid., p. 841.

24 D. Dimant, "Two Discourses from the Apocryphon of Joshua and Their Context (4Q378 3 i-ii)", *RevQ* 23 (2007), pp. 43-61; idem, "The Apocryphon of Joshua—4Q522 9 ii: A Reappraisal", in S.M. Paul et al. (eds.), *Emanuel* (SVT 94; Leiden: Brill, 2003), pp. 179-204; idem, "Between Sectarian and Non-Sectarian: The Case of the Apocryphon of Joshua", in idem et al. (eds.), *Reworking the Bible: Apocryphal and Related Texts at Qumran* (STDJ 58; Leiden: Brill, 2005), pp. 105-134; idem, "Exegesis and Time in the Pesharim from Qumran", *REJ* 168 (2009), pp. 387-389.

the Temple Scroll, and the Apocryphon of Jeremiah, belong to an intermediate sub-group of the Qumran literature. In her view, since these compositions share some ideas and exegetical techniques with the Qumran sectarian scrolls yet lack their peculiar worldview and terminology, they stand between sectarian and non-sectarian Qumran texts.[25] Michaël van der Meer reviewed the significance of the RJ scrolls for the reconstruction of the literary history of the Book of Joshua.[26] Katell Berthelot dealt with the representation of Joshua in the RJ texts.[27] Florentino García Martínez explored their contribution for the study of the formation of the Book of Joshua.[28] Finally, Elisha Qimron currently is preparing a revised edition of selected fragments of 4Q378, 4Q379, 4Q522, and 5Q9.

This overview of the scholarship on the RJ scrolls suggests several directions in which this study should proceed. First, since the majority of these scrolls were edited separately from each other, with some being accompanied by only brief comments, there is a need for a detailed and up-to-date discussion of each of these texts and of all of them as a group. Second, there is a place for a careful analysis of the relationships between the RJ manuscripts. Third, the exegetical traditions embedded in these scrolls have to be placed within the Second Temple exegesis of the Book of Joshua. The present monograph addresses these needs.

The first chapter of this book offers an overview of the Second Temple literature dealing with the figure of Joshua and the events related in the book bearing his name. Its goal is to provide the background against which the RJ scrolls are to be studied.

Chapters 2-7, the bulk of this monograph, are devoted to the analysis of the scrolls 4Q378, 4Q379, 4Q522, 4Q123, 5Q9, and Mas 1039-211. Each scroll is treated in a separate chapter. A brief discussion of the physical peculiarities of a manuscript is followed by a revised Hebrew text, notes explaining and justifying the

---

25 See, especially, Dimant, "Between Sectarian", pp. 105-134; idem, "Criteria for the Identification of Qumran Sectarian Texts", in M. Kister (ed.), *The Qumran Scrolls and Their World* (Jerusalem: Yad Ben-Zvi, 2009), vol. 1, pp. 83-85 (Hebrew).

26 M.N. van der Meer, *Formation and Reformulation* (SVT CII; Leiden, Boston: Brill, 2004), pp. 105-114 (esp. p. 114).

27 K. Berthelot, "Joshua in Jewish Sources from the Second Temple Period", *Meghillot* 8-9 (2010), p. 97-112 (Hebrew).

28 F. García Martínez, "The Dead Sea Scrolls and the Book of Joshua", in N. Dávid & A. Lange (eds.), *Qumran and the Bible: Studying the Jewish and Christian Scriptures in Light of the Dead Sea Scrolls* (Leuven, Paris, Walpole, MA: Peeters, 2010), pp. 97-109; idem, "Light on the Joshua Books from the Dead Sea Scrolls", in H. Ausloos et al. (eds.), *After Qumran: Old and Modern Editions of the Biblical Texts—The Historical Books* (BETL; Leuven-Paris-Walpole, Peeters, 2012), pp. 145-159.

newly proposed readings, a translation, and a commentary.[29] Each chapter concludes with a discussion of broader questions posed by a scroll, particularly, of exegetical matters.

Utilizing the data culled from the study of each scroll, Chapter 8 explores the relationships between the RJ scrolls. The concluding chapter, Chapter 9, assesses the contribution of the RJ scrolls for the study of the ancient interpretation of the Book of Joshua.

---

29 For the detailed physical description of the scrolls the reader is referred to their respective *DJD* editions.

1 Joshua and His Book in Second Temple Jewish Literature

Several Second Temple Jewish writings refer to the figure of Joshua and to the events related in the sixth book of the Hebrew Bible.[30] The following survey of these sources provides the literary and exegetical context for the study of the RJ scrolls.[31] It addresses first the texts that have been known to the scholars prior to the discovery of the Dead Sea scrolls and then proceeds with the new Qumran documents.

1.1 Writings Known before the Discovery of Qumran

Any survey of the Second Temple Jewish writings dealing with the Book of Joshua ought to begin with its translation into Greek. Made sometime around 200 BCE, the Septuagint (henceforth: LXX) version of Joshua often differs from the Masoretic Text (henceforth: MT).[32] The question of whether these differences originate with the translator or his Hebrew *Vorlage* has dominated the modern study of the Greek Joshua.[33] While there is no consensus on the issue among the scholars, several studies of its translation technique suggest that the LXX Joshua follows its Hebrew base text more or less faithfully.[34] While this implies that a significant number of the divergences between the MT and the LXX illuminate the literary processes that shaped this book, many others shed precious light on the translator's interpretation of the Book of Joshua.[35]

---

30 This survey includes works that are dated after the destruction of the Second Temple, such as several of the New Testament writings, Josephus, Pseudo-Philo, and 4 Ezra.

31 See discussions by Elssner, *Josue*, pp. 22-128; N.J. Hofmann, *Die Assumptio Mosis: Studien zur Rezeption massgültiger Überlieferung* (SJSJ 67; Leiden, Boston, Köln: Brill, 2000), pp. 191-227; Berthelot, "Joshua".

32 M.N. van der Meer, "Provenance, Profile, and Purpose of the Greek Joshua", in M.K.H. Peters (ed.), *XII Congress of the International Organization for Septuagint and Cognate Studies, Leiden 2004* (SBL Septuagint and Cognate Studies; Leiden, Boston: Brill, 2006), pp. 55-80, argues that the translation was accomplished in Egypt in the last decades of the 3rd century BCE.

33 For a survey of scholarship see van der Meer, *Formation*, pp. 21-91; E. Tov, "Literary Development of the Book of Joshua as Reflected in the Masoretic Text, the LXX, and 4QJoshª", in E. Noort (ed.), *The Book of Joshua and the Land of Israel* (forthcoming). I thank Prof. Tov for making his article available to me prior to its publication.

34 See, for instance, the description of the LXX translation technique in Tov, ibid.

35 On the exegesis embedded in the LXX Joshua see, among others, J. Moatti-Fine, *La Bible d'Alexandrie: Jésus (Josué): Traduction du texte grec, introduction et notes* (Paris: Cerf, 1996);

Writing in the beginning of the second century BCE, Ben Sira provides a detailed portrayal of Joshua in his "Praise of the Fathers" (44:1-50:24).[36] Joshua, placed between Phineas and Caleb (46:1-8), is praised as "a valiant warrior" and an "aide" (משרת; Ms B[37]) to Moses "in the prophetic office" (46:1).[38] Playing on the meaning of his name, Ben Sira refers to Joshua as "the great savior (תשועה גדלה) of God's chosen ones". As he glorifies Joshua for "fighting the battles of the Lord", Ben Sira selects three episodes: Joshua's brandishing his sword against Ai (Josh 8:18), the miraculous stopping of the sun (10:12-13), and the divine response to Joshua's plea (missing from the biblical account) with the hailstones in the war against the southern Canaanite coalition (10:11).[39] Ben Sira also hails Joshua's faithfulness (מלא אחרי אל [cf. Num 32:12]) and piety (עשה חסד) in the twelve spies' episode (Num 14:6-10).[40] Since he and Caleb stood against the "rebel assembly"

A.G. Auld, *Joshua: Jesus Son of Nauē in Codex Vaticanus* (Septuagint Commentary Series; Leiden, Boston: Brill, 2005).

36 The English translation follows P.W. Skehan & A.A. DiLella, *The Wisdom of Ben Sira* (AB 39; New York: Doubleday, 1987), p. 515, with slight alterations.

37 Joshua is referred to as Moses' servant (משרת) in Exod 24:13, 33:11; Num 11:28; Josh 1:1. In light of the Greek rendering "successor", M.Z. Segal, *The Complete Book of Ben Sira* (Jerusalem: The Bialik Institute, 1997), p. 318 (Hebrew), suggests that the original Hebrew might have read מִשְׁנֵה, while A. Rofé, "Joshua Son of Nun in the History of Biblical Tradition", *Tarbiẓ* 73 (2004), p. 342 note 45 (Hebrew), proposes מורש or מורשת.

38 For the rendering of נבואה as "a prophetic office" see P.C. Beentjes, "Prophets and Prophecy in the Book of Ben Sira", in M.H. Floyd & R.D. Haak (eds.), *Prophets, Prophecy, and Prophetic Texts in Second Temple Judaism* (New York: T&T Clark, 2006), pp. 139-140. On Joshua as a prophet in Ben Sira see further Rofé, "Joshua", ibid; A. Goshen-Gottstein, "Ben Sira's Praise of the Fathers: A Canon-Conscious Reading", in R. Egger-Wenzel (ed.), *Ben Sira's God* (Berlin: de Gruyter, 2002), pp. 250-254; E. Koskenniemi, *The Old Testament Miracle-Workers in Early Judaism* (WUNT 2. Reihe, 206; Tübingen: Mohr Siebeck, 2005), pp. 28-31; J. Corley, "Canonical Assimilation in Ben Sira's Portrayal of Joshua and Samuel", in J. Corley & H. van Grol (eds.), *Rewriting Biblical History* (Berlin: de Gruyter, 2011), pp. 57-77; M. Witte, "Der "Kanon" heiliger Schriften des antiken Judentums im Spiegel des Buches Ben Sira/Jesus Sirach", in E.-M. Becker & S. Scholz (eds.), *Kanon in Konstruktion und Dekonstruktion* (Berlin: de Gruyter, 2012), p. 241.

39 Berthelot, "Joshua", p. 103, observes that, unlike Qumran texts, Ben Sira's description of Joshua emphasizes the latter's miracles and battles. Yet, B.L. Mack, *Wisdom and the Hebrew Epic: Ben Sira's Hymn in Praise of the Fathers* (Chicago: University of Chicago Press, 1985), p. 206, notes that Ben Sira presents Joshua as a "composite figure", serving in a prophetic office, but also a warrior and a ruler. J. Corley, "Joshua as a Warrior in Hebrew Ben Sira", *Deuterocanonical and Cognate Literature Yearbook* (2010), pp. 207-248; idem, "Assimilation", pp. 64-66, suggests that Ben Sira's depiction of Joshua as a prophet, an intercessor, and a warrior reflects an assimilation of his figure with other biblical figures, especially Moses and David.

40 On חסד as piety, rather than loyalty, in Second Temple texts see M. Kister & E. Qimron, "Observations on 4QSecond Ezekiel (4Q385 2-3)", *RevQ* 15 (1992), p. 596.

of 600,000 infantry, they were spared and brought "into their inheritance in the land flowing with milk and honey".

The Jewish historian Eupolemus (c. 150 BCE) mentions Joshua in his now almost completely lost work, *Concerning the Kings in Judaea*.[41] One of its extant quotations presents Joshua as a prophet in a succession of prophets, situating him between Moses and Samuel.[42] He is reported to have prophesied for thirty years and to have lived one hundred and ten years (Josh 24:29).[43] Of all Joshua's deeds this passage mentions only the establishment of the tabernacle in Shiloh (Josh 18:1).[44]

Calling for a zeal for the Torah and the covenant, Mattathias' farewell speech in 1 Maccabees 2:49-70 (end of 2nd century BCE) exhorts his sons to remember the deeds of the ancestors (vv. 50-51).[45] Among other exemplary figures from the past, it mentions Joshua, placing him between Phineas and Caleb (v. 55), as does Ben Sira. Highlighting his obedience to "the Word", 1 Maccabees calls him "a Judge in Israel".[46] Thus it (anachronistically) links Joshua to the succession of the charismatic leaders whose deeds are recorded in the Book of Judges.[47]

---

41 See C.B. Holladay, *Fragments from Hellenistic Jewish Authors: Volume 1: Historians* (SBL Texts and Translations 20; Pseudepigrapha 10; Chico, California: Scholars Press, 1983), pp. 93-104.
42 Frg. 2=Eusebius, *Praeparatio Evangelica* 9.30.1-34.18. On Moses, Joshua, and Samuel as a succession of ruling prophets see W. Horbury, "Monarchy and Messianism in the Greek Pentateuch", in M.A. Knibb (ed.), *The Septuagint and Messianism* (BETL 195; Leuven, 2006), p. 110.
43 The reference to the length of Joshua's life, 110 years, points to Josh 24:29. The thirty years of his prophesying are, apparently, based on Caleb's remark that Joshua was forty years old when sent to spy the land (Josh 14:7). According to Num 14:32, the disobedient wilderness generation spent forty years wandering in the desert. Thus, thirty years remain for Joshua's service as the leader of Israel. See Holladay, *Fragments*, p. 139.
44 J.R. Bartlett, *Jews in the Hellenistic World: Josephus, Aristeas, the Sibylline Oracles, Eupolemus* (Cambridge: Cambridge University Press, 1985), p. 62, suggests that this event is included as it points to the future temple
45 U. Rappaport, "Maccabees, First Book of", *EDEJ*, p. 904, dates it to the last decade of John Hyrcanus' rule (134-104 BCE).
46 The English translation is by J.A. Goldstein, *1 Maccabees* (AB; Garden City, N.Y.: Doubleday, 1974), p. 238. Note also an allusion to Josh 24:14-15 in 1 Macc 2:19-20. Goldstein, ibid., p. 230.
47 See Elssner, *Josue*, p. 59. Several scholars suggest that this description draws a parallel between Joshua and the Hasmonean rulers, such as Judas and, particularly, Jonathan (1 Macc 9:73). See Goldstein, ibid., p. 240; A. Chester, "Citing the Old Testament", in D.A. Carson et al. (eds.), *It is Written: Scripture Citing Scripture* (Cambridge: Cambridge University Press, 1988) p. 151; T. Hieke, "The Role of the 'Scripture' in the Last Words of Mattathias (1 Macc 2:49-70)", in G. Xeravits & J. Zsengellér (eds.), *The Books of the Maccabees: History, Theology, Ideology* (JSJS 118; Leiden: Brill, 2007), pp. 67-68.

2 Maccabees (sometime between 160-124 BCE) alludes to the Book of Joshua in its account of Judas' attack against Kaspin (=Kisfin) in 12:13-16.[48] While the dwellers of this strongly fortified town reviled and blasphemed Judas and his men, the latter "prayed to the great Master of the universe Who overthrew Jericho in the time of Joshua without battering rams or siege engines".[49]

A reference to the crossing of the Jordan, the conquest of the Promised Land and the dispossession of the Canaanite nations is found in the historical summary in Judith 5:15-16 (Maccabean-Hasmonean era).[50] The extermination of the Canaanites is also featured in the Wisdom of Solomon (30 BCE-40 CE), claiming that God provided them with an opportunity to repent and to avoid the divine punishment (12:3-11).[51]

The Assumption of Moses (beginning of the first century CE[52]), presented as a farewell prophetic speech of Moses to Joshua, depicts Joshua as "a man deemed worthy by the Lord to be (Moses') successor for the people", entrusted with "the tabernacle of the testimony" (1:5-7).[53] Expanding on the scriptural account of Joshua's appointment, the Assumption of Moses describes Moses outlining Joshua's role as the one who will lead the people to the Promised Land, apportion it to them, found a kingdom, and establish a local rule (1:8-9, 2:1-2). The bulk of the Mosaic speech to Joshua contains a revelation of the course of history, culminating in the Day of Judgment (2:3-10:10). Following his prophetic discourse, Moses commands Joshua to keep these words and "this book" and "to be strong", as God chose him to be Moses' "successor to his covenant" (10:11, 15). Next comes a non-biblical scene, in which a terrified Joshua tears his clothes and falls to Moses' feet (11:1), questioning Moses about the place of his burial and expressing doubts

---

48 D.R. Schwartz, "Maccabees, Second Book of", *EDEJ*, p. 907. Goldstein, *1 Maccabees*, p. 36, proposes a later date, after 78/77 BCE.

49 Quoted from J.A. Goldstein, *2 Maccabees* (AB; Garden City, N.Y.: Doubleday, 1983), p. 430. It has also been suggested that the description of several battles in 1-2 Macc allude to the Book of Joshua. See Goldstein, *1 Maccabees*, p. 381; B. Bar-Kochva, *Judas Maccabeus: The Jewish Struggle against the Seleucids* (Cambridge: Cambridge University Press, 1989), p. 155; Chester, "Citing", p. 151. For a different view, see K. Berthelot, "The Biblical Conquest of the Promised Land and the Hasmonaean Wars according to 1 and 2 Maccabees", in G. Xeravits & J. Zsengellér (eds.), *The Books of the Maccabees: History, Theology, Ideology* (JSJS 118; Leiden: Brill, 2007), pp. 45-60.

50 B. Halpern-Amaru, "Judith, Book of", *EDEJ*, p. 857.

51 R.D. Chesnutt, "Solomon, Wisdom of", *EDEJ*, p. 1243.

52 J. Tromp, *The Assumption of Moses: A Critical Edition with Commentary* (Leiden: Brill, 1993), pp. 78-85, 116. The English translation is from this edition.

53 On the figure of Joshua in As. Mos. see Hofmann, *Assumptio*, esp. pp. 191-194. According to Tromp, ibid., p. 137, the reference to the Tabernacle reflects a merging of Joshua and Eleazar.

as to whether he can replace Moses (11:5-19). The book in its present incomplete state ends abruptly with Moses reassuring Joshua (12:2-13).

Philo of Alexandria (ca. 20 BCE-ca. 50 CE) in his numerous works refers several times to Joshua and his book.[54] Describing the battle with Amalek (Exod 17:9), he reports Moses' appointment of Joshua, one of his lieutenants, as the military commander (Life of Moses 1.216). Philo notes Moses' altering of Joshua's name (On the Change of Names 121).[55] Dealing with the twelve spies episode (Num 13), he highlights Joshua and Caleb's "courage and hopefulness" (Life of Moses 1.220-236). While praising Moses' virtue as a leader who did not succumb to the natural desire to appoint a successor from among his own children or close family, Philo describes Joshua as Moses' "friend, whom he had known well almost from his earliest year" (On the Virtues 55-70). He is "almost his lieutenant, associated with him in the duties of government". Moses has "carefully tested his excellence in word and deed, and, what was most vital of all, his loyal affection for the nation".[56] For Philo, Joshua is Moses' "disciple", "who modeled himself on his master's characteristics with the love which they deserved".[57]

The New Testament writings (ca. 60-100 CE) contain several references to the Book of Joshua.[58] Thus, Stephen in his speech in Acts 7:45 mentions that the Israelites led by Joshua brought the Tent of Meeting to the Promised Land. The Epistle to Hebrews refers to Joshua's leading the people into the Land in a passage dealing with entering God's rest (4:8). It also mentions the faith demonstrated by the Israelites during the siege of Jericho and the faith of Rahab, who welcomed the spies (11:30-31). There are two more references to Rahab in the New Testament.

---

54 See L.H. Feldman, "Philo's Interpretation of Joshua", *JSP* 12 (2001), pp. 165-178.

55 The English translation of Philo's works is cited from F.H. Colson & G.H. Whitaker, *Philo* (LCL; Cambridge: Harvard University Press, 1966), vols. 1-10.

56 And yet, in On Drunkenness 96 Philo offers an allegorical interpretation of Exod 32:17, where Joshua appears to "represent one's subjective feeling toward the tumult" (Feldman, "Philo's Interpretation of Joshua", p. 170).

57 One may also mention Philo's summary of the conquest of the Promised Land in Hypothetica, presented "not so much by the historical narrative, as by what our reason tells us about them". Philo suggests that the Israelites "were unwarlike and feeble, quite few in numbers and destitute of warlike equipment, but won the respect of their opponents who voluntarily surrendered their land to them". See K. Berthelot, "Philo of Alexandria and the Conquest of Canaan", *JSJ* 38 (2007), pp. 39-56; idem, "The Canaanites Who 'Trusted in God': An Original Interpretation of the Fate of the Canaanites in Rabbinic Literature", *JJS* 62 (2011), pp. 254-259. For another perspective on this topic, see L.H. Feldman, "The Portrayal of Sihon and Og in Philo, Pseudo-Philo, and Josephus", *JJS* 53 (2002), pp. 264-272; idem, "The Command, according to Philo, Pseudo-Phio, and Josephus, to Annihilate the Seven Nations of Canaan", *AUSS* 41 (2003), pp. 14-16; idem, *"Remember Amalek!"* (MHUC 31; Hebrew Union College, 2004).

58 For a discussion see Elssner, *Josue*, pp. 82-104.

Matthew 1:5 lists her name among Jesus' ancestors, while James 2:25 evokes her "works", when she "received the messengers and sent them out another way".

Josephus' rewritten version of the Pentateuch in Jewish Antiquities 1-4 (93/94 CE[59]) provides several insights into his view of Joshua.[60] He first mentions Joshua in his account of the battle with Amalek (Exod 17:9). Josephus explains why Moses selected Joshua as a military commander, describing him as "a man of extreme courage, valiant in endurance of toil, highly gifted in intellect and speech, and withal one who worshipped God with a singular piety which he had learnt from Moses, and who was held in esteem by the Hebrews" (3.49).[61] Josephus observes that having received a "thorough training in the laws and in divine lore under the tuition of Moses",[62] Joshua succeeded Moses "both in his prophetical functions and as commander-in-chief" (4.165).[63]

Further insights into Josephus' interpretation of Joshua and the Book of Joshua can be gleaned from his rewriting of this book in Jewish Antiquities 5.1-120.[64] The most detailed recasting of the Book of Joshua in Second Temple literature, this

---

59 S. Mason, "Josephus, Jewish Antiquities", *EDEJ*, p. 835.
60 On Josephus' portrayal of Joshua see L.H. Feldman, "Josephus' Portrait of Joshua", *HTR* 82 (1989), pp. 351-376; P. Spilsbury, *The Image of the Jew in Flavius Josephus' Paraphrase of the Bible* (TSAJ 69; Tübingen: Mohr Siebeck, 1998), pp. 147-152. Josephus' selective rewriting skips over several references to Joshua in the Pentateuch. He omits Joshua's role during the Sinai revelation (Exod 24:13, 32:17), his constant presence in the Tent (Exod 33:11), Joshua's role in the episode with the seventy-two elders (Num 11), the renaming of Joshua, and the reward for his faithfulness in the twelve spies episode (Num 14:30, 38).
61 The translation is from H.St.J. Thackeray, *Josephus: Jewish Antiquities, Books I-IV* (LCL; London: Heinemann, 1930), p. 343. Other quotations from Josephus are also from the *LCL* edition. On Joshua as possessing four cardinal virtues see Feldman, "Joshua", p. 355.
62 On Joshua as a disciple of Moses, see also J. Ant. 6.84. See further Feldman, ibid., p. 358.
63 On Joshua as a general, see also in War 4.459; J. Ant. 3.59, 4.165, 4.324, 6.84, 7.68, 7.294, 9.207, 9.280, 11.112. Oh his prophetic gift, see further J. Ant. 4.311.
64 On Josephus' rewriting of the Book of Joshua see F.G. Downing, "Redaction Criticism: Josephus' Antiquities and the Synoptic Gospels", *JSNT* 8 (1980), pp. 46-65; Elssner, *Josue*, pp. 114-128; C.T. Begg, "Israel's Treaty with Gibeon according to Josephus", *OLP* 28 (1997), pp. 123-145; idem, "The Transjordanian Altar (Josh 22:10-34) according to Josephus (*Ant.* 5.100-114) and Pseudo-Philo (*LAB* 22.1-8)", *AUSS* 35 (1997), pp. 5-12; idem, "The Ai-Achan Story (Joshua 7-8) according to Josephus", *Jian Dao* 16 (2001), pp. 1-20; idem, "The Rahab Story in Josephus", *Liber Annuus* 55 (2005), pp. 113-130; idem, "The Fall of Jericho according to Josephus", *Estudios Bíblicos* 63 (2005), pp. 323-340; idem, "The Crossing of the Jordan according to Josephus", *Acta Theologica* 26 (2006), pp. 1-16; idem, "Joshua's Southern and Northern Campaigns according to Josephus", *BZ* 51 (2007), pp. 84-97; idem, "The Demise of Joshua according to Josephus", *HTS* 63 (2007), pp. 129-145. Many of Begg's insights are incorporated in his *Flavius Josephus: Judean Antiquities 5–7* (Flavius Josephus: Translation and Commentary 4; Leiden: Brill, 2005).

work frequently omits,[65] summarizes,[66] and rearranges the scriptural account.[67] In several occasions it also expands its base text. This is the case with the description of the Jordan's powerful current at the time of the crossing (5.16), the prayer after the defeat at Ai (5. 39-41), the speeches in the Transjordanian altar episode (5.93-114), and Joshua's epitaph, praising him as "a man not wanting either in intelligence or in skill to expound his ideas to the multitude with lucidity ... stout-hearted and great daring ... a most dexterous director of affairs, adapting himself admirably to every occasion" (5.118).

The account of the biblical history from Adam to David in Pseudo-Philo's Biblical Antiquities (70-150 CE) offers another extensive rewriting of Joshua materials.[68] Of the Pentateuchal references to Joshua, LAB deals only with the twelve spies story (15:3).[69] As it rewrites the Book of Joshua, like Josephus, it omits,[70]

---

65 Among the omitted passages are God's speech to Joshua in Josh 1, three days wait for the spies, Joshua's instructions on the crossing of the Jordan, various details pertaining to the crossing, the appearance of the captain of the Lord's host, the circumcision, the divine instructions before the siege on Jericho, the instructions in the second attack on Ai, and the description of the land allocated to Caleb. Also, Josephus seems to avoid anything that has to do with miracles and magic, e.g., Jordan's water standing in a heap, Joshua's gesture with a sword towards Ai, and the standing still of the sun. On the latter feature see L.H. Feldman, *Josephus's Interpretation* of the Bible (Hellenistic Culture and Society 27; Berkeley: University of California Press, 1998), pp. 210-212.
66 He summarizes the account of the Cave of Makeda (J. Ant. 5.61), Joshua's conquests (5.67), the list of the defeated kings (5.73), tribal allotments (5.81-87), the cities of refuge (5.91), the Levitical cities (5:91), and Joshua's farewell discourses (5.115-116).
67 Thus, the two spies are sent out to Jericho before Joshua's speech to the two and a half tribes (J. Ant. 5.2-3). Joshua departs to the Jordan prior to the arrival of the spies (5.4-15). The ceremony on Mts. Ebal and Gerizim occurs next to the establishing of the Tent at Shiloh (5.69-70). The latter event comes after the conquests in the north of Canaan (5.68). The reference to the "land that yet remains" (Josh 13:1-6; J. Ant. 5.71) comes after the setting of the Tent at Shiloh, during the assembly that takes place there (Josh 18:1; J. Ant. 5.72). All the tribal allotments, including those of Judah and of Ephraim and Manasseh, are given next to the description of the dispatching of the surveyors (5.79). The order of the tribes in the description of the allotments is also different.
68 For the dating see H. Jacobson, *A Commentary on Pseudo-Philo's Liber Antiquitatum Biblicarum* (AGJU 31; Leiden: Brill, 1996), vol. 1, pp. 199-210. For the discussion of LAB's rewriting of the Book of Joshua see F.J. Murphy, *Pseudo-Philo: Rewriting the Bible* (New York: Oxford University Press, 1993), pp. 96-115; Jacobson, ibid., pp. 658-735; B.N. Fisk, *Do You Not Remember? Scripture, Story and Exegesis in the Rewritten Bible of Pseudo-Philo* (JSPSS 37; Sheffield: Sheffield Academic Press, 2001), pp. 282-313; E. Reinmuth, "Zwischen Investitur und Testament: Beobachtungen zur Rezeption des Josuabuches im Liber Antiquitatum Biblicarum", *SJOT* 16 (2002), pp. 24-43; C.T. Begg, "The Ceremonies at Gilgal/Ebal according to Pseudo-Philo", *ETL* 73 (1997), pp. 72-83; idem, "The Transjordanian Altar", pp. 12-18;
69 Joshua's genealogy provided there does not match that of 1 Chr 7:20-27.
70 LAB omits the two spies' journey, the crossing of the Jordan, the account of the circumcision, the celebration of the Passover, the appearance of the captain of the Lord's hosts, Achan's story and the two battles at Ai, the allocation of the cities of refuge and of the Levitical cities.

summarizes,[71] rearranges,[72] and expands the biblical account. For instance, it elaborates on the brief scriptural description of Joshua's succession of Moses. LAB introduces God's covenant with Joshua (20:1), his mourning for Moses (20:2), his clothing himself with Moses' garments, leading to a prophetic inspiration (20:3),[73] and Joshua's Moses-like address to the people (20:3).[74] In its description of the ceremony at Gilgal, LAB includes offerings on the altar at Gilgal, lifting of the ark, praises, and Joshua's blessing of the people (20:9-10). In the case of the Trans-Jordanian altar it amplifies the biblical account with offerings, fasting, prayer, and a destruction of the altar (22:5-7). Joshua's deathbed scene is also expanded: he prophesies to Phineas, kisses and blesses him (25:4-5).[75] Like Josephus, LAB cites the people's epitaph for Joshua, recalling his being "a leader like him (Moses) for forty years" (24:6).

Differing in scope, worldview, and agenda, Jewish Antiquities and Biblical Antiquities employ a similar set of exegetical techniques while recasting scriptural texts.[76] As such, both works belong with a wider group of Second Temple writings commonly designated as the Rewritten Bible.[77]

---

71 The descriptions of Jericho's fall (20:7b), Caleb's allotment (20:10), Joshua's wars, and the apportioning of the land (20:9) are briefly summarized.

72 LAB places the ceremony at Mts. Ebal and Gerizim after the conquest is complete (21:1, 7) and the setting of the Tent of Meeting in Shiloh after the episode with the Transjordanian altar (22:8-9).

73 See J.R. Levison, "Prophetic Inspiration in Pseudo-Philo's 'Liber Antiquitatum Biblicarum'", *JQR* 85 (1995), p. 314.

74 Fisk, *Do You Not Remember*, pp. 282-293, suggests that LAB is influenced here by the biblical depictions of Saul and Solomon as they assumed power.

75 On Joshua as a prophet in LAB see also 21:6, 23:12-13, 24:4.

76 On the rewriting techniques and strategies in Josephus and LAB see Z. Rodgers, "Josephus's Biblical Interpretation", and H. Jacobson, "Biblical Interpretation in Pseudo-Philo's Liber Antiquitatum Biblicarum", in M. Henze (ed.), *A Companion to Biblical Interpretation in Early Judaism* (Grand Rapids, MI, Cambridge, UK: Eerdmans, 2012), pp. 180-199, 436-463.

77 Coined some sixty years ago by G. Vermes to describe the relation of such works as Jubilees and LAB to the biblical text, this term and what it stands for continues to be the subject of intensive scholarly discussion. Some question its usefulness. Others criticize both the descriptive "rewritten" and the canon-oriented "Bible". Still others argue that it represents a technique, rather than a genre. As the scholarly conversation aiming at refining terminology and defining more precisely the criteria for inclusion/exclusion of certain works in this category continues, it seems prudent to retain here the more familiar term "Rewritten Bible". To avoid confusion, I also use here the terms "Hebrew Bible" and "biblical", rather than "Hebrew Scripture" and "scriptural". For a helpful review of scholarship and a pertinent bibliography see D. Machiela, "Once More, with Feeling: Rewritten Scripture in Ancient Judaism - A Review of Recent Developments", *JJS* 61 (2010), pp. 308-320; M.M. Zahn, "Talking about Rewritten Texts: Some Reflections on Terminology", in H. von Weissenberg et al. (eds.), *Rewriting and Interpreting Authoritative Traditions in the Second Temple Period* (Berlin: W. De Gruyter, 2011), pp. 93-119; idem, "Genre and Rewritten Scripture: A Reassessment", *JBL* 131 (2012), pp. 271-288.

Finally, a mention should be made of the reference to Joshua in 4 Ezra 7:107 (end of the first century CE).[78] Asking the angel whether the righteous will be able to intercede for the ungodly ones on the day of judgment (7:102-103), Ezra mentions, along Abraham, Moses, and Elijah, Joshua's intercession on behalf of Israel following Achan's sin.[79]

1.2 Qumran Findings[80]

The overview of the Dead Sea texts dealing with the Book of Joshua begins with two (or, perhaps, three) fragmentary manuscripts of this book.[81] The scroll 4Q47 (4QJosh[a]; 150-50 BCE) preserves Josh 5:2-7, 6:5-10, 7:12-17, 8:3-11a, 14a, 18(?), 10:2-5, 8-11.[82] While in general 4QJosh[a] follows the MT,[83] some of its readings either agree with the LXX[84] or are unique to this scroll.[85] Tov observes:[86]

---

78 K.M. Hogan, "Ezra, Fourth Book of", *EDEJ*, p. 624.

79 A. Lange & M. Weigold, *Biblical Quotations and Allusions in Second Temple Jewish Literature* (Göttingen: Vandenhoeck & Ruprecht, 2011), pp. 113-114, find allusions to the Book of Joshua also in T. Naphtali 5:1 (Josh 10:12-13) and T. Judah 9:4 (Josh 10:31, 34).

80 For a discussion of the representation of Joshua in the Dead Sea scrolls see Hofmann, *Assumptio*, pp. 208-213; Berthelot, "Joshua". On 4Q175 see Chapter 3.

81 For an overview of these scrolls see E. Tov, "Joshua, Book of", *EDSS*, pp. 431-434; van der Meer, *Formation*, pp. 93-105; A. Lange, *Handbuch der Textfunde vom Toten Meer: band 1: Die Handschriften biblischer Bücher von Qumran und den anderen Fundorten* (Tübingen: Mohr Siebeck, 2009), pp. 187-189.

82 E. Ulrich, "4Q47. 4QJosh[a]", in E. Ulrich et al. (eds.), *Qumran Cave 4.IX: Deuteronomy, Joshua, Judges, Kings* (DJD 14; Oxford: Clarendon Press, 1995), pp. 143-152.

83 See remarks by L. Greenspoon, "The Qumran Fragments of Joshua: Which Puzzle are They Part of and Where Do They Fit?", in G. Brooke & B. Lindars (eds.), *Septuagint, Scrolls and Cognate Writings* (Atlanta: Scholars Press, 1992), p. 177; van der Meer, *Formation*, p. 524.

84 Hence, the early description of Joshua scrolls from Qumran as "systematically 'Septuagintal' in character" by F.M. Cross, *The Ancient Library of Qumran* (Sheffield: Sheffield Academic Press, 1994[3]), p. 151 note 84, pp. 180-181; idem, "The Evolution of a Theory of Local Texts", in F.M. Cross & Sh. Talmon (eds.), *Qumran and the History of the Biblical Text* (Cambridge, MA: Harvard University Press, 1975), p. 311.

85 For the view that 4QJosh[a] represents a different, a third (alongside with the MT and LXX), edition of the Book of Joshua see L. Mazor, "The Septuagint Translation of the Book of Joshua— Its Contribution to the Understanding of the Textual Transmission of the Book and Its Literary and Ideological Development", Ph.D. diss., Hebrew University, Jerusalem 1994, p. 49 (Hebrew); E. Tov, "The Growth of the Book of Joshua in Light of the Evidence of the Septuagint", in idem, *The Greek and Hebrew Bible* (SVT 72; Leiden, Boston, Köln: Brill, 1999), p. 396 note 23; Tov, "Joshua, Book of", p. 432.

86 Tov, "Literary Development".

"in small details, 4QJosh[a] ... goes its own way, but in large details the scroll usually follows MT+ except for three major segments."[87]

The three segments in question are the insertion of Josh 8:34-35 (with an appended exegetical expansion) before Josh 5:2, the shorter text of 8:11b-13, and a possible lack of 8:14b-17. This study is particularly interested in the first of the three passages. It has been frequently assumed that 4QJosh[a] places the entire literary unit found in Josh 8:30-35(MT) prior to Josh 5:2.[88] This arrangement is perceived to be superior to that of the MT and LXX (placing it after Josh 9:2). Yet, as van der Meer (now supported by Tov) demonstrates, 4QJosh[a] seems to insert here only vv. 34-35,[89] retaining vv. 30-35 in the same place as the MT.[90] The purpose of the insertion and of the ensuing expansion is exegetical. Reflecting a nomistic interpretation of the crossing story, it presents Joshua reading the Law as Israel crosses the Jordan in fulfilment of the Mosaic commands in Deut 27 (see Chapter 3). Van der Meer describes this insertion as a "harmonization by means of duplication" and compares it to the harmonistic expansions found in the Qumran pre-Samaritan scrolls,[91] 4QReworked Pentateuch,[92] Samaritan Pentateuch (henceforth: Smr), and several passages in the LXX Joshua.[93] Tov also draws a parallel between 4QJosh[a] and 4QReworked Pentateuch scrolls, observing that "both texts contain long stretches that are close to MT+, as well as greatly deviating exegetical segments".[94]

Another Joshua scroll from Qumran, 4Q48 (4QJosh[b]; ca. 50 BCE), contains Josh 2:11-12, 3:15-4:3, 17:1-5, 11-15.[95] While it is close to the MT, this scroll also agrees in several places with the LXX and contains a few unique readings. Finally, the scroll XJoshua (Schøyen MS 2713; 40 BCE-68 CE) of unknown provenance preserves the text of Josh 1:9-12, 2:4-5 which agrees with the MT.[96]

---

87 The abbreviation "MT+" stands for the "combined evidence" of the Masoretic Text, Aramaic Targumim, Peshitta, and Vulgate. See E. Tov, *Textual Criticism of the Hebrew Bible* (Minneapolis: Fortress, 2012³), p. xix.

88 For a survey of scholarship see van der Meer, *Formation*, 485-496.

89 Van der Meer, ibid., p. 513, proposes that the scroll inserts here vv. 32, 34-35 concerned with the writing of the Torah and its reciting, which it attaches to Josh 4:20.

90 Tov, "Literary Development".

91 On the pre-Samaritan texts from Qumran and the Samaritan Pentateuch, see Tov, *Textual Criticism*, pp. 74-93.

92 On the 4QReworked Pentateuch see the recent study of M. Zahn, *Rethinking Rewritten Scripture* (STDJ 95; Leiden, Boston: Brill, 2011).

93 van der Meer, *Formation*, p. 521.

94 Tov, "Literary Developments".

95 E. Tov, "4Q48. 4QJoshb", in E. Ulrich et al. (eds.), *Qumran Cave 4.IX: Deuteronomy, Joshua, Judges, Kings* (DJD 14; Oxford: Clarendon Press, 1995), pp. 153-160.

96 J. Charlesworth, "XJoshua", in J. Charlesworth et al. (eds.), *Miscellaneous Texts from the Judaean Desert* (DJD 38; Oxford: Clarendon Press, 2000), pp. 231-239.

As to the non-biblical Dead Sea scrolls, the sectarian work,[97] Damascus Document (CD; the earliest Qumran copy, 4Q266, is dated to 100-50 BCE), refers to the three traps by which Belial ensnared Israel: fornication, wealth, and "defiling the sanctuary" (IV, 14-18).[98] As it accuses the opponents of being caught in the trap of fornication (IV, 20-V, 6[=4Q269 3 2; 6Q15 1 1-3]), it mentions Joshua:[99]

20.   By fornication, (namely,) taking
21. two wives in their lives, while the foundation of creation is "male and female He created them." (Gen 1:27)
1. And those who entered (Noah's) ark "went two by two into the ark" (Gen 7:9). And of the prince it is written,
2. "Let him not multiply wives for himself." (Deut 17:17) And David did not read the sealed book of the Torah
3. which was in the Ark (of the Covenant), for it was not opened in Israel from since the day of the death of Eleazar
4. and Joshua (ויהושע ויוש'ע)[100] and the elders, because (they) worshiped Ashtoreth. And
5. (the) revealed was hidden[101] until Zadok assumed the office, so David's works were accepted, with the exception of Uriah's blood,
6. and God forgave him for them.

---

97 On the classification of the Qumran scrolls as sectarian and non-sectarian see D. Dimant, "Sectarian and Non-Sectarian Texts from Qumran: The Pertinence and Usage of a Taxonomy", *RevQ* 24 (2009), pp. 7-18, and, in more detail, idem, "Criteria", pp. 49-86. For the limitations of such a classification, see M. Kister, "Some Further Thoughts on Identifying Sectarian Writings at Qumran", in M. Kister (ed.), *The Qumran Scrolls and Their World* (Jerusalem: Yad Ben-Zvi, 2009), vol. 1, pp. 87-90.

98 J.M. Baumgarten, "Damascus Document", *EDSS*, vol. 1, pp. 166-170. The discovery of the Damascus Document in Cairo Geniza preceded that of the Qumran scrolls.

99 What follows is a slightly altered version of the English translation from J.M. Baumgarten & D.R. Schwartz, "Damascus Document", in J.H. Charlesworth et al. (eds.), *The Dead Sea Scrolls: Hebrew, Aramaic, and Greek Texts with English Translations: Damascus Document, War Scroll, and Related Documents* (PTSDSSP; Tübingen: Mohr [Siebeck], Louisville: Westminster John Knox, 1995), p. 18-21.

100 E. Qimron, *The Dead Sea Scrolls: The Hebrew Writings: Volume One* (Between Bible and Mishnah; Jerusalem: Yad Ben-Zvi Press, 2010), p. 11 (Hebrew), observes that the ancient original might have read ישוע, while the medieval scribe proposed two alternative corrections. On the spelling ישוע see comment to 4Q378 22 i 2.

101 The medieval text has ויטמון. A. Rofé, "The End of the Book of Joshua according to the Septuagint", *Shnaton* 2 (1977), p. 224 note 33 (Hebrew; ="The End of the Book of Joshua according to the Septuagint", *Henoch* 4 [1982], pp. 17-35), proposes וַיִּטָּמֵן. L.H. Schiffman, *The Halakhah at Qumran* (Leiden: Brill, 1975), p. 31 note 61, observes (with Rabin) that the active form may substitute a passive in this case. Qimron, *The Dead Sea Scrolls*, p. 11, suggests that something is missing between ויטמון and נגלה.

As the biblical texts adduced to support the argument indicate, "fornication" stands here for polygamy,[102] or, according to some, for both polygamy and remarrying after a divorce.[103] CD seeks to harmonize its view on polygamy, backed by a citation from the "Law of the King" (Deut 17:17), with the fact that King David had numerous wives. It claims that, while the "Law of the King" (Deut 17:18-19) requires the king to make a copy of the Law and "read in it all his life", David was not able to do so, because "it" (either "the sealed book of the Law", also called "the revealed",[104] or the Ark of the Covenant) was not opened since the death of Eleazar, Joshua and the elders.[105] This passage elicits two observations.

First, while according to Josh 24:29, 33, Joshua dies before Eleazar, CD mentions Eleazar's death first. Similarly, whenever the Hebrew Bible mentions these two figures together, it always gives Eleazar pride of place (Num 32:28, 34:17; Josh 14:1, 19:51, 21:1; cf. also 1Q22 I, 11; 4Q522 9 ii 13), apparently, indicating Joshua's subordination to the High Priest (Num 27:18-21). This scriptural precedent, coupled with the preeminence of the priesthood in CD, suggests that its formulation elevates Eleazar over Joshua, rather than reflects a different chronology of events.

Second, the phrase "for (they) worshiped Ashtoreth (אשר עבדו את העשתרת)" may be interpreted as referring to Eleazar, Joshua, and the elders. Yet, since such an understanding would contradict the report found in Josh 24:31 and Judg 2:7-13, it has been plausibly suggested that the verb "worshiped" (עבדו) refers to Israel mentioned earlier (line 3)[106] and that the conjunction אשר should be understood as "because" (cf. Neh 2:3).[107] Hence, CD presents Joshua, along with Eleazar and

---

102 See, for instance, G. Vermes, "Sectarian Matrimonial Halakha in the Damascus Rule", in idem, *Post-Biblical Jewish Studies* (SJLA 8; Leiden: Brill, 1975), pp. 50-56 (and the earlier literature cited there); D.I. Brewer, "Nomological Exegesis in Qumran 'Divorce' Texts", *RevQ* 18 (1998), pp. 568-569.
103 See P.R. Davies, *Behind the Essenes* (Brown Judaic Studies 94; Atlanta: Scholars Press, 1987), pp. 73-85; J.M. Baumgarten, "The Qumran-Essene Restraints on Marriage", in L.H. Schiffman (ed.), *Archaeology and History in the Dead Sea Scrolls* (Sheffield: Sheffield Academic Press, 1990), p. 15; L.H. Schiffman, "Laws Pertaining to Women in the Temple Scroll", in D. Dimant & U. Rappaport (eds.), *The Dead Sea Scrolls: Forty Years of Research* (STDJ 10; Leiden: Brill, 1992), pp. 216-217.
104 As was demonstrated by Schiffman, *Halakha*, p. 30, נגלה ("revelation") refers to the revealed Torah.
105 For a detailed discussion see J.C. VanderKam, "Zadok and the Spr Htwrh Hhtwm", *RevQ* 11 (1984), pp. 565-566. Wacholder's interpretation of the "sealed book of the Torah" as a sectarian Torah fails to convince. B.-Z. Wacholder, "The 'Sealed' Torah versus the 'Revealed' Torah: An Exegesis of Damascus Covenant V, 1-6 and Jeremiah 32, 10-14", *RevQ* 12 (1986), pp. 351-367; idem, *The New Damascus Document* (STDJ 56; Leiden: Brill, 2007), pp. 189-200.
106 L. Ginzberg, *An Unknown Jewish Sect* (New York: Jewish Theological Seminary, 1976), pp. 20-21; Schiffman, *Halakha*, p. 30.
107 VanderKam, "Zadok", p. 567. He also suggests a reading מאשר ("since", "because"), conjecturing that the *mem* could have been lost due to a haplography (והזקנים מאשר). Rofé, "End", p. 224 note 32, amends to כאשר ("when").

the elders, as a guardian of the Law, in whose days the Book of the Torah was consulted (cf. Josh 1:8, 8:34, 24:26).[108] It was only under the High Priest Zadok, when the long neglected Ark of the Covenant was transferred to Jerusalem, that the Book of the Law became available again.[109]

The non-sectarian text 1Q22 (Words of Moses; written in a Middle to Late Hasmonean hand) presents Moses' farewell address to Israel.[110] It opens with a divine speech to Moses, dated to the same day when, according to Deut 1:3, Moses began his farewell discourse (I, 1-2). In this speech God commands Moses to convene the entire congregation, to ascend Mt. Nebo, to stand there together with Eleazar, to expound the Torah first to the leaders, and then to command it to the rest of Israel (I, 2-3). This scenario seems to follow closely the narration of the Sinai revelation, where Moses gathers the people (Deut 4:10), ascends Mt. Sinai along with Aaron (Exod 19:24; 24:1, 9-11), reports God's words first to the elders (Exod 19:7), and stands (Deut 5:4-5) between God and the people as He speaks to Israel.

Yet, when 1Q22 reports Moses' carrying out these divine commands (I, 11-12), it states that, in addition to Eleazar, he also summons Joshua:[111]

11.   And Moses called Eleazar son of
12. [Aaron] and Joshu[a son of Nun   and he spo]ke the words [of the Law
     ]   to complete [

As in CD, Joshua's subordination to the High Priest is indicated by his being mentioned second. His presence while Moses speaks to Israel may point to Deut 3:28, where Moses is commanded to ascend Mt. Pisga, to "give Joshua his instructions, and imbue him with strength and courage".[112] Moreover, given the aforementioned

---

108 The wording of CD may echo Neh 8:17. As in CD, the restoration of the proper celebration of the festival by the returnees from Babylon was prompted by consulting (reading) the Law (vv. 13-14).
109 Rofé, "End", p. 224, suggests that the wording of this passage testifies to the fact that the author was familiar with a text of Josh 24:28-33 as it appears in the Greek translation of Joshua.
110 J.T. Milik, "Dires de Moïse", in O.P. Barthélemy & J.T. Milik, *Qumran Cave I* (DJD 1; Oxford: Clarendon Press, 1955), pp. 91-97. The dating is that of E. Tigchelaar, "A Cave 4 Fragment of Divre Mosheh (4QDM) and the Text of 1Q22 1:7-10 and Jubilees 1: 9, 14", *DSD* 12 (2005), pp. 311-312.
111 The following English translation reflects several improvements on Milik's Hebrew text as proposed in A. Feldman, "Moses' Farewell Address according to 1QWords of Moses", *JSP* (forthcoming).
112 A. Dupont-Sommer, *The Essene Writings from Qumran*. Trans. G. Vermes (Oxford: Blackwell, 1961), p. 307; Tigchelaar, "Divre Mosheh", p. 314, suggest that it is Eleazar and Joshua who address the people in col. II, 1-5. Yet, the phrase "and he spo]ke the words [of the Law", followed by "and you fo[rget all th]at I [command] you today" (II, 4), indicates that there is only one speaker, Moses (cf. II, 5, IV, 3).

parallels to the Sinai revelation, the summoning of Joshua recalls his accompanying Moses during the latter's ascents to Mt. Sinai (Exod 24:13, 15 [LXX and 4Q364 14 4-5 include also Joshua];[113] 32:17-18).

Another non-sectarian composition, 4Q226 (4Qpseudo-Jubilees[b]; 50-25 BCE), deals with several biblical episodes, such as the Aqeda (frg. 7), the Exodus (frgs. 1-2), the commission of Joshua (frg. 4), and the crossing of the Jordan (frg. 6).[114] The extant description of Joshua's leadership in frg. 4 is rather brief:[115]

1. Joshua[116] the so]n of Nun is crossing over bef[ore you
2.   ]   he will do and pay attention[
3.   ]I[   ] to you all the [

Relying on Deut 31:3 for wording, the first line apparently cites God's speech to either Moses or the entire Israel.[117] The phrase "he will do" in the next line may refer to Joshua, implying his compliance with the divine (or Moses') commands (Josh 1:7).

Frg. 6 mentions the crossing of the Jordan:[118]

1.   ] until three [
3.   ] from then. And enter [
4.   ] from the day of their crossing the [Jordan
5.   ]   these beneath the[
6.   ] to their crossing the [Jordan

---

113 An opposite case seems to be found in the scroll 4Q368 1 3-7, where a citation from Exod 33:11-13 apparently lacks Exod 33:13b, reporting Joshua's constant presence in the Tent. See A. Feldman, "Reading Exodus with Deuteronomy in 4QApocryphal Pentateuch A (4Q368 2)", *JAJ* 3 (2012), p. 332 note 12.

114 J.C. VanderKam & J.T. Milik (eds.), *Qumran Cave 4* (DJD 13; Oxford: Clarendon Press, 1994), p. 157. Another copy of this composition seems to be found in 4Q225 (4Qpseudo-Jubilees[a]), yet only 4Q226 preserves fragments dealing with Joshua. For a recent analysis, see A. Livneh, "The Composition Pseudo-Jubilees from Qumran (4Q225; 4Q226; 4Q227): A New Edition, Introduction, and Commentary", Ph.D. diss., University of Haifa, 2010 (Hebrew).

115 The English translation is based on the revised text of Livneh, ibid., p. 126.

116 VanderKam & Milik, "4Q226", p. 162, restore יהושע (cf. יה[ושע of 4QJosh[a]). Livneh, ibid., p. 126 note 532, suggests יה[ושע. However, given the frequent use of the short form ישוע in the Qumran texts, it should also be considered.

117 A similar formulation occurs also in Deut 3:28, yet there a *yiqtol* form is used, יעבר לפני העם הזה כי הוא. Also, the 2nd person formulation of Deut 31:3 suits well the 2nd person address found here.

118 The translation follows the revised Hebrew text by Livneh, "Composition", p. 131.

The reference to "three" can be interpreted as an allusion to the three days remaining until the crossing of the Jordan (Josh 1:11).[119] The 2nd masc. cohortative "and enter (וּבֹאֹהּ)" may have Joshua as the subject.[120] The phrase "from the day of their crossing the[Jordan" appears to be a chronological reference, yet it is unclear what followed. Livneh proposes that the wording "these beneath" points to the setting of the twelve stones "at the spot (תחת) where the feet of the priests bearing the Ark of the Covenant had stood" (Josh 4:9).[121]

The extant fragments of the non-sectarian Aramaic document 4Q559 (4Qpap-Chronologue biblique ar; 100-50 BCE) deal with the chronology of the period from Jacob to Samuel.[122] While the original scope of the composition is unknown, it might have covered the entire biblical history.[123] The badly damaged frg. 4 refers to several events mentioned in the Book of Joshua:[124]

2. [and from their departure]from the La[nd of Egypt until
3. [Kor]ah[rebelled 5]yea[rs and until Joshua son
4. [of Nun crossed the J]ordan[and circumcised the]foreskin of [the]people that was not
5. [circumcised] 35 [years.] In Gilgal[5]y[ears.
6. [In Shiloh and in Sheche]m 20 years. And from the dea[th of Eleazar
7. [and Joshua]Cush-rishathaim, king of[Aram-
8. [Naharaim] 8 [year]s. Othniel s[on of Kenaz

Some of the dates listed in this fragment are not made explicit in the biblical account. Thus, line 5 mentions the period of 35 years culminating in the crossing of the Jordan and the circumcision at Gilgal. Since according to the biblical chronology 40 years have passed from the Exodus (line 2) to the entrance into the Promised Land (line 4), these 35 years are counted from an event that took place 5 years after the Exodus, perhaps Korah's rebellion.[125]

---

119 One may either read here עַד ("until"; VanderKam & Milik, "4Q226", p. 164) or עֹד ("more"; Livneh, "Composition", p. 132).
120 Livneh, ibid., pp. 132-133.
121 Ibid., p. 133. Unless otherwise noted, the English translation of the MT is from the JPS *Tanach*.
122 É. Puech, "559. 4QpapChronologie biblique ar", in idem, *Qumran Cave 4.XXVII: Textes araméens, deuxième partie: 4Q550-575, 580-582* (DJD 37; Oxford: Clarendon Press, 2009), pp. 263-302.
123 M. Wise, "To Know the Times and the Seasons: A Study of the Aramaic Chronograph 4Q559", *JSP* 8 (1997), p. 9.
124 The translation is that of M.O. Wise, M.G. Abegg, and E.M. Cook, *The Dead Sea Scrolls: A New Translation* (San Francisco: HarperCollins, 2005), p. 565, with some modifications that reflect Puech's reconstructed Aramaic text.
125 Thus Wise, "4Q559", pp. 11, 35 (with M. Rand), and Puech, "4Q559", p. 280.

In lines 5-6 the fragment specifies the length of the stay in Gilgal, namely the period of time from the crossing of the Jordan to the transfer of the Tent of Meeting to Shiloh (Josh 18:1). While the Book of Joshua is silent on this matter, Josephus places the setting of the Tabernacle at Shiloh five years after the entrance to the Promised Land (J. Ant. 5.68).[126] He also remarks that the events described in Josh 24:1 took place 20 years later (5.115), most likely counting them from the transfer of the Tent to Shiloh.[127] These data fit well with the remaining text of lines 5-6, where a missing duration of the stay in Gilgal appears, followed by the mention of 20 years that lapsed until the death of Eleazar and Joshua (Josh 24:29, 33).[128]

Several other Qumran scrolls may refer to the Book of Joshua. The scroll 4Q374 2 ii 2-5 seems to allude to the Israelite conquest and settlement of Canaan.[129] A reference to the conquest may also be found in 4Q462 1 6-7.[130] Finally, the description of Noah's division of the earth between his sons in 1QapGen XVI-XVII, XXI, 15-19, which displays affinities in the "vocabulary, phraseology, syntax, and overall structure" to Josh 15:1-19:48,[131] could be an instance of a more subtle use of the Book of Joshua.[132]

---

126 Apparently, this is based on Josh 14:7, 10 stating that the 85 years old Caleb was 40 years old when sent out as a spy (85-40[years in the desert]-40[age when sent out as a spy]=5).

127 Josephus also observes that Joshua served as a general after the death of Moses for 25 years (J. Ant. 5.117).

128 Thus Wise, "4Q559", pp. 41-43. His interpretation is followed, with some modifications, by Puech, "4Q559", pp. 281-282. On the eight years of Cush-rishathaim's oppression of Israel, see Judg 3:8.

129 See the revised text and commentary by D. Dimant, *Connected Vessels: The Dead Sea Scrolls and the Literature of the Second Temple Period* (Asuppot 3; Jerusalem: The Bialik Institute, 2010), pp. 211-223 (Hebrew).

130 Ibid., pp. 182-183 (Hebrew).

131 E. Eshel, "The Imago Mundi of the Genesis Apocryphon", in L. LiDonnici & A. Lieber (eds.), *Heavenly Tablets: Interpretation, Identity and Tradition in Ancient Judaism* (Leiden: Brill, 2007), p. 127; D. Machiela, *The Dead Sea Genesis Apocryphon* (STDJ 79; Leiden: Brill, 2009), p. 86.

132 Other texts from Qumran allude to the Book of Joshua. Thus, CD XX, 14 (עד תם כל אנשי המלחמה) may depend on Josh 5:6 (כל הגוי אנשי המלחמה). If correct, it lacks the noun הגוי (cf. comments by B. Lucassen, "Josua, Richter und CD", *RevQ* 18 [1997-98], pp. 376-378; van der Meer, *Formation*, pp. 334-335). Also, 1QM XVIII, 5 seems to rely on Josh 10:13. Of the other allusions noted by A. Lange & M. Weigold, *Quotations*, pp. 113-114, some seem to reflect a use of lexica found in the book of Joshua (4Q418 43-45 i 4[Josh 1:8]; 1QM VII, 14[Josh 6:4, 6, 8, 13]; 4Q491 1-3 13[Josh 8:19]), while others (1QS VI, 6[Josh 1:8]; 4Q547 8 3[Josh 8:31]; 1QapGen XXI, 7[Josh 16:1]) are doubtful.

1.3 Conclusions

The diverse Second Temple Jewish writings alluding to, quoting from and rewriting the Book of Joshua form the literary and exegetical background against which the RJ scrolls are to be studied. The presumed Hebrew *Vorlage* of the LXX Joshua and Joshua scrolls from Qumran provide a glimpse of Joshua texts that were in circulation when the RJ scrolls were composed. Moreover, these texts, along with the numerous non-biblical compositions, offer a wealth of information shedding light on the ancient interpretation of the Book of Joshua. Among the recurring exegetical motifs and traditions, shared by the Qumran scrolls, both sectarian and non-sectarian, and other Second Temple sources are the representation of Joshua as obedient to God (Sir; 1 Macc; Philo), consulting and observing God's Law (CD; 4QJosh[a]), endowed with a prophetic gift (Ben Sira; Eupolemus; Josephus; LAB), and interceding on behalf of his people (Sir; 4 Ezra). He is often modeled on Moses (Sir; Philo; Josephus; LAB), yet is subordinate to Eleazar (CD; 1Q22). At least one text draws a parallel between Joshua's military victories and the Maccabean campaigns (2 Macc). Several sources are interested in the precise dating of the events described in the Book of Joshua (4Q226; 4Q539; Eupolemus; Josephus). While the ensuing discussion will occasionally note the relevant traditions from the later Rabbinic and Samaritan sources, it is with the aforementioned Second Temple texts in mind that I turn now to the detailed analysis of the RJ scrolls.

2. The Scroll 4Q378

2.1 The Manuscript

The scroll 4Q378 is written in a developed Herodian formal hand. Several of its twenty-nine fragments preserve remains of upper and inter-columnar margins. Relying on these data, as well as on the shape of the fragments,[133] Stegemann reconstructs the original sequence of the fragments as following:[134]

Column	Fragment	Column	Fragment
I	14	X	not extant
II	not extant	XI	22 i
III	13 i	XII	22 ii
IV	13 ii	XIII	26
V	3 i	XIV	20 i
VI	3 ii	XV	20 ii
VII	6 i	XVI	19 i
VIII	6 ii	XVII	19 ii
IX	11		

Yet, given the paucity and the inconclusive nature of the material evidence, this reconstruction is helpful only in those rare instances where the placement of a fragment, based on its physical features, is corroborated by its contents. Still, both the contents of the fragments and Stegemann's reconstruction indicate that in several cases the sequence of the fragments in the *DJD* edition does not reflect their original placement in the scroll.[135]

2.2 The Contents of 4Q378

The extant fragments of 4Q378 contain little narrative (frg. 14 1-4), yet abound with discourses (frgs. 3 i-ii, 6 i, 6 ii 1-4a, 11, 12, 13 i 5-8, 14 4-5, 26) and prayers (frgs.

---

133 On Stegemann's method of reconstruction see his "Methods for the Reconstruction of Scrolls from Scattered Fragments", in L.H. Schiffman (ed.), *Archaeology and History in the Dead Sea Scrolls* (JSOT/ASOR Monographs 2; JSPSup 8; Sheffield: JSOT Press, 1990), pp. 189-220.
134 Newsom, "4Q378", p. 241.
135 As noted by Newsom, "4Q378", p. 241; G. Vermes, *The Complete Dead Sea Scrolls in English* (London: Penguin, 2004), p. 583.

1, 2, 6 ii 4b-8, 7[?], 13 i 1-4, 19 ii[?], 22 i).[136] The only relatively large fragment to preserve a narrative is frg. 14 which reworks the Deuteronomic description of the mourning for Moses (Deut 34:8). From the point of view of the biblical account, this is the earliest episode with which this scroll deals. If 4Q378 follows the scriptural order of events, this fragment should be assigned number 1, rather than 14. The setting of the vast majority of the discourses and prayers is uncertain. The two exceptions are frgs. 3 and 6. The discourse in frg. 3 ii reworks Josh 1:16-18, while frg. 6 i contains an address referring to Achan's transgression (Josh 7).

Event	Bible	Fragment	Stegemann
Mourning for Moses	Deut 34:8	14 1-2	I
Address (by Joshua?) following the thirty days of mourning		14 4-5	I
Joshua's address to Israel		3 i	V
People's response to Joshua	Josh 1:16-18	3 ii	VI
Address mentioning Achan's sin	Josh 7	6 i 5	VII
Address and penitentiary prayer (by Joshua?)		6 ii	VIII

The precise circumstances (and hence the tentative placement) of other speeches and prayers is difficult to determine. As will be argued below, frgs. 11 and 12 may contain a speech by Joshua that is closely related to his discourse in frg. 3 i (Stegemann's col. IX). Frg. 13 i preserves a prayer, apparently, by Joshua, which could have been uttered as he assumed his role as the national leader (Stegemann places it in col. III[137]). The second person address, emphasizing Moses' role at Sinai and during the Exodus, in frg. 26 could be a suitable epitaph for him. This would place it near frg. 14 (although Stegemann believes that it belongs with col. XIII). A prayer in frg. 22 i refers to God's sparing Israel thanks to Moses' intercession and mentions Joshua's investiture. It might be related to the events leading to Joshua's succession to Moses in frgs. 14 and 3 (Stegemann places it in col. XI). Frgs. 19 ii and 20 ii provide no clues that help determining their settings.

While much remains uncertain, the scroll, as we have it now, spans events from Deut 34 to Josh 7.

---

136 As is observed by Newsom, "Psalms of Joshua", p. 58; idem, "4Q378", p. 238.
137 It is unclear whether this placement is based on the contents of the fragment or on its shape, which seems to offer little clues.

2.3 Editions of 4Q378

The scroll 4Q378 was initially assigned to Strugnell for editing.[138] The final edition of the scroll, informed by Strugnell's preliminary transcription and notes, was published by Newsom under the title 4QApocryphon of Joshua[a].[139] Frg. 3 was recently re-edited by Dimant.[140] A new edition of 4Q378's selected fragments is being prepared by Qimron.[141]

2.4 Text and Commentary

Frg. 1

]נדה לפניך[	1
]שׄ∘[]רׄ[	2

Notes on Readings

1 |נדה. The *DJD* edition reads (with Strugnell)]נדה∘[.[142] Yet, a close inspection of the fragment reveals no trace of ink before the medial *nun*.

2 |שׄ∘[]. Newsom reads]הׄשׄ. However, an upper horizontal stroke with a short serif at its left extremity is not consistent with a *he*, as it is inscribed in this scroll (cf. *he* in line 1). Given the uncertainty, one may read with Wacholder & Abegg]שׄ∘.[143] The trace of the first letter is preceded by a letter-size lacuna.

Translation

1.]uncleanness before you[
2.] [] [

Comments

1 |נדה לפניך[. The noun נדה denotes "bleeding, menstruation" (Lev 20:21) and, more generally, "defilement" (Ezra 9:11).[144] The 2nd masc. sg. pronominal suffix in לפניך indicates that this is a 2nd person address, perhaps, a prayer (Newsom).

---

138 Strugnell's transcription of 4Q378 is embedded in Brown et al., *Preliminary Concordance*.
139 Newsom, "4Q378", pp. 241-262. For the preliminary editions of 4Q378 see Newsom, "The Psalms of Joshua", pp. 56-73; idem, "4Q378 and 4Q379", pp. 35-85.
140 Dimant, "Two Discourses", pp. 43-61.
141 Qimron, *The Hebrew Writings: Volume Two*.
142 Brown et al., *Preliminary Concordance*, vol. 3, p. 1384.
143 Wacholder & Abegg, *Preliminary Edition*, vol. 3, p. 167.
144 HALOT, p. 673.

The language of the fragment is reminiscent of Ezek 36:17: "their ways were in My sight (לפני) like the uncleanness of a menstruous woman (כטמאת הנדה)". An even closer formulation occurs in CD II, 1 and 1QS V, 19-20: ו(כול) מעשיהם לנדה לפניו ("and ["and all", 1QS] their deeds were uncleanness to him"). Accordingly, this line may be restored as כטמאת ה[נדה לפניך] or [נדה לפניך]מעשינו/הם ל. The themes of sin and defilement occur in frg. 3 i 1-2 (intermarriage) and frg. 6 i-ii (Achan). The latter alludes to Ezra 9:11 (mentioned above).

Frg 2

[° אֹוׄיׄבׄיׄכה תׄ]   1
[המירותו ל]   2

Notes on Readings

1]תׄ. The *DJD* edition has]ת. The *taw* is represented by the bottom tips of its vertical strokes. Therefore, Strugnell's cautious reading,]תׄ, is adopted here.[145]

Translation

1.] your enemies [
2.] you exchanged it/him [

Comments

1]אֹוׄיׄבׄיׄכה תׄ. As in frg. 1, the 2nd sg. possessive suffix in אֹוׄיׄבׄיׄכה suggests that this might be a prayer.

2]המירותו ל. The referent of the 3rd masc. sg. suffix in this 2nd masc. sg. Hifil *qatal* of מור, "to exchange", is unknown.[146] From a paleographic point of view, the reading המירותי is equally possible. In both Biblical and Qumran Hebrew המיר usually takes a preposition -ב (e.g., Lev 27:10; 1QHa VI, 31). This is also the case in the Rabbinic Hebrew (m. Temurah 1:1; t. Temurah 3:13). Therefore, Newsom's rendering "you exchanged it for" is difficult. Perhaps, the *lamed* in the end of the line may be restored as המירותו ל]ך ב-. Qimron reconstructs ולוא [המירותו.

---

145 Brown et al., *Preliminary Concordance*, vol. 1, p. 71.
146 HALOT, p. 560.

Frg. 3 i+10

]°[

1 [תוע]בותיהם °[לטמאם ול]הזנות[ם

2 [ו]תקח מבנותיה[ם לבניך ותתן מב]נותיך לבניהם   *vacat*

3 ואם] [°°ני[°   ו]מצאוכה צרות רבות וכול

4 [הרעות] והאל[ו]ת הכתובות בספר תורת מושה אי]ש האלוהים
                                                         ו

5 [והסתיר [פנ]י[ו ממכה והייתה לאכלה

6 [והפיצכה יהוה בכול העמים מקצי ה]ארץ ועד קציה והניעכה

7 [בכול הגוים   ועשיתה הר]ע עד לכלה ועד למעול

8 [ביהוה   וידעתה כי בעוזבכה את יהו]ה אלוהיך באו עליךה

9 [כול הקללות האלה   והשבתה אל לבבך בכו]ל הגוים אשר

10 [הדיחכה יהוה אלוהיך שמה   אשר עשיתה

11 [הגוים א]שר משלו בכה

12 [למען]תחיה

13 [אתה וזרעך   כי בכה בחר יהוה אלוהי]ך להיות לו

14 [לעם סגולה   לע]שות לדעת[[

15 [י]הוה] אלוהיך [

Notes on Readings

As the editor indicates, the contents of frg. 10 suggest that it belongs with frg. 3 i. Here it is placed in the upper right corner of the column. A similar placement is suggested now by Qimron.

The extant fragments of 4Q378 preserve no single complete line of a text. The restored lines in frg. 11 (line 5) and frg. 14 (line 2) count 46 and 49 letter-spaces respectively. The reconstructed lines 4 and 6 in this fragment have 47 and 50 letter-spaces respectively.[147]

]°[

1 [תוע]בותיהם. Strugnell reads [א]בותיהם].[148] Newsom follows his reading in the preliminary edition, [א]בותיהם (leaving out the lacuna before the restored *alef*).[149] Yet, in the final edition she proposes [ב]נותיהם (again, leaving out the lacuna). A similar reading (with the lacuna) is offered now by Qimron. On the photographs (PAM 41.779; 43.193) an upper horizontal stroke of *bet* is clearly visible. Above

---

147 Dimant's reconstructed lines have 51 (3 i 4), 57, and 58 (3 ii 5, 10) letter-spaces. See Dimant, "Two Discourses", pp. 46, 53.

148 Brown et al., *Preliminary Concordance*, vol. 1, p. 16.

149 Newsom, "4Q378 and 4Q379", p. 47.

the second letter a bottom tip of a vertical stroke is visible. It might belong to a letter found in the preceding line, yet in this fragment the long vertical strokes of such letters as *qof*, final *kaf*, and *ṣade* do not reach the line below. Hence it seems more likely that this is an addition between the lines.

2 ותׄקח[. Newsom reads תׄקח. It appears that there is a place for another letter before the *taw*. Qimron suggests the same.

3]°ת̊נ°[. The *DJD* edition reads the last letter as a *taw*. Qimron reads only two letters: תעזוב[נׄ]. The traces of the last letter are difficult to read. In fact, they seem to suit better a *he* than a *taw*, as the left vertical stroke is curving to the right at its bottom (PAM 41.779).

4 והאלׄוׄ]ת. Newsom and Qimron fail to notice traces of the fifth letter. On PAM 41.779 a trace of a vertical stroke next to the *lamed* is visible. Thus I propose to read and restore here והאלׄוׄ]ת.

5 פׄנׄ[יׄ]וׄ. The *DJD* edition reads °°°[. While the proposed reading is suggested by the underlying biblical verse (see Comment below), it is also supported by the traces of ink still visible on the photographs (PAM 40.969; 41.779; 43.193). The left extremity of the base stroke in the beginning of the line may well belong to a medial *pe*. It is followed by a base of a medial *nun*. After a blank space, which may easily accommodate a *yod*, a vertical stroke of a *waw* is visible. Qimron suggests פ[נׄיׄוׄ.

7 הר[וׄ עד. Newsom reads ועד. However, the traces of the two diagonal strokes visible in the beginning of the line (esp. PAM 40.969; 43.193) are consistent with an *ayin*. There is a short interval between this *ayin* and the following *ayin* of עד. Qimron has ועד [.

10 אשר[. The editor proposes כׄאשר[. According to the photographs (PAM 40.969; 41.779; 43.193), there are no traces of ink before the *alef*. In fact, the *alef* itself has been only partially preserved. Dimant and Qimron also read אשר[.

12 תׄחׄיה[. The *DJD* edition has יׄה°[. On the photographs (PAM 40.969; 41.779) the upper horizontal and right vertical strokes of a *ḥet* are visible. There is also a tip of a vertical stroke before the *ḥet*, which may fit a *waw*, a *yod* or a *taw*. Qimron reads חׄיה[.

14 לדע]ת. Newsom reads לׄמׄ]ת. Qimron correctly suggests that the second and the third letters are *dalet* and *ayin*. These are well visible on PAM 40.969.

15 יׄ[הוׄה]. The *DJD* edition has]עׄה[. The trace of the frist letter may suit the left extremity of the upper horizontal and the left vertical strokes of a *he*. The traces of the following *waw* or *yod* are clearly visible on PAM 40.969.

Translation

1. their [abo]minations [   ]to make them unclean and to [cause]them[to commit fornication]
2. [and] you will take wives[for your sons] from among [thei]r daughters[and you shall give some of]your [da]ughters to their sons *vacat*
3. and if[ ] [and] many troubles will come upon you and all
4. [the evils] and the curse[s written in the Book of the Teaching of Moses the ma]n of God
5. [and He will conceal]His fa[ce] from you, and you will become food
6. [and YHWH will scatter you from the ends of the] earth to its ends, and he will make you wander
7. [among all the nations   and you will do what is ev]il unto destruction and unto acting unfaithfully
8. [to YHWH   And you will know that because of your foresaking YHW]H your God have come upon you
9. [all these curses   and you will take to heart amidst al]l the nations
10. [where YHWH your God has driven you   ]which you did
11. [the nations w]ho ruled over you
12. [so that]you may live,
13. [you and your seed   for YHWH]your [God has chosen you] to be His
14. [own possession   to obse]rve. To kno[w   ]
15. [Y]HWH[your God]

Comments

1 תוע[בותיהם]. The first two lines of this column are concerned with intermarriage with the indigenous Canaanite population prohibited by the Torah. While New-som restores א[בֹ֗ותיהם, the lacuna in the beginning of the line is large enough to accommodate the reconstruction תוע[בֹ֗ותיהם, "their [abo]minations".

לטמאם֗ ול[הזנות]ם. The three extant letters of the second word, ם[   ]ול, suggest that the Piel infinitive of טמא, "to defile", is followed by another infinitive.[150] Newsom plausibly restores ול[הזנות]ם, a Hifil infinitive of זנה, "to encourage to commit fornication" or, in a metaphorical sense, "to bring someone to practice idolatry".[151] While טמא and זנה occur together elsewhere (see, for instance, Ps 106:39),[152] this line may echo Exod 34:15-16 (cf. line 2).

---

150 HALOT, p. 376.
151 Ibid., p. 275.
152 On the use of Psalms 105-106 in the Dead Sea scrolls see G.J. Brooke, "Psalms 105 and 106 at Qumran", *RevQ* 14 (1989), pp. 285-290.

ו]ת̇קח מבנותיה̇]ם לבניך ותתן ותיך מב]נׄותיך לבניהם 2. This line makes clear that this is a
2nd person address. The Torah prohibits intermarriage in Exod 34:15-16 and Deut
7:3-4. The scroll seems to take up the narrative style of Exodus 34. Yet, the phrase
מב]נׄותיך לבניהם indicates that it reads Exod 34:15-16 in light of Deut 7:3-4. For
while the plural מבנותיה̇]ם, ב]נׄותיך, and לבניהם point to Exod 34, it is Deut 7 that
prohibits marrying both Cananaite males and females (cf. Ezra 9:12).

Col. i does not name the speaker. However, col. ii suggests that this is Joshua. As
in Josh 23:11-26, 24:19-20, he appears to address Israel, warning them of their future
violation of the divine laws, including the prohibition of intermarriage (Josh 23:12).

ואם] 3. Most certainly, a verb signifying abandoning either God or his commandments followed.

ו]מׄצאוכה צרות רבות וכול / [הרעות] ... אי]ש האלוהים 3-4. Line 3 alludes to one of the
key biblical passages underlying this column, Deut 31:14-21. In this passage God
reveals to Moses (in the presence of Joshua) that Israel will forsake Him and
therefore will be punished. The scroll relies here on Deut 31:17 for wording (cf. v.
21). It rephrases ומצאהו as ו]מׄצאוכה to make it fit a 2nd person address and applies
the adjective רבות to the noun צרות, instead of רעות (for the phrase צרות רבות see
Ps 71:20; 4Q398 14-17 ii 2). The restoration וכול / [הרעות (Dimant) is supported by
Deut 31:18. Qimron prefers הקללות] / וכול. The reference to אלות seems to point
to Deut 30:7.

הכתובות בספר תורת מושה אי]ש האלוהים. The reconstruction follows Deut 29:20
(Dimant). The expression ספר תורת מושה (Qimron prefers ספר מושה) occurs in
Josh 8:31, 23:6, while Josh 1:8 mentions ספר התורה הזה. Moses' description as
איש האלוהים (cf. frg. 26 2) may point to Deut 33:1.[153] Qimron suggests that a phrase
יבואו אליך followed in line 5.

ו
והסתיר [פׄנׄ]יׄו ממכה והייתה לאכלה 5. This line paraphrases Deut 31:17a. Adapting it to
the 2nd person discourse, the scroll rephrases the 3rd masc. pl. pronoun מהם as a 2nd
masc. sg. ממכה and the 3rd masc. sg. *qatal* והיה as a 2nd masc. sg. והייתה.[154] While
the MT has here a Qal infinitive of אכל, לאכל, the scroll reads a noun לא̇כלה, "for
food" (for the expression היה לאכלה see Gen 1:29; Lev 25:6). As Dimant notes, a
similar reading is found in Smr, LXX, S, and T[N] ad loc. 11QT[a] LIX, 7-8, elaborating
on the punishment for breaking the covenant, rephrases Deut 31:17 in a similar
way. Dimant restores here with this passage ולבז ולמשיסה] / והייתה לא̇כלה.

---

153 On this appellation see A.P. Jassen, *Mediating the Divine: Prophecy and Revelation in the Dead
Sea Scrolls and Second Temple Literature* (STDJ 68; Leiden: Brill, 2007), pp. 113-121.
154 On the long 2nd masc. sg. *qatal* afformative תה–, see E. Qimron, *The Hebrew of the Dead Sea
Scrolls* (HSS 29; Atlanta: Scholars Press, 1986), p. 43.

והפיצכה יהוה בכול העמים מקצי ה[ארץ ועד קציה והניעכה 6. This line depends on Deut 28:64 (cf. 4Q216 II, 15[=Jub 1:13]). Dimant notes that the scroll abbreviates the biblical formula מקצה הארץ ועד קצה הארץ, reading קציה, instead of the Deuteronomic קצה הארץ (cf. Gen 47:21). Yet, unlike this biblical formula, the scroll has a plural קציה (unless one takes the *yod* as a *mater lectionis* for *ṣere*[155]), which might be a plural of קָצֶה ("edge, end, extremity", as in Ezek 33:2) or קץ ("end").[156] 11Q20(11QT^b) XVI [frg. 30], 4 (based on Deut 13:8) reads מקצי הארץ ועד קצי הארץ. Thus, while Newsom and Dimant supplement the line with מקצה ה[ארץ ועד קציה, it is proposed here to restore מקצי ה[ארץ ועד קציה.

והניעכה [בכול הגוים. Dimant observes that the 3rd masc. sg. Hifil *weqatal* נוע, "toss about, shake, cause to wander", points to Amos 9:9.[157] The reconstruction follows this verse. Qimron suggests [יהוה בגויים / והניעכה.

ועשיתה הר[ע]ֹ עד לכלה ועד למעול / [ביהוה אלוהיך 7-8. The preceding line describes the divine punishment of Israel. However, the verb מעל, "to be untrue, violate one's legal obligations",[158] is never used in the Hebrew Bible with reference to God, but describes human disloyalty (cf. Lev 26:40; Neh 1:8).[159] Apparently, the scroll shifts here to the description of Israel's abandonment of God. לכלה is a Piel construct infinitive of כלה, "to complete, to bring to an end, to destroy".[160] Newsom and Dimant interpret it in a nominative sense, rendering עד לכלה as "unto destruction" (cf. Josh 24:20). Alternatively, it could imply fullness, completion (as in 2 Chr 31:1).[161] The preceding word may be restored either as a noun כי עשיתה (ה)רֹֻ[ר]ע [cf. Pr 2:14; 2 Chr 12:14; 4Q370 I, 2]) or as a Hifil form of רעע, "to do an injury, hurt", ועד למעול / הר[ו/ו/ל.ֹ[162] The beginning of line 8 could have read מעל ביהוה אלוהיך / [מעל ביהוה אלוהיך (cf. Lev 5:21) or ביהוה אלוהיך] / ועד למעול (Dimant; cf. Josh 22:31).

וידעתה כי בעוזבכה את יהו[ן]ה אלוהיך באו עליךה / [כול הקללות האלה 8-9. This line depends either on Deut 28:15 or 30:1 (alluded to in the next line). The scroll rephrases the Deuteronomic (28:15) *weqatal* ובאו (30:1 has כי יבאו והיה), pointing to the future, as a *qatal* באו, referring to the past (Newsom). Newsom restores the line

---

155 See E.Y. Kutscher, *The Language and Linguistic Background of The Isaiah Scroll (1QIsaᵃ)* (Leiden: Brill, 1974), p. 154; E. Qimron, "A Grammar of the Hebrew Language of the Dead Sea Scrolls", Ph.D. diss., The Hebrew University, Jerusalem, 1976, pp. 57f. (Hebrew); idem, *Hebrew*, p. 19.
156 HALOT, pp. 1118-21.
157 BDB, p. 631.
158 HALOT, pp. 612-13.
159 Qimron, *The Hebrew Writings: Volume Two*, also notes that למעול does not fit the context and parses it as an infinitive of עלה with an additional *mem* (cf. Neh 8:6; Jer 48:15).
160 HALOT, pp. 476-77.
161 BDB, p. 478.
162 Ibid., p. 949.

as עלידה באו אלוהיך יהו]ה קללות כל כי והיה. Dimant proposes הגיד אשר הרעות וכול
עלידה באו אלוהיך יהו]ה and notes that it is unclear whether the curses have already been fulfilled (cf. 4Q398 11-13 1-4) or not (which would fit the times of
Joshua). This difficulty may be resolved by restoring this line with Qimron as
אלוהיך יהו]ה את בעוזבכה כי וידעתה (cf. Josh 24:16, 20).

עלידה. As Dimant observes, 4Q378 seems to prefer longer forms of the objective
pronominal suffixes (yet, see לפניך [frg. 1 1]) and short forms for the possessive
suffixes (except for אֹוּבִֿיֹכֹה [frg. 2 1]). She suggests that the form עלידה reflects the
hesitation of the scribe.[163] Tov notes that the letter *he* is somewhat smaller than
usual in 4Q378 and proposes that this is a scribal correction introduced upon the
completion of writing.[164]

9 שמה אלוהיך יהוה הדיחכה] / אשר הגוים בכו]ל לבבכה אל והשבתה. This line paraphrases
Deut 30:1. The reconstruction is that of Dimant, who notes that, as in the biblical
verse, the change from an "admonitory tone in ll. 1-9 to a more positive tenor in
ll. 10-15" reflects people's repentance.[165] Compare a similar change in attitude in
11QT[a] LIX, 9-10. Qimron restores with Deut 15:6 and line 11 אשר. / משלו בך].

10 עשיתה אשר]. This phrase most likely refers to the Israelites' repentance over
the wicked deeds committed in the past.

11 בכה משלו שר א]הגוים. As is the case with עשיתה (line 10), while the scroll employs here a *qatal* form, משלו, the line evidently refers to the future events. The
wording is reminiscent of Ps 106:41. However, the scroll may also allude here to
Deut 30:7, stating that once Israel repents, God will put those curses on the nations who persecuted them. Thus the line might have read: האלות כול את יהוה ונתן
בכה משלו א]שר הגוים על האלה.

12-13 וזרעכה אתה] / תִֹחִיה] למען. The verb תִֹחִיה] seems to point to Deut 30:19.

13-14 סגולה לעם] / לו להיות אלוהיך]ך יהוה בחר בכה כי. The scroll appears to employ here
the expression סגלה לעם לו להיות (Deut 7:6, 14:2, 26:18). Dimant restores סגולה לעם]
/ לו להיות אלוהי]ך יהוה אל תשוב כי. Alternatively, one may restore (with Deut 7:6)
העמים מכול סגולה לעם] / לו להיות אלוהי]ך יהוה בחר בכה כי.

14 לדע]ת לע]שׂות. Apparently, a Qal infinitive of ידע opens a new clause.

---

163 Dimant, "Two Discourses", p. 48.

164 E. Tov, "Some Reflections on Consistency in the Activity of Scribes and Translators", in
U. Dahmen & J. Schnocks (eds.), *Juda und Jerusalem in der Seleukidenzeit: Herrschaft—Wider-
stand—Identität: Festschrift für Heinz-Josef Fabry* (Bonner Biblische Beiträge 159; Göttingen: V&R
Unipress, 2010), p. 329.

165 Dimant, "Two Discourses", p. 52.

The Scroll 4Q378

15 [אלוהיך] [וה]י. The reconstruction follows the formula found in line 8 (cf. the reconstructed lines 10 and 13).

Frgs. 3 ii+4

[	3 ויוצא[אותנו ממצרים
ככול אשר]	4 ועתה היום [הזה
מושה]	5 שמענו למושה כ[ן נשמע אליכה
שרי האלפים שרי]	6 איש ישר וגדול[ ]
ולשופטים]	7 המאיות שרי הח[ח]משים ושרי העשרות
כל איש אשר ימרה את פיך ולוא]	8 ולשוטרים [ ]ל[ ]
אל תערץ]	9 ישמע ולוא[ ] יעשה את כל אשר תצונו יומת
לוא]	10 ואל תחת חזק וא[מץ כי את]ה תנחיל את[העם הזה
ועתה קום לך]	11 ירפכה ולוא י[עזב]כה ועתה ת[חזקנה ידי]ך[
[	12 למסע ל[פנינו

Notes on Readings

5 שמענו. Strugnell reads [ו]שמענו.[166] The *DJD* edition and Qimron have [ו]שמענו. The examination of the fragment reveals no traces of ink before the *shin* (PAM 40.969; 41.779; 43.193). The short blank space before the *shin* may result from a defect on the parchment (Dimant).

10 את]ה. The phrase את]ה תנחיל את[is preserved on frg. 4, placed by Newsom (following Strugnell) in lines 10 and 11 of frg. 3 ii. Of the first letter only a bottom tip of a vertical stroke survives. Strugnell reads and restores with Josh 1:6 את]ה.[167] However, Newsom rejects his reading and suggests כ[י, "since the additional width required for that word (i.e. את]ה) causes problems for the restoration of line 11".[168] Yet, as Dimant rightly observes, while the problems with the restoration of line 11 are easily resolved, the unwarranted omission of אתה "produces a curtailed version of the verse" quoted here.

Translation

3. and He brought]us] out[from Egypt	
4. And now[, this very] day, [	just as]
5. [And] we obeyed Moses s[o we will obey you	Moses]

---

166 Brown et al., *Preliminary Concordance*, vol. 4, p. 1886.
167 Ibid., vol. 3, p. 1391.
168 Newsom, "4Q378 and 4Q379", p. 42.

6. a man upright and great [the leaders of thousands, the leaders of]
7. hundreds, the leaders of f[ifties and the leaders of tens   and as the judges]
8. and as the officers [   ] [whoever rebels against your command and does not]
9. obey and does not[do whatever you command him, shall be put to death   do not be terrified]
10. and do not be dismayed. Be strong and of go[od courage, for yo]u will cause [this people] to inherit [He will not]
11. abandon you or forsake [you. And now, let] your hands be strong[And now arise, go] on [your]
12. journey a[t the head of us

Comments

3 ויוצא̇א̇] אותנו ממצרים. This column contains Israel's response to Joshua's speech in col. i. The 3rd masc. sg. Hifil *wayyiqtol* of יצא most likely refers to the Exodus from Egypt (cf. Deut 4:20). Following Newsom's lead, Dimant restores the line with Deut 4:20 ויוצא̇א̇] אותנו ממצרים להיות לו לעם נחלה. This reconstruction has been partially adopted here. The reference to God's deliverance from Egyptian bondage may constitute a part of the people's affirmation that they will keep God's commandments. This element of their response may be modeled on Israel's answer to Joshua (also referring to Exodus) in Josh 24:17.

4 הזה] ועתה היום. The reconstruction is by Qimron. This locution is unattested in biblical Hebrew. Compare a similar combination of the biblical construction כיום הזה with עתה, ועתה כיום הזה, in 4Q504 XIX, 5-6. Most likely, this phrase opens a new clause. The wording ועתה occurs in the divine address to Joshua in Josh 1:2, while the expression היום [הזה reminds of Joshua's farewell admonishion to Israel to choose "today" (היום) whom they will serve (Josh 24:15).

5 מושה]   כ̇ן נשמע אליכה / שמענו למושה כ̇] ככול אשר[. The scroll rewrites the reply of the Transjordanian tribes to Joshua in Josh 1:17 as if spoken by the entire nation of Israel (Newsom). The interchange of prepositions, (למושה→אל משה) ל→-אל, is well attested to in the Qumran scrolls.[169] Dimant's reconstruction כ̇]ן נשמע אליכה רק [מושה עם היה כאשר עמכה יהוה יהיה (60 letter-spaces) appears to be too long.

6 איש ישר וגדול. Moses' soubriquet איש ישר וגדול, being a combination of two biblical expressions איש תם וישר (Job 1:1) and איש גדול (2 Kgs 5:1), is most likely an expansion of Josh 1:17 quoted in the previous line. The use of the adjective גדולˈ points to Exod 11:3 (Dimant).

---

169 See, for instance, Kutscher, *Isaiah*, p. 408.

שרי האלפים שרי] / המאיות שרי הח]משים ושרי העשרות 6-7. It appears that in their response to Joshua the people refer to the appointment of officers by Moses (Exod 18:21, 25; Deut 1:15; Dimant). Perhaps, they promise to obey Joshua, Moses' appointee, as they have obeyed other officers he has appointed. Alternatively, it may well be that the respondents here are the officials, who describe themselves as Moses' appointees. Compare Josh 1:10, where Joshua addresses שטרי העם (see also Josh 23:3, 24:1).[170] Unlike the MT of Exod 18 and Deut 1, the scroll has המאיות and הח]משים with a definite article (cf. Num 31:14). It reads שרי without the *waw* conjunctive as in Exod 18:21, 25(MT; thus also Deut 1:15[Smr]). For the spelling המאיות with a *yod* see 2 Kgs 11:4 (*Ketib*); 1QM III, 17; 11QTᵃ XLII, 15.

ולשופטים] / ולשוטרים 8. Josh 1:10 records Joshua's address to שטרי העם. Deut 1:15 also lists these among the officers appointed by Moses. As to the reconstruction ולשופטים, in Josh 23-24 (echoed elsewhere in this fragment) Joshua summons the entire Israel לשפטיו ולשטריו (23:2, 24:1; Newsom).[171]

כל איש אשר ימרה את פיך ולוא] / ישמע ולוא] יעשה את כל אשר תצוונו יומת 8-9. The scroll depends here on Josh 1:18. Dimant restores ולוא] / ישמע ולוא] יעשה. If correct, the addition of ולוא] יעשה makes explicit the need to carry out Joshua's orders, the notion that is implicit in the MT ישמע, denoting not simply hearing, but also obeying (for שמע and עשה see Exod 24:7; cf. also ולא שמעו ולא עשו [2 Kgs 18:12]). Perhaps, this addition echoes v. 16: כל אשר צויתנו נעשה.

אל תערץ] / ואל תחת חזק ואן]מץ כי את]ה תנחיל את] העם הזה 10. This is an expansion of Josh 1:18: רק חזק ואמץ. The scroll utilizes the wording of the divine encouragement to Joshua in vv. 6 and 9. Dimant restores the beginning of the line with Deut 31:7-8 ואתה אל תירא] / ואל תחת.

לוא]/ ירפכה ולא ̊י ̊ע ̊ז ̊ב]כה 11. The phrase לוא]/ ירפכה ולא ̊י ̊ע ̊ז ̊ב]כה ועתה ת]ה ̊ז ̊קנה ידיך] occurs in Moses' farewell address to Joshua in Deut 31:8, as well as in the divine address to Joshua in Josh 1:5. If the scroll depends here on Josh 1, then it reworks vv. 1:5-6 in a reverse order (Dimant). Yet, it is equally possible, that it replicates the sequence of Deut 31:7-8, where the promise לא ירפך ולא יעזבך follows the encouragement חזק ואמץ ... ואתה תנחילנה אותם.

---

170 Compare also the reworking of this scene in the Samaritan Cronicle of Abu 'l-Fatḥ, where Joshua first addresses the leaders of Israel, who then assemble the entire nation. See P. Stenhouse, *The Kitāb Al-Tarīkh of Abu 'L-Fatḥ* (Studies in Judaica 1; Sydney: The Mandelbaum Trust, 1985), p. 8-9.

171 Note also that the LXX to Deut 1:15 (ושטרים לשבטיכם) renders the word לשבטיכם as τοῖς κριταῖς ὑμῶν=לשפטיכם.

ת[חֹזקנה ידיך]. While this phrase is not found in Deut 31 and Josh 1, it occurs frequently in the Hebrew Bible (2 Sam 2:7). The scroll might have read (with 2 Sam
2:7) ואתה ת[חֹזקנה ידיך] (Dimant) or ועתה ת[חֹזקנה ידיך].

ועתה קום לך] / למסע ל[פנינו 12. The scroll may allude to Deut 10:11 (Newsom), re-
phrasing it as the people's encouragement to Joshua. In Josh 1:2 God commands
Joshua to cross the Jordan using an imperative קום ועתה. Qimron suggests ל[פני העם.

Frg. 5

1	[° לש]
2	[לוא בֹ°]

Translation

1.] [
2.]not [

Frg. 6 i

3	[הֹ כי באשֹ[מה]
4	[גדולה אנחנו נש[אֹ תפלה עלחטאתינו
5	אל תלכו אחרי הב]עֹלים אל תדמו לאחדֹ [י]וֹרדי
6	[שאול ל]עֹולם עלילותיו כי לעלמיה
7	[ ]שמכה הוי אחי עליכמה
8	]ישמ[ו]רֹכֹמֹה וכֹאֹב לבֹנֹוֹ ירֹחֹם

Notes on Readings

4 עלחטאתינו. Newsom reads על חטאתינו, yet notes that there is no space between
the two words.

5 הב]עֹלים. The *DJD* edition has]לים°[. On the photographs (PAM 40.969; 41.779)
the traces of both right and left strokes of *ayin* are visible.

לאחדֹ. Newsom reads לאחֹ[י]. Of the fourth letter only a vertical stroke survives. It
may belong to a *waw/yod*, but also to a *dalet* (Qimron). There is a blank space
next to the *dalet*, indicating that this is the last letter of this word.

8]ישמ[ו]רֹכֹמֹה. The *DJD* edition reads]דֹ [ ]מֹ[ה. Qimron suggests]הֹוֹמֹה[. There are
traces of three letters before the medial *mem*. The hook-shaped top of the first
letter (PAM 40.969) is most likely a *waw* or a *yod*. The next letter is clearly a *resh*

(see PAM 40. 969; 41.779). The following vertical stroke may belong to a medial *kaf*. There is no lacuna between this letter and the medial *mem*, as can be seen on PAM 43.193.

יֹרֹחֹם. Newsom reads יֹדבר. Qimron suggests יֹאֹהֹב or יֹרֹחֹם. The reading is difficult. The upper horizontal stroke of the second letter may belong to a *bet*, a *dalet* or a *resh*. The traces of the third letter seem to suit better those of a *ḥet*. There seems to be a trace of ink above the third letter (to the left of it). It is unlclear whether this is a letter added between the lines. It is also difficult to determine whether the fragment preserves traces of the fourth letter.

Translation

3. [   ] for [we are] in [deep]guil[t]
4. [let us offe]r[up] a prayer on behalf of our sins
5. [Do not go after the Ba]als. Do not be like one of those [g]oing down
6. [to Sheol   f]orever His deeds; for forever
7. [   ]your name. Woe to you my brothers
8. [He will gua]rd you and like a father to his son He will have compassion

Comments

3 [גדולה אנחנו] / [מה]כי באש[. This column may contain Joshua's admonitory discourse related to Achan's violation of *ḥerem* (see line 5; Newsom).[172] The reconstruction follows Ezra 9:7 (Qimron). Another possible restoration would be כי באש[מתינו] / [הגדולה (with Ezra 9:13).

4 נש[א] תפלה על חטאתינו. The first word is restored as a 1st pl. Qal imperative of נשא, "to lift up", following the recurring biblical expression נשא תפלה (e.g., Isa 37:4; Jer 7:16).[173] While Biblical Hebrew prefers a construction תפלה בעד, the scroll uses the preposition על. The noun חטאתינו can be read as a sg. or pl. form of חטאה, "sin". The former reading would imply that the scroll employs a *yod* as a *mater lectionis* for *ṣere*, חטאתֵינו. Since Joshua and the people took no part in Achan's transgression, the inclusive language, "our sins", may reflect the notion of corporal/communal responsibility (as in Josh 7:1a).[174]

---

172 Newsom is followed by Tov, "Rewritten Book", p. 249, and Qimron, *The Hebrew Writings: Volume Two*.

173 HALOT, p. 724.

174 Given an allusion to Ezra's prayer in lines 3-4, one may note the similarities between the descriptions of Joshua's grief in Josh 7:6 and that of Ezra in Ezra 9:3-4.

שאול] / **[י]ורדי** **5-6**. אל תלכו אחרי הב[עלים אל תדמו אל לאחד]. As the first word is likely to be restored as הב[עלים, "the Baals", the speaker seems to exhort his adressees to abstain from Baal worship. The scroll might have utilized here such a biblical phrase as ללכת אחרי הבעלים (1Kgs 18:18). The pl. masc. participle of ירד in construct, [י]ורדי, may be restored with one of the following expressions יורדי בור (Isa 38:18), יורדי דומה (Ps 115:17), יורדי עפר (Ps 22:30) or יורדי שאול (Job 7:9; 1QHᵃ XVI, 29; Qimron). Qimron compares the construction לאחד] / [י]ורדי שאול to the wording of Deut 15:7 and suggests that it refers to Achan (cf. the reference to Achan as איש אחד in Josh 22:20). Rabbinic and Samaritan sources claim that the items taken by Achan were previously used in an idolatrous worship.[175] If the scroll espoused a similar view, this would explain the link between the exhortation against Baal worship and Achan's sin.

ל[עולם עלילותיו כי לעלמיה. ל[עולם. The first word may be restored as ל[עולם or מ[עולם. The 3ʳᵈ masc. sg. possessive pronoun in עלילותיו, "deeds, actions", seems to refer to God, as in הודיעו בעמים עלילותיו (Isa 12:4; Ps 105:1; 1Chr 16:8) or הגידו בעמים עלילותיו (Ps 9:12).[176] Perhaps, this line read something like ל[עולם הגידו עלילותיו (cf. Ps 75:10) or זכרו ל[עולם הודיעו עלילותיו (cf. Ps 105:8). Qimron restores הודו לאלוהים ל[עולם עלילותיו.

כי לעלמיה. This appears to be an Aramaic counterpart of the Hebrew לעולמים, לְעָלְמַיָּא (Dan 2:44), spelled phonetically with a *he* instead of an *alef* (as in 4Q542 1 i 1). This phrase occurs once again in frg. 26 6. The conjunction כי indicates that the scroll went on providing a reason for telling/remembering God's deeds. Compare כי לעולם חסדו (4Q177) to כי לעולם יברכם (Ps 119:152), כי לעולם יסדתם (e.g., Ps 106:1), 1-4 i 10).

שמכה הוי אחי עליכמה 7]. The first word is apparently a noun שם, "name", with a 2ⁿᵈ masc. sg. possessive suffix (thus also Qimron). The abrupt change from a sg. addressee to a pl. may be understood in several ways. The speaker might have used 2ⁿᵈ sg. and 2ⁿᵈ pl. interchangeably (cf. אוי לך [6 ii 4]) as he addressed the people. More likely, שמכה concludes a brief prayer (or exclamation addressed to God). Newsom restores [א]שמכה, yet the short blank space before *shin* reveals no trace of the *alef*'s left stroke (cf. *alef* in לאחד [line 5] and אחי [line 7]).

הוי אחי עליכמה. For the formula הוי על see Jer 50:27 and Ezek 13:3. While in line 4 the speaker refers to "our sins", here the woe is pronounced on the addressees

---

175 See Pirke de Rabbi Eleazer 37; Tanḥuma Vayeshev 2. For the Samaritan tradition see the Arabic Book of Joshua in O.T. Crane, *The Samaritan Chronicle or the Book of Joshua, the Son of Nun* (New York: John Alden, 1890), pp. 52-54.
176 HALOT, p. 833.

only (but, see col. ii 4). Still, by employing the phrase אחי (cf. its use by David in
1 Sam 30:23; 1 Chr 28:2) the speaker identifies himself with the audience.

8 ישמ֯[ו֯ר֯כ֯מ֯ה וכ֯אב לב֯נ֯ו י֯ר֯ח֯ם. While in the previous line the speaker pronounces a
woe on the addressees, here he speaks of God's protection (cf. Num 6:24) and
father-like compassion to his people (Ps 103:13). In the Hebrew Bible רחם usually
takes a direct object. Yet, in Ps 103:13, which seems to underlie the wording of this
line, it occurs with a preposition על. The construction רחם ל- either reflects the
use of ל- as a direct object identifier or an interchange ל-←על.¹⁷⁷ For the father-son
relations between God and Israel see Isa 1:2; Jer 31:9; Mal 1:6; 4Q377 1 i 6; 4Q382
104 3.¹⁷⁸ Note particularly the wording כ֯א[ב לבנו] in 4Q392 6-9 5.

Frg. 6 ii

	1 [ ]י֯ח֯נני ויתננ֯]י [
[	2 ל֯עמ֯ו֯ד לפני אלוה ו֯ל֯פ֯נ֯י֯]ן כל העדה
]ידע	3 לבי כי אלהים יבחן מל֯]י
ועוונתינו רבו]	4 ויבחן vacat אוי לי כ֯]י
[	5 מעלה לרא֯שי]נו
	נ ו
[	6 הכרתי ואמ֯ר]
[	7 עליכה אדני וב]
[	8 ולא כתו֯ר֯כ֯ה]
[	9] ל] [ ]ללl]

Notes on Readings

1 י֯ח֯נני[. Newsom reads ב]חנני. On PAM 42.819 a bottom tip of a vertical stroke is
visible to the right of *ḥet* (Strugnell reads ח֯ני[]).¹⁷⁹ Perhaps, this is a *waw* or a *yod*.
Qimron suggests י]ח֯וננ, yet the letter preceding the first medial *nun* is clearly a *ḥet*.

4 כ֯]י. Newsom has]ו°. On the photographs (PAM 41.779; 42.819; 42.974; 43.193)
only an upper tip of a vertical stroke is visible. Qimron proposes כ֯]י.

---

177 For examples of על (MT)←ל- (DSS) interchange see Kutscher, *Isaiah*, p. 408.
178 See further Y. Kaduri (Kugel), "Biblical Interpretation at Qumran", in M. Kister (ed.), *The Qumran Scrolls and Their World* (Between Bible and Mishnah; Jerusalem: Yad Ben Zvi Press, 2009), p. 392–394 (Hebrew).
179 Brown et al., *Preliminary Concordance*, vol. 3, p. 1420.

ג ו

6 הכרתי ואמרֹ|. Newsom reads הכרֹיתי ו^יאמרֹ|. In her opinion, "the scribe did not delete the taw to produce הכרנו ונאמר ('We acknowledged and said')".[180] According to the photographs (esp. PAM 40.969; 42.974), the second letter added above the line is clearly not a *nun*, but a *waw* or a *yod* (cf. the shape of the *waw* in ולֹא [line 8]). Also, there is no evidence that the scribe intended to delete the *taw*, reading הכרני, just as he did not intend to delete the *alef*. The main difficulty is to determine whether he added a *waw* or a *yod*. The context seems to favor the reading וא'מרֹ (cf. וה^חינה [1QHᵃ XIX, 32], where the *ḥet* is written above the *he*, and not the *nun*).

8 כתורֹלֹכֹה|.The first letter may be read either as a *bet* or a medial *kaf*.

9 ללֹל|. There is a trace of another *lamed*, unnoticed in the *DJD* edition (PAM 41.779; 42.819).

Translation

1. [   ] He will show favor to me and He will appoint me[   ]
2. to stand before God and before[the entire congregation   ]
3. my heart, for God will test [my]wor[ds   He will know]
4. and He will test. *vacat* Woe is me fo[r   our iniquities have risen]
5. higher than our heads[   ]
6. you have acknowledged me and I said[   ]
7. upon you, O Lord, and [   ]
8. and not as your appearance[   ]
9. [ ] [ ] [   ]

Comments

1 יֹחֹנני ויתנֹנֹי|. The speaker here may well be the same person as in col. i, i.e. Joshua (Newsom). Yet, while the previous column contains an admonition, here he speaks of his personal standing with God (lines 1-4a) and offers a prayer (lines 4b-8). יֹחֹנני[is a 3ʳᵈ masc. sg. Polel *yiqtol* of חנן, "to favor someone" (written defectively).[181] The *waw* of ויתנֹנֹי is read here as a *waw* conjunctive. The now lost beginning of the line might have read something like [לֹא] / [כֹי or [הוא] / [כֹי.

180 Newsom, "4Q378", p. 248. In the preliminary edition she adds, "Perhaps the intention was to create a double reading, reflecting the scribe's uncertainty about the correct text". Newsom, "4Q378 and 4Q379", p. 46.
181 HALOT, p. 334.

לעמׂׂד לפני אלוה ולׂפׂנׂיׂן כל העדה 2. While in the biblical parlance 'standing before God' frequently refers to the cultic responsibilities of priests and Levites, in the case of Joshua this phrase may point to the description of his appointment as Moses' successor in Num 27:19-22 (והעמדת אתו לפני אלעזר הכהן ולפני כל העדה; cf. also Deut 1:38). The restoration follows Num 27:19. Qimron's reconstruction, כי אין] / לעמׂׂד לפני אלוה ולׂפׂנׂיׂן מלאכיו, seems to disagree with the affirmative language of line 1.

לבי כי אלהים יבחן מלׂן י 3. The beginning of the line might have read יבחן] לבי /י (Jer 12:3; Ps 17:3), ראה] לבי /י (Jer 20:12), or (with Qimron) ידע] / לבי (Ps 139:22). The reconstruction יבחן מלׂ]י (cf. Job 19:23) is that of Qimron (following Newsom's suggestion).

ידע] / ויבחן vacat אוי לי כׂן י 4. The verbs ידע] / ויבחן (Qimron; cf. Jer 6:27) have God as their subject. A blank space next to ויבחן indicates a change in a train of thought. In fact, lines 4b-8 contain a prayer. For the phrase אוי לי כי see Isa 6:5 (cf. הוי על in col. i 7). The pronouncement of woe in both columns supports the assumption that the speaker remains the same. If the entire fragment is related to the Achan's sin, by pronouncing a woe upon himself Joshua demonstrates that he shares the communal responsibility for the transgression. Compare 4Q522 9 ii 10-11, where he admits that he sinned by establishing a covenant with the Gibeonites (Josh 9).

ועוונתינו רבון] / מעלה לראשינׂנו 5. The reconstruction follows Ezra 9:6 (Qimron). For the use of מעלה ל-, instead of the biblical למעלה, compare 4Q403 1 i 28; 11Q5 XII, 12. The line may also be restored as the speaker's personal confession,] ועוונתי רבון] / מעלה לראשי.

הכרתי ואמרׂן 6. I suggest to read here הכרתׂי וא'מׂרׂ. The 2nd masc. sg. Hifil qatal of נכר, "to recognize, acknowledge",[182] הכרתׂי, has God as its subject, while ואומׂר introduces a statement by the speaker.

עליכה אדני ובן 7. This phrase makes clear that this is a prayer (cf. Ps 31:15).

ולא כתורלכׂהן 8. The word כתורלׂכׂה may be parsed as a Qal infinitive of תור, "to spy out" (cf. Num 13:25), or, more likely, as a phonetic spelling of תׂאׂר, "appearance, form" (cf. 1QIsaᵇ LII, 13; 11QPsᵃ XXI, 11; XXVIII, 9; Sir[Ms. M] 43:9, 18).[183] A similar

---

182 BDB, p. 648.

183 Ibid., pp. 1676-77. See further H. Dihi, "The Morphological and Lexical Innovations in the Book of Ben Sira", PhD diss., Ben-Gurion University of the Negev, Beer-Sheva 2004, pp. 705-709 (Hebrew).

interpretation is proposed by Qimron. Still, the precise meaning of this line is unclear.

Frg. 7

[אֱלֹהִים [	] 1
יה]וה אבי̊נ̊]ו	] 2
]ל̊[	] 3

Notes on Readings

2 אבי̊נ̊]ו. Newsom reads אבות̊. The upper tip of a vertical stroke visible on the photographs (PAM 41.779; 43.191) may be read in various ways. According to PAM 41.779, it curves backwards, as in a medial *nun* (cf. the medial *nun* in והניעכה [3 i 6]).

Translation

1   ]God [
2   YH]WH [our] father
3   ] [

Comments

2 יה]וה אבי̊נ̊ו. For this phrase see Isa 63:16, 64:7. Apparently, this is a prayer.

Frg. 8

]א ∘[	1
]שה ועד ה∘[	2
]ה̊שכילו ועד̊[	3
]∘[	4

Translation

1.] [
2.] and until [
3.]they understood and until[
4.   ] [

Comments

3 ה̊שכילו[. Hifil forms of שכל, "to understand, make wise", occur in Josh 1:7, 8 with reference to Joshua.[184] Here the context has been lost.

---

184 HALOT, p. 1328.

Frg. 9

]הֵמֿה[	1
]לֿ ובֿיֿ[	2

Translation
1.   ]they[
2.   ]   [

Frg. 11

]כי יהוה [אלהיכ]מה בֿחֿ]ר[	1 [
לה]עֿמיד דבריו אשר דבר	2]בכם
הנשבע לאברהם לתת	3]לאבותיכמה
]לו ולזרעו אחריו ארץ]טובה ורחבה ארץ נחלי מים	4
]עינות ותהומות יוצאים בב]קעה ובהר ארץ חטה ושעֿו]רה[	5
]גפן תאנה רמון זית שמן ו]דבש כי ארץ זבת חלב ודבֿשֿ	6
]היא לוא תחסר כול בה אב]נֿיה ברזל ומה]רֿ]יֿה נחושה	7
א]יֿן לחקור וירשֿ]תם	8]תחצוב	[
]יֿםֿ[ ]וש]	9 [	[

Notes on Readings
The fragment may contain remains of the top margin (Newsom).

1]בֿחֿ]ר[. The editor reads]מֿ°, yet correctly observes that the extant base and vertical strokes are consistent with a *bet*. A trace of a following vertical stroke may belong to a *resh* ([בֿרֿ]ככמה) or (with Qimron) to a *ḥet*.

5 ושעֿו]רה[. This is Qimron's reading. Newsom reads ושעֿר]ה[. The vertical stroke visible on the fragments can be read both as a *waw* and a *resh*.

9]יֿםֿ[. Abegg & Wacholder read]יֿם[.[185] The *DJD* edition has]יֿ[. On the photographs the upper part of a final *mem* is clearly visible next to a *yod* (e.g. PAM 41.779; cf. the final *mem* in לאברהם [line 3]).

Translation
1. [   ]for YHWH [you]r [God] ch[ose]
2. [you   to] establish his word which he spoke
3. [to your fathers   ] who swore to Abraham, to give

---

185 Abegg & Wacholder, *Preliminary Edition*, p. 172.

4. [to him and to his descendants after him] a good and a broad[land], a land of streams of water

5. [of fountains and springs, flowing forth in the v]alley and in the mountain, a land of wheat and barle[y]

6. [vines, fig trees, pomegranates, olive trees and] honey, for [it is] a land flowing with milk and honey

7. [in which you will lack nothing.]Its [sto]nes are iron and from its moun[tain]s copper

8. [you will mine   wit]hout measure and [you] will take possession

9. [   ] [ ] [   ]

Comments

1 בכם] / בֹּחֹ[ר] [אלהיכ]מה אלהוה [כי יהוה]. This is another 2nd person address, presumably, by Joshua. Its setting is unknown, yet the topic suggests that this discourse precedes the crossing of the Jordan. For the possibility that it is closely related to the speeches in frg. 3 see Discussion. Qimron restores בֹּחֹ[ר] / [באבותיכם. Yet, the scroll seems to refer here to God's choosing of the nation of Israel (cf. Deut 7:7), as the following line presents this act as a fulfillment of the divine promise to the fathers.

2 לאבותיכמה] / דבר אשר דבריו לה]עֹּמיד. This line follows Deut 9:5b. Hence, the reconstruction לאבותיכמה (MT reads אבותיך, yet cf. LXX [τοῖς πατράσιν ὑμῶν] and Tᴶ·ᴺ [לאבהתכון]). Reflecting the Late Biblical Hebrew preference for עמד, the scroll replaces the Deuteronomic למען הקים את הדבר with להעמיד דבריו.[186] It also uses דבר instead of נשבע.

3-4 לו ולזרעו אחריו] / לתת לאברהם הנשבע. While the biblical formulations of the Promise of the Land usually mention the names of the three patriarchs (e.g., Gen 50:24; Exod 33:1; Deut 1:8), the scroll names Abraham alone, probably, as the first and the primary recepient of the promise (cf. 2 Chr 20:7 and the passage in 4Q252 2 8 based on this verse).[187] The antecendent of the Nifal masc. sg. participle of שבע, "to swear", has not been preserved.[188] Qimron restores וירשתם את הארץ] הנשבע לאברהם (cf. Josh 5:6). The restoration לתת [לו ולזרעו אחריו is based on Deut 1:8.

---

186 See A. Hurvitz, "The Linguistic Status of Ben Sira as a Link between the Biblical and the Mishnaic Hebrew: Lexicographical Aspects", in T. Muraoka & J.F. Elwolde, *The Hebrew of the Dead Sea Scrolls and Ben Sira* (STDJ 26; Leiden: Brill, 1997), pp. 78-85; Dihi, "Innovations", pp. 514-516.
187 On the Abrahamic traditions in the Dead Sea scrolls, see the recent discussion by R.G. Kratz, "Friend of God, Brother of Sarah, and Father of Isaac: Abraham in the Hebrew Bible and in Qumran", in D. Dimant & R.G. Kratz (eds.), *The Dynamics of Language and Exegesis at Qumran* (Tübingen: Mohr Siebeck, 2009), pp. 79-105 (and the literature cited there).
188 BDB, p. 989.

ארץ |טובה ורחבה ארץ נחלי מים / |עינות ותהומות יוצאים בב|קעה ובהר 4-5. Citing Deut 8:7, the scroll reads with Smr, 4QDeut[f,j,n], and LXX ורחבה טובה[, apparently under the influence of Exod 3:8.[189] See Discussion.

ארץ חטה ושעו[רה] / |גפן תאנה רמון זית שמן ו|דבש 5-6. Here the scroll follows Deut 8:8. The available space in the beginning of line 6 cannot accommodate the MT's וגפן ותאנה ורמון ארץ זית שמן ודבש. Perhaps, the fragment lacks the word ורמון, thus obtaining two pairs of descriptives ארץ חטה ושער[ה] |גפן ותאנה (reading גפן with Smr and LXX). Alternatively, the scroll may lack the word ארץ, as well as the *waw* before גפן, תאנה (with Smr, 4QDeut[n] and LXX) and רמון (with LXX): וגפן ותאנה ורמון וזית שמן ו[דבש]. Qimron's restoration |גפן תאנה רמון זית שמן ו[דבש seems to be a little long.

כי ארץ זבת חלב ודבש / |היא 6. The inclusion of this formula, borrowed from Exod 3:8 (as in line 4), could have been prompted by the mention of דבש in both Deut 8:8 and Exod 3:8 (this expression occurs also in Josh 5:6). The scroll seems to omit ארץ אשר לא במסכנת תאכל בה לחם.

לא תחסר כול בה אב|נ|יה ברזל ומה|ר|ה נחושה / |תחצוב 7-8. The restoration follows Deut 8:9, omitting the phrase ארץ אשר to accommodate the passage to the lacuna's size (Qimron omits only בה). While the MT has ומהרריה, a form that frequently occurs in a hymnic context (e.g., Deut 33:15[Smr מהרי]),[190] this line has (with 4QDeut[f,j,n] and 5QDeut) a more common form, ומה[ר]יה.[191] The scroll also either transposes (Qimron) or entirely omits the verb תחצב and uses נחושה instead of the MT's נחשת. ברזל and נחושה occur together in numerous biblical passages. Newsom points to a similar formulation in Job 28:2.

א|ין לחקור 8. The phrase א|ין לחקור is synonymous to the recurring biblical expression אין חקר, frequently rendered as "unsearchable,"[192] with no end/measure" (thus also Qimron).[193] Apparently, it describes the abundance of the Promised Land.[194]

---

189 See E. Eshel, "4QDeut[n]—A Text That Has Undergone Harmonistic Edition", *HUCA* 62 (1991), p. 142.

190 Cf. M. Weinfeld, *Deuteronomy 1-1* (AB; New York: Doubleday, 1991), p. 387.

191 Cf. Eshel, "4QDeut[n]", p. 136. Compare 1QIsa[a] to Isa 42:11 reading הררים, while the MT has הרים. Kutscher, *Isaiah*, p. 372, considers הררים to be a later form than הרים.

192 HALOT, p. 348.

193 See H. Yalon, *Studies in the Dead Sea Scrolls* (Jerusalem: Shrine of the Book, America-Israel Cultural Foundation, Kiryat Sefer, 1967), pp. 35-36 (Hebrew).

194 The suggestion by Newsom, "4Q378", p. 252, that this line alludes to Job 28:2-3 "contrasting the normal difficulty of mining with the situation in Canaan, where iron and copper may be obtained without the heavy work of mining (אין לחקור)", seems to be less plausible.

וירש֯[תם. Since this fragment quotes from Deut 8, the verb וירש֯[תם may point to
Deut 8:1, the verse that may underlie the reference to the promise to the Fathers
in lines 2-3.

Frg. 12

ת[פארת]   1

ומלאתם פני] כל תבל בתים]   2

[נֿתן יהוה אלוהֿ]יכם   3

[אֿלֹוהֿ]ים   4

Translation
1.   sp]lendour [
2.   and you will fill the face of] the entire earth with houses [
3.   ]YHWH your Go[d] gave [
4.   ]Go[d

Notes on Readings
2 בתים. Thus reads Qimron. Newsom suggests בתום.

Comments
1 ת[פארת. This fragment seems to belong with the description of the Promised
Land in frg. 11. The restoration ת[פארת, "glory, splendour, radiance",[195] is that
of Newsom.

2 ומלאתם פני] כל תבל בתים. The reference to houses may point to Deut 8:12 (cf.
also 6:11 and Josh 24:13). Qimron restores the phrase כל תבל, with תבל denoting
"mainland" (cf. 4Q369 1 ii 7),[196] as כל תבל [תנובת] (with 1QS X,15). Yet, it seems
more likely that the scroll reworks here Deut 8:12 employing the language of Isa
14:21 (וירשו ארץ ומלאו פני תבל ערים).

3 נתן יהוה אלוהֿ]יכם. Apparently, this is a reference to God's gift of the Promised
Land to His people (Exod 12:25; Deut 1:21).

195 HALOT, pp. 1772-73.
196 Ibid., pp. 1682-1683.

Frg. 13 i

לפ[נ]יכה	1 [
ע[ל פני	2 [
כל ה[מ]מ֗ל֗כות	3 [
הו[ש֗ע את עמי	4 [
כחסדי[ך הטובים	5 [ישראל
למ[ד]֗ני לדעת	6 [
]כ֗ים	7 [
]ת֗י֗	8 [

Notes on Readings

1 לפ[נ]יכה. The *DJD* edition offers no reading of the first letter. The extant base stroke seems to suit well a medial *nun*.

6 למ[ד]֗ני. The last letter may also be read as a *waw* (thus Newsom).

8]ת֗י֗. Newsom reads]ת֗י֗ו֗, yet there are no traces of a third letter on the photographs (PAM 40.969; 41.779; 43.193).

Translation

1. [	befo]re you
2. [	on] the surface of
3. [	all the]kingdoms
4. [	deli]ver my people
5. [Israel	according to] your good [mercies]
6. [	te]ach me to know
7. [	]
8. [	]

Comments

1 לפ[נ]יכה. Lines 4-6 suggest that this 2nd person address is a prayer.

3 כל ה[מ]מ֗ל֗כות. If the speaker is Joshua, this might be an allusion to Deut 3:21-22.

4 הו[ש֗ע את עמי / ישראל]. The first word is clearly a form of ישע. Qimron reconstructs הו[ש֗ע, a 2nd masc. sg. Hifil imperative of ישע, "to help, save".[197] The restoration את עמי / [ישראל] echoes 2 Sam 3:18. If the speaker is Joshua, the use of ישע may

---

reflect a pun on his name, "YHWH is salvation". Similar puns are found in Sir 46:1 (Ms B) and Mat 1:21.

5 הטובים כחסדי]ך. The adjective הטובים may point to such biblical phrases as טובים דבריך (2 Sam 15:3) or משפטיך טובים (Ps 119:39). The proposed restoration follows 4Q185 1-2 ii 1 (cf. כטוב חסדך הצילני [Ps 109:21]). A similar reconstruction is suggested now by Qimron.

6 למ]דֹני לדעת. The first word may be restored as a 2nd masc. sg. Piel imperative of למד, לַמְּד]ֹני (Qimron prefers לַמְּ]דֹנו). Compare לַמֵּד דעת in Ps 94:10, 119:66. Qimron restores לדעת / תורתך]. A fitting occasion for such a prayer by Joshua would be his assumption of leadership after Moses' death.[198] Compare LAB 20:2, where Joshua is commanded to clothe himself with Moses' garments of wisdom and belt of knowledge.[199]

Frg. 13 ii

	]ּי 3

Frg. 14

[ ] ויבכו בני [ישראל את מושה בערבת מואב]	1 [
[על ירדן] ירחו בבית הישימות] עד אבל השטים שלושים יום]	2
[ויתמו ימי בכי]אֹבל מושה ובני ישֹ]ראל	3
הברית א]שֹר כרת יהוה ל°[	4]
פח]דֹך ויראתך [	5]

Notes on Readings

1 | ויבכו בני [. Newsom reads **]ויבכו בני[**. Yet, according to the photographs (PAM 41.779; 43.193) there is a blank space before ויבכו and after בני.

Translation

1. [   ]And the [Israel]ites wept [for Moses in the plains of Moab]
2. [by the Jordan at] Jericho in Beth-Yeshimoth[by Abel-Shittim for thirty days]
3. [And the days of weeping and]mourning for Moses [ended] and the sons of Is[rael

---

[198] Stegemann's reconstruction places this fragment in the third column of the scroll (frg. 14 dealing with the mourning for Moses is Stegemann's col. I).

[199] On sapiential motifs in the LAB's reworking of the Book of Joshua, see Fisk, *Do You Not Remember*, pp. 282-283.

4. [the covenant wh]ich YHWH made with [   ]
5. [dre]ad of you and fear of you [   ]

Comments

1 [ויבכו בני] ישראל את מושה בערבת מואב. This line depends on Deut 34:8a. The description of Moses' death indicates that this fragment might have preceded frgs. 3 and 6. Stegemann suggests that it belongs with the first column of the scroll.

2 [על ירדן] ירחו בבית הישימוֹתֿ] עד אבל השתים שלושים יום. The reconstruction is based on Num 33:48-49 (Newsom). The area from Beth-Yeshimoth to Abel-Shittim was the Israelites' last stop before crossing the Jordan. It is there that the thirty days of the mourning for Moses took place. This, as well as the usage of the phrase בערבת מואב by both passages, might have contributed to the insertion of the geographical data from Num 33:48-49 into Deut 34:8 either by the scroll or its *Vorlage*. A similar reading of Deut 34:8 with Num 33:48 is found in LXX: ἐν Ἀραβὼθ Μωὰβ ἐπὶ τοῦ Ἰορδάνου κατὰ Ἰεριχώ. Newsom notes that the scroll's reading facilitates "the word-play between the name Abel-shittim (אבל השתים) and the reference to the mourning (אבל) for Moses". While the MT reads מבית הישמת, the scroll has בבית (cf. the preposition ב- in בערבת מואב).

3 [ויתמו ימי בכי]אֿבל מֹשה ובני יׁש]ראל. The first part of the line follows Deut 34:8b. Yet, the phrase ובני יׁש]ראל does not appear in the ensuing text of Deut 34.

4 [הברית א]שֿר כרת יהוה לֹ]. The fragment may refer to the covenant with the Fathers or with Israel (for the construction ל- כרת see Exod 23:32; Deut 7:2). Since God is referred to in the 3rd person, lines 4-5 may contain Joshua's address to Israel after the completion of the mourning for Moses.

5 פח]דֿךֿ ויראתך. This phrase points to Deut 2:25. Whereas in this passage God encourages the people to cross the Arnon river, here it may be used with reference to the crossing the Jordan. Qimron reconstructs [היום הזה אחל לתת פח]דֿךֿ ויראתך] על פני העמים .

Frg. 15 i

Frg. 15 consists of two fragments joined together.[200] Yet, the shapes of their edges do not fit well. Thus, they are presented here separately.

---

200 The joint is not depicted on the existing photographs. On the *DJD* plate XIX only one of the two fragments appears.

Frg. a (PAM 41.779):

הׄ∘∘[כי]‏ 1

[לׄוא ימוש מתחתיו תׄ]‏ 2

Notes on Readings

1 הׄ∘∘[. The *DJD* edition reads הׄ[. According to PAM 41.779, there are traces of two more letters before *he*.

Translation

1.   ]   [
2.   ]it will not depart from under him[

Comments

2 לׄוא ימוש מתחתיו. The subject of ימוש, a Qal *yiqtol* of מוש, "to withdraw from a place" (cf. Josh 1:8),[201] and the antecedent of מתחתיו are unknown.

Frg. b i (PAM 43.195; 43.547)

∘∘קׄ[   ]1

[הׄ כי מעשה ידים   ]2

דׄ∘ [   ]לׄ[   ]3

Notes on Readings

1 ∘∘קׄ[. The *DJD* edition reads ף∘[. On the photographs (PAM 43.195; 43.547) there is a vertical stroke projecting below the imaginary base line, as in a *qof* or in a final *pe*. To the left of it bottom tips of two strokes are visible. One may either read here ∘ףׄ∘[or ∘∘קׄ[(in this case, the tiny trace of ink to the right of the vertical stroke belongs to the *qof*'s upper stroke). Since there is only one instance of using a final letter in a medial position in this scroll (3 i 8), the second reading has been adopted here.

Translation

1. [   ]
2. [   ] for work of hands
3. [   ][   ]

---

201 HALOT, p. 561.

Comments

2 כי מעשה ידים. The phrase מעשה ידים occurs frequently in the Hebrew Bible (e.g., Deut 4:28, 27:15, 31:29; cf. 11QTᵃ LIX, 3 [see Comments to frg. 3 i 5, 9 noting parallels to 11QTᵃ LIX, 7-10]) with reference to idolatry (Newsom).

Frg. b ii

]° 2

Frg. 16

בֻּ֯נ֯י[	] 1
מ֯ס֯פֿ֯ר[	] 2
ה֯ כי[	] 3

Notes on Readings

2 מספר[. Strugnell reads נ֯ס֯פֿ֯ר[.[202] The *DJD* edition has נ֯°פֿ֯[. On the photographs (PAM 41.779; 43.195; 43.547) a right vertical stroke, a base stroke descending to the left, and a trace of the upper diagonal stroke of a medial *mem* are visible. The extant traces of the second letter may belong to a *samech*. Its base, as well as the bottom tips of the vertical strokes, is still visible.

Translation

1. [ ]sons of
2. [ ]number
3. [ ] for

Comments

2 מ֯ס֯פֿ֯ר[. This word may be read in several ways: as a masc. sg. Piel participle of סִפֵּר, "to make known, to announce", as a noun מִסְפָּר, "a number", or as a noun סֵפֶר with the preposition מ-, "from a book".

Frg. 17

ו°[	] 1
בֻּ֯ן נום[	] 2
ה°[	] 3

Comments

2 נום בן[. While Newsom renders נום as a form of נום, "to fall asleep",[203] it is possible that this is a phonetic spelling of Joshua's patronimic, נון. Similar interchanges in the representation of a nasal vowel, such as לשון/לשום, are attested to in the Rabbinic sources.[204]

Frg. 18 i

°[2

Frg. 18 ii

כֹֿא°[1
אף שׁ] 2
כי אתה א] 3
י[שראל ול°°[4
הֿ[ ] 5

Translation

1. [
2. even [
3. for you [
4. [I]srael and [
5. [ ] [

Comments

3 כי אתה. This phrase suggests that this fragment contains a 2nd person address (cf. Deut 31:7, 23; Josh 1:6).

Frg. 19 i

וֹעֿ] °[   ] 1
עתיה[   ] 2
אֿ[ ]ל[   ] 3

---

203 HALOT, p. 680.

204 Z. Ben-Ḥayyim, "The Samaritan Tradition and Its Relation to the Language of the Dead Sea Scrolls and to the Rabbinic Hebrew", *Leshonenu* 22 (1958), pp. 232-233 (Hebrew). Note also Kutscher's remarks in his *Isaiah*, pp. 61, 91. My thanks are to Dr. Noam Mizrahi who pointed out this phenomenon to me.

54 —— The Scroll 4Q378

Comments

עתיה] 2. Perhaps, restore, יד[עתיה, "I knew her" (cf. Ezek 11:5).

Frg. 19 ii

```
[ ]°[ ] 2
3 יֹעֲמִיד אלהיֹ[ן]ם דבריו
4 ואנחנו הברנו בכֹחֹ ]
5 וכעבדים אל יד אדוֹנֹ[י]הם
6 ובציא במדבר למקנה לֹכֹ]ה
7 [ובכ]ל שדֹי א[נ]חזתנו ]לֹ[עולם
```

Notes on Readings

3 יֹעֲמִיד. Newsom reads וֹ[י]עֲמִיד. Qimron rightly corrects it to יֹעֲמִיד.

4 בכֹחֹ]. The *DJD* edition has בכֹ[ן, yet according to the photographs (PAM 41.779; 43.195; 43.547), there is a blank space after the *ḥet*. Qimron reads בנח[לתנו. However, the upper horizontal stroke of the third letter resembles that of a medial *kaf*.

7 שדֹי. Strugnell and Newsom read שרי. It is sometimes difficult to distinguish between *resh* and *dalet* in this scroll. Yet, in this case the shape of the letter is similar to that of a *dalet*, as it is inscribed in וכעבדים in line 5.

Translation

3. Go[d] will establish[his words
4. And as for us we grew strong in power [
5. and like slaves to the hand of [their] lord[
6. and in the dry land, in the desert, as an acquisition to yo[u
7. [and in all the] fields of[our] in[heritance] for[ever

Comments

3 יֹעֲמִיד אלהיֹ[ן]ם דבריו. For the reconstruction compare frg. 11 2.

4 ואנחנו הברנו בכֹחֹ. Newsom parses the verb הברנו as a Hifil form of ברר, "sift, cleanse", and renders the line as "And as for us we cleansed".[205] Yet, Qimron suggests that this is a form of ברא,הִבְרָנוּ (cf. 1 Sam 2:29: להבריאכם [MT]; 4QSamᵃ III,

---

205 HALOT, p. 163.

27 has here להבריך), "we grew strong".[206] The construction בכה may be rendered as "in power" (cf. מת[חֹ]זק בֹּכֹוח [1QHᵃ XX, 38) or restored as בכה [יד/ו (cf. Isa 10:13) or בכה [גבורתך/ו (1QS XI, 19). The speaker is unknown, but it may be Joshua. Line 6 is reconstructed as a prayer.

5 וכעבדים אל יד אדונֹ]יהם. This line depends on Ps 123:2. The scroll omits the word עיני and transposes the preposition -כ to עבדים.

6 ובציא במדבר למקנה לֹכֹ]ה. The noun ציא is a phonetic spelling of צִיָּה, "dry landscape, dry region".[207] The synonymous במדבר stands in apposition to ובציא. Newsom reads the word למקנה as a noun מִקְנֶה, "livestock", with the preposition -ל.[208] Perhaps, the scroll alludes here to the biblical imagery of Israel as God's flock (Ezek 34) and refers to the journey from Egypt to the Promised Land. Yet, it is likewise possible to read here לְמִקְנָה, "as an acquisition".[209] In Exod 15:16 Israel is presented as God's acquisition (cf. also Ps 74:2). In this case, the scroll refers to the events of Exodus as the time when Israel became God's own possession. Thus, it is proposed to restore לְךֹ]ה, "for you", namely God. If this reconstruction is correct, this is a prayer.

7 ובכ]ל שדֹי א]חזתנו לֹ]עולם. The reconstruction follows that of Qimron with slight alterations. For the expression שדה אחזתו, with אחזה denoting "property", see Lev 27:16.[210] The restoration לְ]עולם echoes the depiction of the Promised Land as אחזת עולם (Gen 17:8, 48:4).

Frg. 20 i

vacat]	] 5
אֹשֹר[	] 6

Notes on Readings

5 According to the photographs (PAM 41.779; 43.195; 43.547) there is an uniscribed surface in line 5.

206 HALOT, p. 154; M. Sokoloff, *A Dictionary of Jewish Palestinian Aramaic of the Byzantine Period* (Ramat Gan: Bar Ilan University Press, Baltimore and London: The Johns Hopkins University Press, 2002), p. 112.
207 HALOT, p. 1022. For the use of *alef* as a *mater lectionis* in DSS see Qimron, "Dissertation", pp. 66-67; idem, *Hebrew*, p. 23.
208 HALOT, p. 628.
209 Ibid.
210 Ibid., p. 32.

Translation

6 [   ]which

Frg. 20 ii

1] [א הֹ[
2] [בינה לו]
3] [כֹיֹ כן הוא °[
4 לאמור] [לֹ]
5 ולתת הון ל[
6 ל[ ] [אֹֹדֹ°[

Notes on Readings

2 הֹ[. Newsom offers no reading for the traces of the first letter. On PAM 41.779 the left vertical and the upper horizontal strokes of a *he* are visible (Abegg & Wacholder).[211]

3 כֹיֹ [. The *DJD* edition has כֹיֹ[. However, according to the photographs (esp. PAM 41.779; 43.195; 43.547), there is a blank space before the medial *kaf*.

6 אֹֹדֹ[. The editor suggests °°אֹ[. According to PAM 43.547 what she reads as traces of two letters is, in fact, a vertical stroke of a *dalet* and a serif on the left extremity of its upper horizontal stroke.

Translation

1. [   ] [
2. [   ] understanding to him [
3. [   ]for thus he [
4. saying[ ] [
5. and to give wealth to[
6. [   ]   [

Comments

2 בינה לו[. If read as a noun, בִּינָה denotes an "understanding" (cf. Dan 10:1).[212] Perhaps, restore, וית]ן בינה לו (for נתן בינה see Job 38:36) or אי]ן בינה לו (Qimron [with Pr 30:2]). It is also possible to read בינה as a Qal masc. sg. imperative of בין, "understand, pay attention, consider" (cf. Job 9:11).[213]

---

211 Abegg & Wacholder, *Preliminary Edition*, vol. 3, p. 175.
212 HALOT, p. 123.
213 Ibid.

3 כֹּ֗י כן הוא [. The word כן may denote "righteous, honest", as well as "thus, in the same manner". Accordingly, the line may be rendered either as "for honest is he" (cf. Gen 42:33) or as "for thus he" (cf. 1 Sam 8:8).

5 לתת הון לו. The noun הון denotes "wealth, property".[214] For a possible use with a reference to a bribe, see 4Q160 7 3. For the phrase נתן הון see Pr 6:31; Song 8:7; 1QpHab IX, 6.

Frg. 21

[גלוה ות∘]	1
[הֹנֹה האלהים]	2
[ת וַיירד] [ ]∘ [	3

Notes on Readings

1 גלוה[. The *DJD* edition has גליה[. Since *waw* and *yod* are frequently indistinguishable in this scroll, one may also read גלוה[. See Comment.

2 הֹנֹה[. Newsom reads הֹנ∘[. According to the photographs (PAM 41.779; 43.195; 43.547) the shape of the third letter is more consistent with a *he*, than with a *ḥet*. As to the first letter, the traces that are visible on PAM 41.779 resemble a *he*.

3 ת[ ]∘ [. The editor proposes את [. The traces of the first letter seem to be more consistent with a *bet* or a *dalet*. Still, given the uncertainty, no reading is offered here. There seem to be a letter-size lacuna between this letter and the *taw* (see esp. PAM 41.779).

4 וַיירד[. Newsom reads הירד[. However, what she takes to be a right vertical stroke of a *he*, has a characteristic hook-shaped top and is separated from the following letter of the same shape by a short blank space as between two adjacent letters (PAM 41.779).

Translation
1.] they disclosed her/it [
2.]this is the God[
3.] and he went down [

---

214 HALOT, p. 242.

Comments

1 גלוה[. Perhaps, a 3rd masc. pl. *qatal* Piel of גלה, "uncover, disclose", with a 3rd fem. sg. objective suffix.[215] One may also consider a reconstruction ה[ג]לוה, a 3rd masc. pl. Hifil form of גלה, "to deport", with a 3rd. fem. sg. objective suffix.[216]

2 [הֹנה האלהים. For the language compare Isa 40:9; Ps 54:6.

3 [ויירד. The subject of this *wayyiqtol* form of ירד is unknown.

Frg. 22 i

top margin

[משה אלהי ולא הֹכחדתֹם באשממתם	]1
ונתת את [עֹמֹך ביד ישוע משרת עבדך משה	]2
ונתת מהו[דך ביד משה על ישוע למען עמך	]3
בריתכ]הֹ אשר כֹ[רת]הֹ עם אברהם	]4
עושה [חֹסד לאֹלפים [ ]°[	]5

Notes on Readings

1 משה [. Newsom reads [משה. However, there is a blank space before the medial *mem*.

4 בריתכ]הֹ. Qimron reads and restores in this way. Strugnell reads בר]יֹתֹי,[217] while the *DJD* edition offers no reading.

5 [°[. Newsom reads [שׁ[. However, the traces of the letter(s) visible on the fragment are illegible.

Translation

1. [   ] Moses, O my God, and you did not efface them in their guilt
2. [and you gave]your people into the hand of Joshua, the minister of your servant Moses
3. [and you gave of your spl]endour by the hand of Moses to Joshua for the sake of your people
4. [you]r[covenant] which yo[u ma]de with Abraham
5. [   ] [showing]mercy to thousands

215 HALOT.
216 Ibid., p. 191-92.
217 Brown et al., *Preliminary Concordance*, vol. 1, p. 520.

Comments

1 משה אלהי ולא הֻכחדתֻם באשמתם. This is a prayer referring to both Moses and Joshua in the 3rd person.[218] The identity of the speaker is not made clear. The recollection of Joshua's appointment in lines 2-3 makes Eleazar a possible candidate (Newsom; Tov).[219] This line seems to refer to the period of Moses' leadership. The phrase ולא הֻכחדתֻם באשמתם (cf. Ezra 9:13; 2Chr 24:18) points to an event(s), when Israel was spared, apparently, due to Moses' intercession, such as the Golden Calf (Exod 32; Newsom) and the twelve spies (Num 14) episodes. Tov's suggestion that the object of the verb הֻכחדתֻם, a 2nd masc. sg. Hifil *qatal* of כחד, "to efface",[220] are the Gibeonites (Josh 9), does not tally well with the mention of Moses.[221] Qimron restores ותשמע אל [משה.

2 משה עבדך משרת ישוע ביד עֹמֹד] ונתת את. For the restoration ונתת את [עֹמֹד ביד compare 2 Sam 10:10. Qimron reconstructs כי דברתה להושיע את [עֹמֹד. For the spelling ישוע see Neh 8:17; CD V, 4; 1Q22 I, 12; 4Q175 21; 4Q379 22 ii 7; 4Q522 9 ii 14; 5Q9 1 1. Num 11:28 and Josh 1:1 refer to Joshua as Moses' minister. Moses is called God's servant in multiple passages. Both appellations occur in close proximity to each other in Josh 1:1.

3 ונתת מהו]דך ביד משה על ישוע למען עמד. The fragment may allude to Num 27:16-23. The reconstruction ונתת מהו]דך follows v. 20. If correct, the scroll ascribes הוד, "splendour, majesty" (in Num 27:20 usually rendered as "authority") not to Moses, as in the biblical verse, but to God.[222] The phrase ביד משה seems to point to Moses' laying of hands on Joshua (vv. 19, 23). Qimron offers an alternative reconstruction צויתה בחס]דך.

4 בריתכ]ה אשר כֹ]רתֹה עם אברהם. The reference to the Covenant with Abraham (cf. Ps 105:8-9[=1Chr 16:15-16]) occurs also in frg. 11 3. It is unknown whether the fragment listed the names of all the three patriarchs, or of Abraham alone, as in frg. 11 3. Qimron restores להקים את בריתכ]הֻ.

5 עושה]חסד לאלפים. This is Qimron's restoration (with Exod 20:6; Deut 5:10; cf. also נצר חסד לאלפים [Exod 34:7]). The occasion for this prayer is unknown. Joshua's assumption of leadership after Moses' death (frg. 3) could provide a suitable setting (note, however, that Stegemann places this fragment in col. XI). Other possible occasions which could prompt a recollection of God's mercies, Joshua's

---

218 Thus Joshua cannot be the speaker here, as Berthelot, "Joshua", p. 99, proposes.
219 Tov, "Rewritten Joshua", p. 248.
220 HALOT, p. 469.
221 Tov, "Rewritten Joshua", p. 249.
222 HALOT, p. 241.

appointment, and the Covenant with Abraham are the crossing of the Jordan and the siege of Jericho.

Frg. 22 ii

]° 3
]לו[4
]מֿ[5
]° 6

Notes on Readings

4]לו. The *DJD* edition has]לוֹאֿ. However, there are no traces of the third letter on the photographs (PAM 41.504; 41.779; 43.195; 43.547).

5]מֿ. Newsom reads]אוֹ. On the photographs (PAM 41.504; 41.779; 43.195; 43.547) the base, the vertical and the upper horizontal strokes of the medial *mem* are clearly visible. There are no traces of another letter next to it.

Frg. 23

]בֿהֿם ולוא יועלֿו 1
]ה כי להֿ 2
]בימים °°הֿ 3

Notes on Readings

3]הֿ°°. Newsom reads הֿהמֿ]ה. However, the surviving traces of ink do not support this reading. It is unclear whether there are traces of three or four letters. The first one (or two?) is illegible. The next letter might be either a *resh* or a *waw/yod*. The last letter is clearly a *he* (see esp. PAM 43.547).

Translation

1.]in them and [they] will do no good[
2.] for [
3.]in the days [

Comment

1]בֿהֿם ולוא יועלֿו. Newsom reads ולוא יועלֿ], yet in view of the plural בֿהֿם the restoration יועלֿ[ו, a 3ʳᵈ masc. pl. Hifil *yiqtol* of יעל (spelled defectively, as in Jer 2:8, 12:13), "to profit, benefit", seems fitting.[223] The phrase לא יועילו frequently occurs in the Hebrew Bible with reference to idolatry (cf. 1 Sam 12:21; Jer 2:8, 12:13).

---

223 HALOT, p. 420.

Frg. 24

‏[תו]	1
‏[הֿ ונֿ]	2
‏א[ת אשמֿ]ת	3
‏]∘ ∘[	4

Notes on Readings

2 ‏תו[. Newsom reads]∘ ת[. However, according to the photographs (PAM 43.195; 43.547) the second letter is clearly a *waw* or a *yod*. Moreover, there is no blank space between the two (Abegg & Wacholder).[224]

4]∘ ∘[. There is a blank space between the traces of the two letters.

Translation

1.] [
2.] [
3. th]e gui[lt of
4.] [

Comments

3 ‏א[ת אשמֿ]ת. The second word seems to be a form of the noun ‏אשמה, "guilt".[225] The theme of guilt is featured in frg. 6 i-ii.

Frg. 25

‏שנא∘[‏[	1
‏]∘ ∘[	2

Notes on Readings

1 ‏שנא∘[. Newsom reads] ‏שנא[. According to the photographs (PAM 43.195; 43.547), there is a blank space before the *shin*, indicating that this is the first letter of this word. Next to the *alef* a trace of a vertical stroke is visible. Perhaps, it is a *waw* or a *he*. It has been also noted by Abegg & Wacholder who read]∘‏אשנ[.[226]

---

224 Abegg & Wacholder, *Preliminary Edition*, vol. 3, p. 176.
225 HALOT, p. 96.
226 Abegg & Wacholder, *Preliminary Edition*, vol. 3, p. 176.

Frg. 26

1 [יוד]ע [ד]ֿעת עליון ומֿ[חזה שדי יחזה

2 דברי תור]ה הֿ[ג]ֿיד לנו איש האלהים מפי יֿ]הוה

3 [ועדת עליוֿן הֿקֿ[ש]ֿיבו לקול מֿ[ן השמים

4 [°°ו ובֿ]   [אֿלהים עליוֿ]ן

5 [מפתים גדולים ובחמה יעצר] מגפה

6 [אֿיש הֿ[ח]סֿדים ועד לעלמיה זכור]

7 [°תֿ° עד למ]

8] vacat

9 [אֿ[°]   [°°]   [יֿכֿהֿ]

Notes on Readings

1 יוד]ע. Newsom reads [יוד]ֿע. However, there are no traces of ink before the *yod* on the photographs (PAM 40.615; 41.779; 43.195; 43.547). Qimron also reads [יוד]ע. **ד]ֿעת**. The *DJD* edition has [דֿעת. Yet, there is no blank space before the *dalet*, which has been partially destroyed by the hole in the leather. Thus one should read with Strugnell [דֿעת.[227]

2 הוה]ֿי. Newsom offers no reading for a trace of a vertical stroke surviving in the end of the line. Perhaps, one may read here a *yod* or a *he* (Qimron).

3 ועדת [. The *DJD* edition has [ועדת. However, there is a letter-size blank space before this word. Strugnell reads [ועדת.[228]

4 °°ו[. The editor reads [מֿיו. The last letter is clearly a *waw* or a *yod*. Yet, the preceding traces of one or two letters are illegible. Abegg & Wacholder also read [°ֿי.[229]

6 אֿיש[. Newsom reads א[יֿש. On the photographs (PAM 40.615; 41.779; 43.195; 43.547) the left stroke of an *alef* is partially visible. Qimron also reads in the same way.

Translation

1.] (one) kno[wing] the knowledge of the Most High and[(one) seeing]the vi[sion of the Almighty

2. the words of Tora]h the man of God made [k]nown to us from the mouth of Y[HWH

3.] and the congregation of the Most High g[ave] ear to the voice f[rom heaven

227 Brown et al., *Preliminary Concordance*, vol. 2, p. 787.
228 Ibid., vol. 4, p. 1524.
229 Abegg & Wacholder, *Preliminary Edition*, vol. 3, p. 177.

4.] [ ]God Most Hig[h
5.]great signs and in wrath he stopped[the plague
6.]man of pi[o]us deeds. And forever remember [
7.] until [
8.] *vacat*
9.] [ ] [ ]your[

Comments

1 יודֿ]ע]דֿעת עליון ומֿ]חזה שדי יחזה. This line uses the language of Num 24:16, describing Balaam, to depict Moses (Newsom). The wording of this passage fits Moses rather well, as he is said to "behold the likeness of the Lord" (Num 12:8). The next line seems to suggest that Moses' "seeing]the vi[sion of the Almighty" has to do with his role during the giving of the Law at Sinai (cf. 4Q377 2 ii 10-11). If the proposed reconstruction, based on Num 24:16, is correct (see also Num 24:4), then the fragment reads ומֿ]חזה, instead of the MT's מחזה. It is unclear whether scroll cited also Num 24:16a (שמע אמרי אל וידע דעת עליון). If it did, one may consider reading וֿיֿדֿ]ע[(as in 4Q175 10), as *waw* and *yod* are frequently indistinguishable in this scroll.

2 הוה[יֿ מפי האלהים איש לנו יֿ]גֿ[ד הֿ]ה תור]דברי. Lines 2 and 3 seem to refer to the Sinai revelation. This line focuses on Moses' transmitting the divine words to the people. Among the possible reconstructions are דבר יהו]ה הֿ]גֿ[יֿד לנו (with Deut 5:5), מצו]ה הֿ]גֿ[יֿד לנו (Qimron), and דברי תור]ה הֿ]גֿ[יֿד לנו (cf. Deut 28:58; 1Q22 I, 4, II, 9). Moses is also called איש האלהים in frg. 3 i 4. For the restoration מפי יֿ]הוה see Jer 23:16; 4Q377 2 ii 11.

3 השמים מֿ]ן לקול יֿבו הֿ]קֿ[שֿ הֿ]קֿ[שֿ עליון ועדת. Newsom restores הֿ]קֿ[שֿ]יֿבו לקול מֿ]שה (for the phrase הקשב לקל see Jer 6:17; for קול מושה cf. CD I, 16). In light of the Deuteronomic הֿ]קֿ[שֿ]יֿבו לקול (4:36), it is proposed to reconstruct here קלו את השמיעך השמים מן. מֿ]ן השמים. If correct, while line 2 speaks of Moses' reporting God's words to Israel at Sinai, this line refers to their listening to the divine voice.[230] The phrase עדת עליון, synonymous to the biblical 'עדת ה (e.g., Josh 22:16, 17), replaces the Tetragrammaton with the appellation "Most High" employed also in the next line.

4 עליון אֿ]לֿהים. For this collocation see Ps 57:3, 78:56.

---

230 This fragmentary passage may have tried to reconcile the diverging biblical reports on the modes of the divine communication with Israel at Sinai, as does, for instance, 4Q377 2 ii. On the latter see A. Feldman, "The Sinai Revelation according to 4Q377 (Apocryphal Pentateuch B)", *DSD* 18 (2011), pp. 155-172.

5 מפתים גדולים ובחמה יעצר] מגפה. The phrase מפתים גדולים seems to refer to the events of Exodus (cf. Deut 6:22, 29:2). The reconstruction יעצר] מגפה is that of Qimron. He suggests that the scroll alludes here to Moses' role in stopping a plague resulting from divine wrath, as in Num 17:13.

6 א̇[יש ה̇]ח]ס̇דים ועד לעלמיה זכור. The soubriquet א̇[יש ה̇]ח]ס̇דים is borrowed from the blessing of Levi in Deut 33:8 (cf. 4Q175 14). The Deuteronomic לאיש חסדך may be vocalized as לאיש חַסְדָ(י)ךָ or לאיש חֲסָדָ(י)ךָ. Both appellations are applied to Moses in 4Q377 2 i 8, 12 (the latter occurs also in 4Q398 14-17 ii 1 with reference to David).[231] Assuming that א̇[יש ה̇]ח]ס̇דים is not a defective spelling of איש החסידים ("one of the pious ones"), it is rendered here as "a m[a]n of pious de[e]ds". While the referent is not explicit, the context, as well as the usage of this soubriquet in 4Q377, suggests that the scroll refers here to Moses, the grandson of Levi.[232]

ועד לעלמיה זכור. This phrase seems to open a new phrase. For the construction ועד לעלמיה see frg. 6 i 6. The verb זכור is apparently a Qal imperative. It indicates that the fragment contains an admonitory discourse. The identity of the speaker is unknown, yet it may well be Joshua or Eleazar. Such a discourse, featuring Moses' unique role, would form an appropriate eulogy for him (cf. frg. 14),[233] yet the setting of this speech remains elusive (Stegemann places this fragment toward the end of the scroll, in col. XIII).

Frg. 27

top margin

ל[מען	] 1
[בר	] 2

Translation

1 [so] that

2 [ ]

---

231 See Feldman, "Revelation", p. 168.

232 Aramaic Targums (T^Ps-J,F,N) interpret this passage as referring to Aaron. A similar interpretation seems to underlie Sif. Deut. 349 (ed. Finkelstein, p. 408). On the other hand, in Lev. Rab. 1:4 (ed. Margaliot, p. 15) it is applied to Moses.

233 Compare Joshua's eulogy for Moses in the Arabic Book of Joshua in Crane, *Samaritan Chronicle*, pp. 31-33

Frg. 28

]אני[	1
]°זן לה[	2
]°לֹה ל°[	3

Translation
1.   ]I[
2.   ]   [
3.   ]   [

Frg. 29

]°°°[	1
]°י מאבנ[י	2

Notes on Readings
2]°י[. Newsom reads]י[. On PAM 43.195 a trace of a letter preceding the *yod* is visible.

Translation
1.   ]   [
2.   ] from the stone[s

Comments
2 מאבנ]י. This might be an allusion to Josh 4:1-9 or 8:30-35.

2.5 Discussion

The foregoing analysis of 4Q378 suggests several topics for further study. First, its account of the transition from Moses' leadership to that of Joshua diverges from the biblical one both in its scope and details. Second, the scroll's representation of Joshua and Moses deserves further consideration. Third, the scriptural quotations and allusions in 4Q378 should be scrutinized in order to learn about its *Vorlage(n)*. Finally, its placement within the wider corpus of Qumran literature has to be explored.

2.5.1 Joshua's Succession in 4Q378

The biblical description of Joshua's succession is rather brief. Deut 34:9 remarks on the Israelites' obedience to Joshua. Joshua 1 opens with a divine address to

Joshua (1-9), followed by the account of his preparations for the crossing of the Jordan (10-18). The author of the scroll seems to have envisioned a somewhat different scenario. This scenario seems to have included Joshua's address to Israel following the mourning for Moses (frg. 14 4-5?),[234] his prayer (frg. 13 i?), and, most importantly, two discourses (frg. 3 i-ii), which Dimant demonstrated to be Joshua's address to the people (frg. 3 i) and their response to him (frg. 3 ii).[235]

Since the second discourse (frg. 3 ii) alludes to Josh 1:16-18, it seems that both speeches are to be located within the narrative framework of Josh 1. Yet, while the people's reply employs phraseology found in Josh 1:16-18, there seem to be no verbal links between Joshua's discourse in frg. 3 i and his speeches in Josh 1:10-15. Rather, the tone and the language of Joshua's address in frg. 3 i echo his speeches in Josh 23-24, where he warns against abandoning God and describes the punishment that will befall the unfaithful (esp. 23:11-16, 24:19-20). Among several verbal allusions to Josh 23-24, the reference to Israel's future intermarriage with the nations, featured in frg. 3 i 1-2, seems to point to Joshua's warning in Josh 23:12.[236]

Even more obvious is the dependence of Joshua's speech in frg. 3 i on the Mosaic prophetic warnings from Deut 28 and 31.[237] This reiteration of Moses' admonitions by Joshua may point to the opening words of Joshua's address to the Trans-Jordanian tribes in Josh 1:13: "Remember what Moses the servant of the Lord enjoined upon you". While it refers to their promise to Moses to assist the ten tribes in the conquest of the land to the west of Jordan, this phrase could have served as a peg on which the author of 4Q378 hung Joshua's speech.

Deuteronomy 28 features not only curses, but also blessings for obedience. Similarly, Joshua's discourses in Josh 23-24 warn of divine punishment, yet also recount the divine blessings (23:5-6, 9-10, 15, 24:20), including the abundance of the "good" Land (23:13, 24:13). The description of the Land in Josh 24:13, 16,

---

234 Compare the reworking of the Book of Joshua in J. Ant. 5 which opens with a recapitulation of Moses' death and the subsequent mourning.

235 Dimant, "Two Discourses", pp. 58-59.

236 Compare LAB 21:1 where Joshua alludes to Exod 34 and foretells Israel's future mingling with the nations. Note also Jub 30:14-15 invoking intermarriage as the reason for Israel's being punished by plagues and curses. On intermarriage in Second Temple sources see C. Werman, "Jubilees 30: Building a Paradigm for the Ban on Intermarriage", HTR 90 (1997), 1-22; S.J.D. Cohen, *The Beginnings of Jewishness* (Berkeley, Los Angeles, London: University of California Press, 1999), pp. 241-262; C.E. Hayes, "Intermarriage and Impurity in Ancient Jewish Sources", HTR 92 (1999), pp. 3-36; idem, *Gentile Impurities and Jewish Identities: Intermarriage and Conversion from the Bible to the Talmud* (New York: Oxord University Press, 2002); H. Harrington, "How Does Intermarriage Defile the Sanctuary", in G.J. Brooke et al. (eds.), *The Scrolls and Biblical Traditions* (STDJ 103; Leiden: Brill, 2012), pp. 177-195.

237 As noted by Newsom, "4Q378", p. 238.

reminiscent of Deut 8:7, 12, may help link Joshua's discourse in frg. 3 i to a second person address found in frg. 11 (and frg. 12) describing the treasures of the Promised Land and citing Deut 8. Since both Deut 28 and Josh 23-24 serve as literary models for Joshua's address in 4Q378, it seems likely that the speech in frgs. 11-12 should also be attributed to Joshua. Perhaps, it either followed or preceded the verbal exchange recorded in frg. 3.[238]

The people's answer to Joshua in frg. 3 ii expands the response by the Transjordanian tribes to Joshua in Josh 1:16-18. Reworking it into a full-blown address by the entire nation, the scroll employs phraseology found in the description of Joshua's commission in Deut 31 and in the people's reply to Joshua in Josh 24.[239] It also refers to Moses' appointment of the officers (Exod 18; Deut 1), apparently suggesting that Joshua is to be obeyed because he is also Moses' appointee.[240]

The scroll 4Q378 is not the only Second Temple text to rework Josh 1 (cf. J. Ant. 5.1-4).[241] Of particular interest for this study is Pseudo-Philo's account of the transition of the leadership from Moses to Joshua (LAB 20). As 4Q378, LAB expands the biblical story with an admonitory Moses-like speech by Joshua, featuring reward and punishment (20:3-4):

> "Behold now, all you tribes, be aware today that if you go in the ways of your God, you will prosper. If however you do not heed his voice and you be like your fathers, your affairs will be ruined and you yourself will be crushed and your name will perish from the earth..."[242]

---

238 Stegemann assigns frg. 11 to col. IX. Yet, the shape of the fragment suggests that it might have come next to frg. 3. Prof. Annette Steudel observes that the physical evidence in this case is inconclusive and both Stegemann's sequence of the fragments and the one proposed here are equally plausible (personal communication). I am grateful to Prof. Steudel and her students who took time to check this issue for me.

239 D.M. Howard, "All Israel's Response to Joshua: A Note on the Narrative Framework of Joshua 1", in A.B. Beck et al. (eds.), *Fortunate the Eyes that See* (Grand Rapids, Michigan, Cambridge, U.K.: Eerdmans, 1995), pp. 81-91, argues that Josh 1:16-18 is, in fact, a response by the entire Israel. This interpretation is mentioned also by R. Polzin, *Moses and the Deuteronomist: A Literary Study of the Deuteronomic History: Part One: Deuteronomy, Joshua, Judges* (New York: The Seabury Press, 1980), p. 79.

240 In the Temple Scroll (11QTª LVII, 3-5) the appointment of the officials is one of the prerogatives of the king. The author of 4Q378 might have also regarded Moses' appointment of the officials as one of the expressions of his authority and therefore mentions it as an example of people's obedience to Moses.

241 See Begg's notes in his, *Josephus*, p. 3.

242 Jacobson, *Pseudo-Philo*, p. 124.

As in 4Q378 3 ii, the people respond to him, accepting his divinely ordained leadership (LAB 20:5):

> "The people said to him, "Behold, we see today what Eldad and Medad prophesied in the days of Moses, saying, 'After Moses' death, the leadership of Moses will be given to Joshua the son of Nun.' Moses was not jealous, but rejoiced when he heard them. From then on all the people believed that you would exercise leadership over them and apportion the land to them. Now even if there is a conflict, be strong and resolute, because you alone will be ruler in Israel".

Not only do both 4Q378 and LAB include in the people's response a justification of Joshua's assumption of Moses' office, but they also recast the Transjordanians' reply to Moses, "be strong and resolute", as the entire nation's response.

Some of the exegetical strategies utilized by 4Q378 in reworking Josh 1 are shared by a Samaritan work, the so-called Arabic Book of Joshua. According to this work, following God's address to Joshua (paralleling Josh 1:1-8), the latter assembled priests, Levites, officials, and the entire Israel. In his address to them he recalled their past violations of God's will and urged them to renew the covenant with God. Joshua recounted the blessings and warned them of the divine punishment "written in the book of Wrath and Curse". Heavily influenced by Joshua's farewell speeches and Mosaic Deuteronomic discourses, this address is followed by people's response expanding on the Transjoranian tribes' answer in Josh 1:16-18:

> "The congregation of the children of Isrâîl answered him ... saying: „O our master and our lord, we hear and will obey the command of God–Mighty and Powerful–and of His true and faithful Prophet, and also thy command, O king ... and there will be no opposition to what ye order, and no deviation from what ye say either to the right or to the left ... and whoever shall rebel and deviate, and act treacherously, let upon him be the Curse and Wrath, for after this manner did our master Mûsa, the Prophet–peace be upon him–agree with us and impose conditions upon us, and put us under oath, and covenant with us ... and we answered him as we have answered you."[243]

While each of these texts reworks Josh 1 in its own way, all of them envisioned the transition from Moses to Joshua as accompanied by an extensive verbal ex-

---

243 Crane, *Samaritan Joshua*, p. 38. See also a shorter version of Joshua's address and people's response in the Chronicle of Abu L'Fath in Stenhouse, *Kitāb*, p. 9.

change between Joshua and the people, focusing on the obedience to God and the nation-wide acceptance of Joshua's leadership.

2.5.2 Joshua and Moses in 4Q378

By modeling Joshua's speeches in frg. 3 ii (and, possibly, in frgs. 11, 12, 14 5) on the Mosaic discourses, 4Q378 draws parallels between the two men, a tendency well attested already in the biblical account.[244] As it depicts Joshua reiterating Mosaic prophetic warnings (frg. 3 ii), the scroll presents him as a prophetic figure, indeed, as a prophet like Moses (Deut 18:18).[245] Frg. 22 i may even put Joshua almost on par with Moses, as he seems to receive there a share of God's "splendor (הוד)", and not that of Moses, as in Num 27:20. Yet, Moses is not the only biblical figure who serves as a model for Joshua in this scroll. Joshua's admonitory address and prayer in frg. 6 i 3-4, ii 5 allude to Ezra's penitential prayer in Ezra 9. The request for knowledge in frg. 13 i 6 recalls Solomon's plea for wisdom and knowledge in 2 Chr 1:10.

At the same time, the scroll highlights the unique role of Moses. It refers to him as "a man upright and great" (3 ii 5-6), a play on Job's description as "blameless and upright" (Job 1:1), "the man of God" (26 2), "man of pi[o]us deeds" (26 6), and the one who "kno[ws] the knowledge of the Most High and[sees]the vi[sion of the Almighty" (26 1). The latter designation is borrowed from Balaam's description in Num 24:16 and is re-applied in 4Q378 to Moses within the context of the Sinai revelation where he transmits God's words to the people.[246]

---

244 On the parallels in the biblical depiction of Moses and Joshua, see E. Assis, "Divine versus Human Leadership: An Examination of Joshua's Succession", in M. Poorthuis & J. Schwartz (eds.), *Saints and Role Models in Judaism and Christianity* (Jewish and Chrsitian Perspectives Series 7; Leiden, Boston: Brill, 2004), pp. 26-42 (esp. pp. 37-42); S.B. Chapman, "Joshua son of Nun: Presentation of a Prophet", in J.J. Ahn & S.L. Cook (eds.), *Thus Says the Lord: Essays on the Former and Latter Prophets in Honor of Robert R. Wilson* (New York: T & T Clark, 2009), pp. 13-26; Corley, "Canonical Assimilation", p. 63.
245 On Joshua as a "prophet like Moses" in the biblical account and in Ben Sira, see Chapman, ibid., pp. 20-21; Corley, "Canonical Assimilation", pp. 63-64, 71-72.
246 Jassen, *Mediating*, pp. 249-250, suggests that the application of Num 24:16 to Moses identifies him "as a recipient of revelation like Balaam", namely of a sapiential revelation. Thus, he classifies 4Q378 as an "apocryphal-sapiential text". Yet, this classification, as well as Jassen's interpretation of this line, is difficult, primarily because he leaves it unclear in what way 4Q378 recasts the Sinai revelation as a sapiential revelation. It seems more likely that the use of Num 24:16 reflects an attempt to magnify Moses. For the comparison of Moses and Balaam in the Rabbinic literature see Sif. Deut. 357 (ed. Finkelstein, p. 430). See further L.H. Feldman, "The Rehabilitation of Non-Jewish Leaders in Josephus' Antiquities", in idem, *Judaism and Hellenism*

2.5.3 Biblical Quotations and Allusions in 4Q378

In several instances the scroll's citations and praphrases of biblical passages may suggest a *Vorlage* diverging from the Masoretic Text.[247] These can be grouped as following:

1. Variations in the use of prepositions and conjunctions:

   Num 24:16 (frg. 26 1) דחיזו 4Q175 10 אשר מחזה M Smr מחזה **[** מחזה G S V T[N] ומ]חזה) SmrT T[O,Ps-J]

   Num 33:49 (frg. 14 2) מבית M 2QNum[b] G (ἀνὰ μέσον) S V SmrT T[O,Ps-J,N] **|** בבית

   Josh 1:17 (frg. 3 ii 5) אל משה M **|** למושה

2. Morphological variations:

   Deut 8:9 (11 7) ומהרריה M Smr **|** 5QDeut 4QDeut[f,j,n] ומה]ר[יّه

   Deut 8:9 (11 7) נחשת M Smr 4QDeut[f,j,n] 5QDeut **|** נחושה

   Deut 31:17 (3 i 5) לא'כלה Smr G ([καὶ ἔσται] κατάβρωμα) S (ܠܡܐܟܘܠܬܐ) T[N] לאכל M **|** (לאוכלה) 4QDeut[c] LIX, 7 11QT[a] (למזון)

3. Minuses:

   Frg. 11 5-7 citing Deut 8:8-9 contains a shorter text than the MT (see Comments ad loc.)[248]

4. Pluses:

   In frg. 14 1-2 geographical data from Num 33:48-49 are introduced into a citation from Deut 34:8:

   1 [   ] ויבכו בני [ישראל את מושה בערבת מואב]
   2 [על ירדן] ירחו בבית הישימות֗ עד אבל השטים שלושים יום]

Reconsidered (SJSJ 107; Leiden: Brill, 2006), p. 588 note 8. On the ancient interpretations of the figure of Balaam, see G.H. van Kooten & J. van Ruiten, *The Prestige of the Pagan Prophet Balaam in Judaism, Early Christianity and Islam* (Leiden: Brill, 2008).

247 On the quest for the *Vorlagen* of the Rewritten Bible texts see, for instance, G. Brin, "The Bible as Reflected in the Temple Scroll", *Shnaton* 4 (1979-80), pp. 182-225 (Hebrew); E. Tov, "The Temple Scroll and Old Testament Textual Criticism", *Eretz-Israel* 16 (1982), pp. 100-111 (Hebrew); G.J. Brooke, "Some Remarks on 4Q252 and the Text of Genesis", *Textus* 19 (1998), pp. 1-25; J.C. VanderKam, "The Wording of Biblical Citations in Some Rewritten Scriptural Works", in E.D. Herbert & E. Tov (eds.), *The Bible as Book: the Hebrew Bible and the Judaean Desert Discoveries* (London: British Library; New Castle, DE: Oak Knoll Press, 2002), pp. 41-56; Tov, *Textual Criticism*, pp. 114, 189-190.

248 Frg. 11 7-8 may omit the word תחצב (see Comments ad loc.), an omission unattested in other ancient textual witnesses.

Deut 34:8

ויבכו בני ישראל את משה בערבת מואב **שלשים יום** ויתמו ימי בכי אבל משה

Num 33:48-49

ויחנו בערבת מואב **על ירדן** ירחו ויחנו על הירדן **מבית הישמת עד אבל השטים** בערבת מואב

A similar expansion is found in LXX to Deut 34:8, which adds after "ἐν Ἀραβὼθ Μωὰβ" the phrase "ἐπὶ τοῦ Ἰορδάνου κατὰ Ἰεριχὼ".

The citation from Deut 8:7 in frg. 11 4 includes the adjective ורחבה, apparently under the influence of a similar formulation from Exod 3:8:

Deut 8:7 (11 4) ורחבה Smr 4QDeut[f,j,n] G SmrT] > M V S T[O,Ps-J,N]

The same fragment also includes the phrase כי ארץ זבת חלב ודבשׁ / היא in the quotation from Deut 8:8-9 (line 6). This phrase is also borrowed from Exod 3:8.

The allusion to Exod 34:16 in frg. 3 i 2 reflects a text expanded with the language of Deut 7:3:

[ו]תֿקח מבנותיהֿ[ם] לבניך ותתן מב[נֿ]ותיך לבניהם

Exod 34:16

ולקחת מבנתיו לבניך

Deut 7:3

בתך לא תתן לבנו ובתו לא תקח לבנך

In a similar fashion, the LXX to Exod 34:16 adds "καὶ τῶν θυγατέρων σου δῷς τοῖς υἱοῖς αὐτῶν".[249]

Newsom observes that Deuteronomy is the most frequently cited biblical book in 4Q378. Hence, it is not surprising that most of the items listed above come from the citations and paraphrases of Deuteronomy. Noting that the reading of Deut 8:7 in frg. 11 4 agrees with LXX, she suggests that the scroll's *Vorlage* of Deuteronomy might have been "septuagintal in character".[250] Certainly, some of the scroll's readings of Deuteronomy are shared by LXX (3 i 5 [Deut 31:17], 11 4 [Deut 8:7]; 14 1-2 [Deut 34:8]). Yet, in two of those cases the scroll also agrees with other textual witnesses, while the third (14 1-2 [Deut 34:8]) follows LXX only partially. Also, 4Q378 contains several unique readings. In light of these data it seems prudent to avoid associating the *Vorlage(n)* of 4Q378 with any particular contemporary textual witness of Deuteronomy. Still, one feature common to many of the divergent readings of 4Q378 (or of its *Vorlage*) has to be noted: the tendency

---

249 Compare also the reading of Exod 34 with Deut 7 in 4Q368 2 and 11QT[a] II. See further Feldman, "Reading Exodus", pp. 329-338.

250 Newsom, "4Q378", p. 238. Vermes, *Dead Sea Scrolls*, p. 547.

to harmonization.[251] Several other ancient textual witnesses of Deut attest to a similar tendency (e.g., the pre-Samaritan Qumran scrolls, the LXX, and the Samaritan Pentateuch),[252] including a Qumran copy of the Book of Deuteronomy.[253]

2.5.4 The Provenance of 4Q378

Some scholars suggest a sectarian provenance for this scroll. Thus, Talmon ascribes 4Q378 (together with 4Q379) to the Qumran community.[254] Tov also tends to classify this scroll as sectarian or, at least, as copied by a member of *Yaḥad*.[255] Dimant, basing her arguments primarily on the contents of 4Q379 and 4Q522, argues that the RJ scrolls belong to an intermediary category of scrolls, between sectarian and non-sectarian (see Chapter 3). Yet, none of the scholars furnishes any concrete evidence for positing a sectarian (or close to sectarian circles) authorship for 4Q378. Since this scroll exhibits no sectarian terminology or worldview, it seems to belong with the wider corpus of the non-sectarian writings found at Qumran (Strugnell; Newsom).[256]

---

251 On harmonizations see E. Tov, "The Nature and Background of the Harmonizations in Biblical Manuscripts", *JSOT* 10 (1985), pp. 3-29.

252 For the discussion of the pre-Samaritan texts from Qumran and the SP see Tov, *Textual Criticism*, pp. 74-93. On the individual scrolls see further J.E. Sanderson, *An Exodus Scroll from Qumran: 4QpaleoExodᵐ and the Samaritan Tradition* (Harvard Semitic Studies; Atlanta, Georgia: Scholars Press, 1986); N. Jastram, "A Comparison of Two "Proto-Samaritan" Texts from Qumran: 4QpaleoExodᵐ and 4QNumᵇ", *DSD* 5 (1998), pp. 264-289; G.J. Brooke, "Deuteronomy 5-6 in the Phylacteries from Qumran Cave 4", in S.M. Paul et al. (eds.), *Emanuel* (VTSup 94; Leiden: Brill, 2003), pp. 59-68. On the harmonizations in the Greek translation of Deuteronomy see E. Tov, "Textual Harmonizations in the Ancient Texts of Deuteronomy", in N.S. Fox et al. (eds.), *Mishneh Todah* (Winona Lake, Indiana: Eisenbrauns, 2009), pp. 15-28.

253 See Eshel, "4QDeutⁿ", pp. 117-154. On the Deuteronomy manuscripts from Qumran see further J.A. Duncan, "Deuteronomy, Book of", *EDSS*, vol. 1, pp. 198-202; Lange, *Handbuch*, pp. 83-106.

254 Talmon, "Mas 1039-211", pp. 115-116.

255 Tov, "Rewritten Joshua", pp. 254-255. He notes the phrase ל[הון תתלו (frg. 20 ii 5) and observes several orthographic and morphological features (long possessive suffixes, verbs of קטלתה type, and a plene spelling מושה) associating its scribe with Qumran scribal practices. Still, he excludes 4Q378 from his later list of the scrolls exhibiting these practices. See E. Tov, *Scribal Practices and Approaches Reflected in the Texts Found in the Judean Desert* (STDJ 54; Leiden, Boston: Brill, 2004), p. 341.

256 J. Strugnell, "Moses-Pseudepigrapha at Qumran: 4Q375, 4Q376, and Similar Works", in L.H. Schiffman (ed.), *Archaeology and History in the Dead Sea Scrolls* (JSPSS 8; Sheffield: Sheffield Academic Press, 1990), p. 221; Newsom, "Psalms of Joshua", p. 59.

2.5.5 Conclusions

Replete with non-biblical discourses and prayers, the extant fragments of the non-sectarian scroll 4Q378 rewrite some of the events related in Deut 34-Josh 7, from the mourning for Moses to Achan's transgression. Among other episodes, the scroll expands on the brief biblical account of the transition from Moses' leadership to that of Joshua. Ellaborating on Joshua 1, it offers an extensive verbal exchange between Joshua and Israel. Joshua's address to the people, reminiscent of his farewell speeches in Josh 23-24, relies heavily on the Mosaic Deuteronomic discourses thus portraying him as a prophet like Moses. Some of the scroll's non-scriptural expansions of Joshua have parallels in both contemporary and later Jewish, as well as Samaritan, sources. These may reflect similar exegetical strategies and a dependence on a common pool of interpretive traditions. Exhibiting a vast array of exegetical techniques common to the Rewritten Bible works, 4Q378 also contains scriptural quotations and allusions diverging from the Masoretic Text. Thus, this scroll emerges as an important witness to both the text and the interpretation of Deuteronomy and Joshua in Second Temple times.

3 The Scroll 4Q379

3.1 The Manuscript

The scroll 4Q379 is written in a Hasmonean semi-cursive hand. Most of its forty-one fragments are small and provide little physical data for reconstructing their original sequence. Stegemann suggests that the fragments of 4Q379 may come from the middle portion of the scroll and tentatively arranges them into eight columns:[257]

Column	Fragment	Column	Fragment
I	18	V	3 ii, 13, 22 i
II	1-2	VI	22 ii
III	12	VII	19
IV	3 i and 17	VIII	4

In several cases this arrangement is corroborated by the contents of the fragments. In those cases it is preferable to the sequence suggested by the numbering of the *DJD* edition. Yet, it remains highly tentative and in a few cases seems to contradict the contextual evidence.

3.2 The Contents of 4Q379

Like 4Q378, this scroll contains a limited amount of a narrative (frgs. 3 i, 12, 16, 26, 31 ii?), yet abounds with speeches (frgs. 3 i, 4, 6, 13, 19, 22 ii 7-15, 32), prayers, and praises (frgs. 1-2, 5, 7, 10, 14, 15, 17, 18, 22 i-22 ii 1-6, 27). It deals with the crossing of the Jordan (frg. 12), the fall of Jericho (frgs. 3 i, 22 ii 7-15), and the conquest of Ai (frg. 26?). In one instance the setting for a non-biblical liturgical expansion is made clear by its juxtaposition to Joshua's curse, thus relating it to the fall of Jericho (frg. 22 i-ii 6).

Event	Bible	Fragment	Stegemann
Crossing of the Jordan	Josh 3-4	12	III
Fall of Jericho	Josh 6	3 i	IV
Joshua's praise		22 i-22 ii 1-6	V-VI
Joshua's curse	Josh 6:26	22 ii 7-15	VI
Conquest of Ai	Josh 8:12, 16	26?	

---

257 Newsom, "4Q379", p. 263.

The setting of other liturgical additions is unclear. Still, the speeches in frgs. 4, 6, 13 and the praises in frgs. 15, 17 (cf. frg. 16) may be linked to the crossing of the Jordan.

As this table indicates, the numbers assigned to some of the fragments in the *DJD* edition do not reflect their original sequence in the scroll. Frg. 12 (and, perhaps, also frgs. 4, 6, 13, 15-17) seems to precede frg. 3. Similarly, while Stegemann's sequence of frgs. 12, 3, 22 is corroborated by their contents (but not necessarily the assignment of the fragments to particular columns), his placement of the admonition from frg. 13 with Joshua's praise from frg. 22 i (col. V), of the 1st person praise from frg. 17 with the instructions concerning Jericho from frg. 3 i (col. IV), and of the speech related to the crossing of the Jordan in frg. 4? (col. VIII) after Joshua's curse in frg. 22 ii (col. VI) seems to be doubtful.

3.3 Editions of 4Q379

Initially assigned to Strugnell for editing, the scroll 4Q379 was finally published by Newsom as 4QApocryphon of Joshua[b].[258] Dimant recently re-edited frgs. 12 and 22.[259] Qimron currently is preparing a new edition of selected fragments of 4Q379.[260]

3.4 **Text and Commentary**

Frg. 1[261]

וֹתשמחהו בֹֹשנֹיֹםֹ] עשר בנים[	1
הׄ[ת את לוי ידידכֹ]ה וברכת ל[עֹולמים	2
ו[את ראובן ואת י[הודה	3
וא[ת גדׄ ואת דן וא[ת	4
ו	
שנים עשר מט]תֹ{ׄ}[ ]ישראל	5
] עד [	
ל[עֹלמי ומן]	6
]ל °°°[	7

---

258 Newsom, "4Q379", pp. 263-288. For preliminary editions see idem, "Psalms of Joshua", pp. 56-73; idem, "4Q378 and 4Q379", pp. 35-85.

259 Dimant, "Between Sectarian", pp. 105-134; idem, "Exegesis", pp. 387-389.

260 Qimron, *The Hebrew Writings: Volume Two*.

261 Frg. 1 (PAM 40.991) was acquired by the Museum of the Flagellation. See P.A. Spijkerman, "Chronique du Musée de la Flagellation", *Liber annus* 12 (1961-62), pp. 324-325.

Notes on Readings

2 ידידכ]ה. The short vertical stroke next to the *dalet* (PAM 40.991) may belong either to a *yod* (ידי̊ד]ה) or to a final *kaf*. Qimron prefers the latter option.

5 ט̊{ם}מ. The letter next to the *ṭet* has been deleted. The scribe blacked it out and wrote a *waw* above the interval between the deleted letter and the right vertical stroke of the *taw*.

Translation

1.   ]And You gladdened him with twe[lve sons
2.   ]forever Levi, Y[our] beloved[
3.   and] Reuben and J[udah
4.   and] Gad and Dan and[
5.   ]twelve tribes [of Israel
6.   ]forever and from ^{until}[
7.   ] [

Comments

1 ו̊תשמחהו ב̊שנים̊] עשר בנים. The fragment contains a prayer naming Jacob's sons. Hence, the reconstruction ב̊שנים̊] עשר בנים (Newsom). The speaker and the occasion are unknown. Joshua would be a likely candidate, while the events related to the crossing of the Jordan, featured in several fragments of this scroll, could be a possible setting. Newsom narrows it down to the errection of the twelve stones (one for each of the twelve tribes) at Gilgal (Josh 4) and notes its similarity to frg. 17 4-5. Less probable is Tov's identification of this prayer with the apportioning of the land to the Levites (Josh 21).[262] The verb ותשמחהו, a 2nd masc. sg. Piel *qatal* of שמח, "to gladden", has God as a subject (for שמח ב- see Ps 92:5), while the 3rd masc. sg. suffix refers to Jacob.[263] Qimron reconstructs in the beginning of the line ותשמחהו] את יעקוב.

2 וברכת ל]עׄולמים את לוי ידידכ]ה. The scroll seems to name Levi first of Jacob's twelve sons. The appellation 'God's beloved' alludes to Moses' blessing of Benjamin in Deut 33:12 (Newsom).[264] The phrase ל]עׄולמים may also point to Deut 33:12, חפף עליו כל היום. The beginning of the line might have read וברכת ל]עׄולמים (with 11QPsᵃ XXII, 2).

---

262 Tov, "Rewritten Joshua", p. 248.
263 HALOT, p. 1335.
264 Ibid., p. 390.

3 ואת ראובן ואת י[הודה. Most of the biblical tribal lists place Simeon next to Reuben (Gen 29:31-33; Gen 49:3-7; Num 1:5-6, 20-23, 13:4-5). The letter *yod* at the end of the line indicates that the scroll has a different sequence. Although the restorations י[שׂשׂכר or י[וסף are possible, the allusion to Deut 33:12 in line 2 suggests that the fragment may follow the order of the names as found in the Mosaic blessings of the tribes. Deut 33:6-7 omits Simeon and mentions Judah next to Reuben.[265] The restoration ואת י[הודה follows that sequence (Newsom), although frg. 2 indicates that 4Q379 includes Simeon too. The names in lines 2-4 are preceded by *nota accusativi*, which may point to the same missing verb (e.g., a form of ברך) in line 2.

4 וא[ת גד ואת דן וא[ת. Dan is mentioned after Gad in Gen 49:16-19 and Deut 33:20-22.

5 שׁנים עשׂר מט]{°}ת[|ישׂראל. The reconstruction (Newsom) follows the synonymous biblical phrase שׁנים עשׂר שׁבטי ישׂראל (Exod 24:4; Ezek 47:13). Apparently, the scroll identifies here Jacob's twelve sons with the twelve tribes of Israel.

6]לעֹלמי ומן עד[. The absence of the *nomen regens* next to the construct לעֹלמי is puzzling.[266] Perhaps, the supralinear addition עד should have been written above the interval between לעֹלמי[and ומן (Newsom), לעֹלמי עד (cf. 1QSb III, 21; frg. 14 3 has לכל עלמי עד). It is also possible, yet less likely, that the scribe omitted the final *mem*,]לעֹלמים. Qimron restores עד]לעֹלמי.

Frg. 2

```
ואת שׁמֹ[עון        1
          ]°[           2
```

Translation
1.]and Sim[eon
2.   ] [

---

265 On the order of the tribes in Deut 33 see J.H. Tigay, *Deuteronomy* (JPS Torah Commentary; Philadelphia: Jewish Publication Society, 1996), pp. 541-542.

266 E. Tigchelaar, "Assessing Emanuel Tov's 'Qumran Scribal Practice'", in S. Metso et al. (eds.), *The Dead Sea Scrolls: Transmission of Traditions and Production of Texts* (STDJ 92; Leiden, Boston: Brill, 2010), pp. 203-204, notes the defective, MT-like, orthography of 4Q379, placing it within a small group of non-biblical scrolls employing such an orthography. He suggests that the use of the MT-like orthography may reflect a "strategy of authorization".

Comments

1 ‏[וא]ת שׁמֹ[עון. This fragment most likely belongs with frg. 1. It indicates that the scroll, unlike Deut 33, whose order of tribal names it seems to follow, includes Simeon in its list of Jacob's sons.[267] See Comment to frg. 1 3.

Frg. 3 i

‏[עדֹיֹעֹדֹ	‏[1
‏[אֹת יהוה	‏[2
‏[אֹזֹ ירימו בחֹנֹים	‏[3
‏[ºבֹ̇י יהוה ולא	‏[קולם 4
‏ולא יתגֹאֹלו בכל [	‏[5
‏והיתה העיר [חֹרֹם לו לעולֹמֹ] ºº	‏[6
‏[ ]לֹ[ ]	‏[7

Notes on Readings

It is likely that the uninscribed space in the end of lines 5 and 6 belongs with the left inter-columnar margin.[268] Apparently, the vacats in lines 1-4 also represent the same margin. For a diagonal pattern of a text/margin compare 4QJudg[b].[269]

1 עדֹיֹעֹדֹ[. The *DJD* edition reads (with Strugnell) ‏עֹרֹוֹעֹר[.[270] The letters *dalet* and *resh*, as well as *waw* and *yod*, are frequently indistinguishable in this scroll. While both ‏עֹרֹוֹעֹר and ‏עדֹיֹעֹדֹ are graphically possible, the toponym seems to be less fitting on contextual grounds.

3 אֹ[. The editor offers no reading for the upper tip of a vertical stroke in the beginning of the line. Yet, it is consistent with the left stroke of an *alef*.

Translation

1. [   ]for ever and ever
2. [   ] YHWH

---

267 On the exclusion of Simeon see Tigay, *Deuteronomy*, pp. 541-542.

268 Stegemann's suggestion that frg. 3 "may come just above and to the left of frg. 17 in the same column" (Newsom, "4Q379", p. 265) seems implausible. Both fragments preserve remains of the left margin and have a similar diagonal pattern of damage at their left side. These suggest that they belong to diferent columns, while the distance between these remain unclear.

269 See G.J. Brooke, "Some Remarks on the Reconstruction of 4QJudges[b]", in D. Minutoli & R. Pintaudi (eds.), *Papyri Grecae Schøyen: Essays and Texts in Honour of Martin Schøyen* (Papyrologica Florentina XL; Firenze: Edizioni Gonneli, 2010), pp. 107-115.

270 Brown et al., *Preliminary Concordance*, vol. 4, p. 1562.

3. [   ]then the tested ones will raise
4. [their voices   ] of YHWH and not
5. [   ] and they shall not defile themselves with any
6. [and the city will be]a dedicated thing to him forever[ ]
7. [   ] [   ]

Comments

1 עד־ⁱעֹ֗דׄ[. The phrase עד עדי (Isa 26:4; Ps 83:18) is written as one word (cf. frg. 22 ii 9, 13).

3 קולם] / אֹ֗ ירימו בחֹנׄים. Line 6 suggests that this fragment deals with the fall of Jericho (Josh 6). It is somewhat unclear whether this is a 3rd person narration of the events or, more likely, Joshua's discourse expanding on Josh 6:16-19. The reconstruction follows the recurring biblical expression קול הרים. The verb ירימו may be parsed either as a *yiqtol* (if a 3rd person narrative) or as a jussive (if a discourse). It may refer to the people's cry or the sounding of the trumpets by the priests immediately before the fall of Jericho's walls (Josh 6:5, 16, 20 [cf. וכהרים קול בחצצרות, 2 Chr 5:13]). The passive Qal participle of בחן, "to examine, to put to the test", בחֹנׄים, refers to either to the Israelites in general or, better, to the aforementioned priests (cf. the use of this term in the sectarian texts, e.g., CD XIII, 3[with reference to a priest]; 1QM XVII, 1).[271]

4 בׄי יהוה ולא. The scroll might have read או[יֹ֗בׄי יהוה (1 Sam 30:26; Ps 37:20), עו[זֹ֗בׄי יהוה (Isa 1:28) or או[הֹ֗בׄי יהוה (Ps 97:10).

5 ולא יתגֹ֗אֹ֗לו בכל. Using a Hitpael jussive or a *yiqtol* form of גאלׄ, "to defile oneself" (Dan 1:8; 1QM IX, 8),[272] this line seems to refer to the divine prohibition of taking anything from Jericho (Josh 6:18).

6 והיתה העיר [חֹ֗רֹ֗ם לו לעולֹ֗ם. The first word seems to be a noun חרם (Newsom), "what is banned", occuring several times in Josh 6-7 (for ל- חרם cf. Josh 6:17).[273] The reconstruction follows Josh 6:17. The phrase לעולֹ֗ם may point to the Deuteronomic command prohibiting a rebuilding of an idolatrous city, תל עולם (Deut 13:17). Qimron restores יו[חֹ֗רֹ֗ם.

Frg. 3 ii

]° 6

---

271 HALOT, p. 119.
272 Ibid., p. 169-170.
273 Ibid., p. 354.

Frg. 4

[גְּבֹוֹל ארץ]   1[

[כנען]   ואתם עמדים] וראים נפלאֹתֹוֹ   2

[במצולה]   תפאר]תֹ וגדולה   3

[אשר ל[אֹ היתה כמוה   4

[לם כי אמש   5

[°°°° °   6

Notes on Readings

3 תפאר]תֹ. The editor reads ֹח[. However, the shape of a vertical stroke visble on PAM 43.218 is more consistent with a *taw*, than with a *ḥet*.

4 ל[אֹ. The *DJD* edition offers no reading for the diagonal stroke descending from right to left. Yet, Strugnell correctly reads it as a left stroke of an *alef*.[274]

5 אמש. Qimron notes that the *alef* has been corrected.

Translation

1. [   ]border of the land of
2. [Canaan   and you are standing] and seeing his wonders
3. [in the deep   glor]y and greatness
4. [which there was n]o like her
5. [   ] for yesterday

Comments

1 [גְּבֹוֹל ארץ] / [כנען. The wording of lines 1 and 5 suggest that this might be Joshua's address to Israel closely related to the crossing of the Jordan.[275] If correct, this fragment must have preceded frg. 3. The phrase [גְּבֹוֹל ארץ] / [כנען (Qimron) may refer to Jordan, which constitutes the eastern border of the Land of Canaan (cf. Num 34:2-12; see also Num 33:51, 35:10; Josh 22:10-11). See Discussion.

2 [במצולה] / ואתם עמדים] וראים נפלאֹתֹוֹ. Newsom plausibly reads נפלאֹת(י)ו, "his won-ders" (yet, cf. the orthography of [גבורתיו in frg. 22 i 2).[276] The 3rd masc. sg. posses-sive suffix refers to God, while the participle וראים has Israelites as its subject (cf. Ps 107:24). נפלאֹתֹוֹ may stand for God's wonders performed during the crossing of

---

274 Brown et al., *Freliminary Concordance*, vol. 2, p. 883.
275 Since this fragment's left margin preserves remnants of the stitches, Stegemann places it at the end of the sheet that was joined to frg. 3. Yet, it is equally possible that this fragment comes from a sheet that preceded frg. 3.
276 See Qimron, *Hebrew*, p. 59.

the Jordan, as in Josh 3:5. Alternatively, it may remind the audience of the divine miracles during the Exodus (e.g., Exod 3:20; note also Micah 7:15). The reconstruction follows Ps 107:24 and 2 Chr 20:17.

תפאר[תֿ וגדולה 3. Read וגדולה, "and greatness" (cf. frg. 36 1). The restoration תפאר[תֿ, "glory, splendour, radiance", is based on Esther 1:4.[277] The scroll seems to refer to the divine attributes/acts revealed during the crossing of the Jordan. Qimron restores אימתכם הולכת[תֿ וגדולה (cf. Josh 2:9).

אשר ל[אֿ היתה כמוה 4. The reconstruction (Qimron), following Exod 9:24, 11:6, seems to refer to God's acts (יֿשועה?) at the crossing of the Jordan.

כי אמש 5. This phrase may refer to the day of the sanctification mentioned in Josh 3:5.

Frg. 5

]∘∘חֿיתם א∘[	1
אֿ]לֿהֿיֿ מה אֿק]רֿא	2
]לֿ[ ]∘∘∘∘[	3

Notes on Readings

1 חֿ∘[. The *DJD* edition reads חֿיתם[. On the photograph (PAM 43.218) an illegible trace of ink is visible before *ḥet*.

2 אֿלֿהֿיֿ[. Newsom reads]∘לֿ∘[. The shape of the upper horizontal stroke of the third letter is similar to that of a *he*. The trace of the first letter is difficult to decipher. The last letter may be read both as a *waw* and a *yod*. In light of the context it is proposed to read with Strugnell אֿ]לֿהֿיֿ[(this reading is mentioned also by Newsom).[278] **אֿק]רֿא.** The *DJD* edition has אשֿ∘. However, the traces of the second letter as they are seen on the photographs (PAM 41.778; 43.218), do not resemble those of a *shin*. A vertical stroke projecting below the imaginary bottom line suggests that this is a *qof*. Strugnell also reads thus.[279]

Translation
1.   ]   their [
2.   ]my God, What shall I procl[aim?
3.   ]   [   ][

---

278 HALOT, pp. 1772-1773.
278 Brown et al., *Preliminary Concordance*, vol. 4, p. 1706.
279 Ibid.

Comments

2 אראק] מה אלֹהֹי אֹ[. The 1st sg. possessive suffix in אֹלֹהֹי[indicates that this is a prayer. The phrase מה אקרא seems to be borrowed from Isa 40:6.

Frg. 6

]° °°[	1
בז]אֹת תדעו אשר אין לֹן[	2
]מה כי כל עֹזֹו ר°°[	3
]° ° ° °° לֹו °[	4

Notes on Readings

3 עֹזֹו. The *DJD* edition reads עֹזֹי. Both readings are possible, as *waw* and *yod* are difficult to distinguish in this scroll.

Translation

2.   by t]his you shall know that there is no [
3.   ] for all His might   [
4.   ]   to him   [

Comments

2 בז]אֹת תדעו אשר אין. This might be an allusion to Joshua's speech in Josh 3:10. If correct, this fragment may belong with frg. 4. Newsom notes a similarity with Josh 23:13.

3 כי כל עֹזֹו. Read either עֹזֹו, from עֶזּוּז, "might, power" (cf. Ps 78:4), or עֹזֹו/עֹזֵֹי(יֹ)/עֹזֵי, from עָזּוּז, "mighty one".[280] The usages of both nouns in the Hebrew Bible suggest that the 3rd masc. possessive suffix refers to God.

Frg. 7

]° אלהי[	1
]°°[ ]°[	2

Translation

1.]God of [
2.] [ ] [

---

280 HALOT, p. 808.

Comment

1 אלהי[may also be rendered as "]my God".

Frg. 8

]° יֿן[	1
]עִ֯ין[	2
]לֿ[	3

Frg. 9

]תֿ֯ןֿ°[	1
]לֿ[	2

Frg. 10

]°°[	]	1
]רוֿן °°°°°° ולֿא		2
]בענותי וֿבישֿרי֯ן		3
]מצאתי לי שֿמֿהֿ		4
]°[		5

Notes on Readings

3 וֿבישֿרי֯ן. The *DJD* edition reads]וֿבישֿרתֿ. However, the vertical stroke next to a *resh* may well be a *yod*.

4 לי. Newsom reads לו, yet לי seems to suit better the context. The *waw* and *yod* are frequently indistinguishable in this scroll.

שֿמֿהֿן. The editor reads ה°°°. There are remains of two letters before *he*. The first one is clearly a *shin*. Its three strokes are well visible on the photographs (PAM 41.784; 43.218). Wacholder & Abegg plausibly suggest that the second letter is a medial *mem*.[281]

---

281 Wacholder & Abegg, *Preliminary Edition*, vol. 3, p. 180.

Translation

1. [   ] [
2. and not   [
3. in my humility and in my uprightness[
4. I found there[
5. [   ] [

Comments

3 בענותי ובישרי[ן‎. The 1ˢᵗ sg. possessive suffixes in בענותי, "in my humility",[282] and ובישרי[ן‎, "in my uprightness" (cf. Pr 14:2; 1 Kgs 9:4),[283] indicate that this is a prayer, perhaps, by Joshua.[284] If read as בענותו ובישרו, this phrase may refer to Moses (cf. Num 12:3; 4Q378 3 ii 6).

4 מצאתי לי שׁמׁה[‎. The object of the verb מצאתי is unknown.

Frg. 11

[מׁׄוׄ באׄ[ׄ°	1
[ם הגביהו °°°°°[	2
[ם והיו להם]	3
[°°°] [° °° °]	4

Translation

1.]   [
2.]   he exalted him [
3.] and they had [
4.] [   ] [

Comments

2 הגביהו‎. Read either a 3ʳᵈ masc. sg. Hifil *qatal* of גבה, "to make high, to exalt", with a 3ʳᵈ masc. sg. pronominal suffix or a 3ʳᵈ masc. pl. Hifil *qatal* or imperative of the same root.[285]

---

282 HALOT, p. 855.
283 Ibid., p. 450.
284 Berthelot, "Joshua", p. 99.
285 HALOT, p. 171.

Frg. 12

1 [ו]הֿֿיורדים תמֿו בֿיֿֿם
2 [הערבה   והמים] היורדים עמֿדו נֿֿד
3 [אחד   וכול ישראל עֿֿבֿרו ביבשׄהֿ בֿחדש
4 [הרא]שֿֿון בשנת האֿֿ]חת ו]אֿֿרֿבעים שנה לצאֿתם מאֿֿר]ֿץ]
5 מֿצֿרים היֿאֿֿ השנה ליובלים לתחלת ביאתם לארץ
6 כנֿעֿן והיורדן סלֿא מֿֿ]ם] על כל גדותיו ושוטף
7 [ב]מֿֿֿימיו עֿֿד החדש השֿֿֿ]לֿי]שֿֿי עד חֿֿֿדֿשֿ קציר חטים
8] [לֿֿ] [ ]ㅇㅇㅇ[ ] [ㅇㅇ[להㅇ] [לֿֿ] [ㅇㅇㅇ ישראלֿ]

Notes on Readings

1 ו]הֿֿיורדים. Newsom reads הֿֿיורדים [, yet there is no blank space before the *he*. In fact, its right vertical stroke has been lost due to the damage incurred by the fragment.

תמֿו. The *DJD* edition has ㅇㅇㅇㅇו. Dimant suggests ㅇㅇㅇשֿֿבֿי. According to PAM 40.618, the first letter is a *taw* (cf. *taw* in ביאתם [line 5]). Its upper diagonal stroke is clearly visible on this photograph. The second letter is consistent with a medial *mem*. What Dimant reads as the right stroke of a *shin* is, in fact, an upper horizontal stroke of a medial *mem*. The last letter, represented by a vertical stroke with a hook-shaped top, is a *waw*.

בֿיֿֿם. The *DJD* edition offers no reading for the three letters in the end of the line. The first letter, represented by a base stroke, seems to be a *bet* or a medial *mem*. The following bottom tip of a vertical stroke is most likely a *waw* or a *yod*. The vertical stroke curving to the left and projecting below the imaginary bottom line belongs to a final *mem*.

3 ביבשֿהֿ. Newsom reads ביבשֿה. As Qimron points out, the traces of the last letter better suit a *taw*. On PAM 41.778; 43.218 one can clearly see the left vertical stroke of the *taw* curving left at the bottom.

4 האֿֿ]חת. Thus reads Newsom. Dimant notes that a tiny tip of a third letter is visible on PAM 41.778. I was not able to locate any traces of a third letter on this image.

5 ביאתם. This is Strugnell's reading.[286] Newsom suggests בואתם. Dimant and Qimron affirm Strugnell's reading.[287]

---

286 Brown et al., *Preliminary Concordance*, vol. 1, p. 477.
287 Dimant, "Between Sectarian", p. 109.

7 עֹּ. The *DJD* edition has מֹּ. The traces of the two letters are virtually illegible. Yet, as Dimant convincingly argues, the reading עֹּ is contextually more appropriate.[288] Qimron notes that the traces are illegible and reconstructs עֹ. See Comments.

הש̇[לי]ש̇י. Strugnell reads הר̇[בי]ע̇י.[289] Newsom suggests [ ]ה[ ]°י. The trace of a diagonal stroke next to the *he* resembles a right stroke of a *shin* (PAM 40.618; 41.778; 43.218). The letter preceding the final *yod* is also a *shin*. What Strugnell reads as a right stroke of an *ayin* is, as Dimant observes, a vertical stroke of a *lamed* inscribed in the next line.[290]

8 לה]. Qimron reads להב̇[. I was not able to find any traces of the third letter on the photographs.

Translation

1. [and those]flowing downstream ceased in the Sea
2. [of the Arabah   and the waters] flowing downstream stood in a [single] heap
3. [and all Israel cr]ossed over on dry ground in the [fir]st month
4. of the forty-f[irst] year of their exodus from the lan[d]
5. of Egypt. This is the year for Jubilees, from the beginning of their entrance to the land of
6. Canaan. And the Jordan was full of wat[er] over all its banks and overflowing
7. [with] its waters until the th[ir]d month, until the month of the wheat harvest.
8. [ ] [ ]   [   ] [   ][ ]   Israel[

Comments

1 הערבה] / היורדים תמ̇ו בלֹּם ו[ה̇. This fragment narrates the crossing of the Jordan. The reconstruction follows Joshua 3:16b.

2 אחד] / נֹד̇ עמ̇דו היורדים [והמים. This line reworks Joshua 3:16a. The verb עמדו, employed here instead of the biblical קמו, may point to Joshua's words in v. 13. Thus the scroll ties together the description of God's future miraculous act and its fulfillment. The replacement of קמו with עמ̇דו may also reflect a preference for עמד in the late Biblical and Qumran Hebrew (cf. frg. 22 ii 10; see also Comment to 4Q378 11 2).

3 ביבשת / עב̇רו ביבשת וכול ישראל. The scroll paraphrases Josh 3:17 using the noun ביבשת, found in Joshua's recapitulation of the events in Josh 4:22 (note also its use in Exod 14:16, 22, 29, 15:19), instead of בחרבה.

---

288 Dimant, "Between Sectarian", p. 109.
289 Brown et al., *Preliminary Concordance*, vol. 4, p. 1735.
290 Dimant, "Between Sectarian", p. 109.

בחדש / [הרא]שׁוֹן בשנת הא[ח]ת ו[אַ]רְבעים שנה לצאתם מאׄר[ץ] / מִצְּרים **3-5**. The scroll expands Josh 3:17 with chronological data culled from Josh 4:19 and Deut 1:3, 34:8 (see Discussion). The counting of years from the Exodus is well attested (for the wording see Exod 16:1). For the mention of the units before the decades compare Gen 47:28; Lev 25:8. As to the sequence בשנת ... שנה, see Gen 7:11; 1 Kgs 16:8.

היא השנה ליובלים לתחלת ביאתם לארץ / כנֹעַן 5-6. The pronoun היא opens a nominal clause explicating the nature of the forty-first year after Exodus (for the construction -ל היא השנה cf. 2 Kgs 18:9). The phrase היִׄא השנה ליובלים identifies it as the year from which the computation of the Jubilee years begins. The apposition לתחלת ביאתם לארץ / כנֹעַן, alluding to Lev 25:2, clarifies that the crossing of the Jordan, i.e. the entrance into the Land of Canaan proper, makes the Torah's jubilean laws effective. See Discussion.

ביאתם. The noun בָּאָה, "entrance, coming", is attested to in Biblical (Ezek 8:5), Qumran (e.g., 4Q332 3), and Rabbinic Hebrew.[291]

והיורדן מלא מ[י]ב] על כל גדותיו ושוטף / [ב]מִׄימיו 6-7. This line reworks Josh 3:15. The name of the river, ירדן (MT), is spelled יורדן.[292] The addition of the word מים produces the expression [מ]מׄלא מי[ם], as in Ps 65:10. Together with ושוטף / [ב]מִׄימיו (cf. Ps 124:4), it emphasizes the abundance of water in the Jordan. Compare the description of the Jordan overflowing with waters in Nisan in 1 Chr 12:16.

עַׄד החדש הש[לי]שִׁי עד חֹדֶשׁ קציר חטים. This phrase is an elaboration of the biblical כל ימי קציר (Josh 3:15) explicating the period of time implied. The phrase עַׄד החדש הש[לי]שִׁי extends the period of the Jordan's overflowing with water to the third month of Sivan. The phrase עד חֹדֶשׁ קציר חטים, an apposition to עַׄד החדש הש[לי]שִׁי, explains that Sivan is the month of the wheat harvest. Similarly, 4QJosh[b] 2-3 2(=Josh 3:15) reads בימי קציר[חטים] (for this phrase see Gen 30:14; Judg 15:1; cf. 2 Sam 24:15[LXX]; Judith 8:2), while LXX ad loc. has ὡσεὶ ἡμέραι θερισμοῦ πυρῶν (= כימי קציר חטים?).[293] See Discussion.

Frg. 13

ל[גֹ]לים לפניו ואתם לש̇ניה תה̇י[ו]	1
[אי]ן לכם מנוֹסה בתבל ראו מֹה[ן] עשה לנו	2
[°][]°ל °° והמים לנׄוׄ °°°° ל[	3
°[וֹהֹלל]	4

---

291 HALOT, p. 106; M. Jastrow, *Dictionary of the Targumim, the Talmud Bavli and Yerushalmi, and the Midrashic Literature* (New York: Judaica Press, 1982), p. 159; M. Bar-Asher, "Two Phenomena in Qumran Hebrew. Synchronic and Diachronic Aspects", *Meghillot* 1 (2003), p. 170 (Hebrew).
292 Qimron, *Hebrew*, p. 39.
293 Tov, "4Q48", pp. 155-157.

Notes on Readings

1 לֹשׁניה. Wacholder & Abegg read thus.[294] Newsom suggests לֹשׁ∘ה. She notes that "the damaged letter might be read as aleph or perhaps yod, but neither suggestion yields a plausible meaning for the context". Still, according to the photographs (PAM 41.778; 43.218), the vertical stroke with a hook-shaped top is most likely a *waw* or a *yod*. Qimron suggests לֹשׁנים, yet according to PAM 41.778, the last letter is clearly a *he*.

תהֿי]ו. Newsom offers no reading for the third letter. A bottom tip of the vertical stroke visible on PAM 41.778 may well belong to a *waw* or to a *yod*. Qimron reads תחצ]ו. On the photographs (PAM 41.778; 43.218) the second letter seems to have a vertical horizontal stroke projecting to the left beyond the left vertical stroke, as in a *he*.

2 מנוסֿה. The *DJD* edition has מנו∘ה. The editor observes that *samech* is possible, "although the context does not favor such a reading". Still, on the photographs (PAM 41.778; 43.218) the vertical strokes and the base of a *samech* are clearly visible. Strugnell and Qimron also read thus.[295]

מֿה]. Newsom offers no reading for the last letter of this line. The upper tip of the vertical stroke visible on PAM 43.218 may belong to several letters. Given the contents it is proposed to read here a *he*.

3 לֹנו. The editor reads לה. Qimron (personal correspondence) suggests לנו, a reading supported by PAM 43.218.

4 On the photograph PAM 43.218 frg. 39 is placed to the left of וֹהֿלל. The shape of the fragment, as well as its contents, does not support this placement.

Translation

1.   to]a rubble before Him. And you will b[eco]me[a saying[
2.   ]you have no place of refuge in the world. See what[He has done for us
3.   ]   and the waters to us in   [
4.   ]   and a praise [

Comments

1 ל]גלים לפניו ואתם לֹשֹׁניה תהֿי]ו. Lines 1-2 seems to contain an admonition, perhaps, by Joshua.

294 Wacholder & Abegg, *Preliminary Edition*, vol. 3, p. 181.
295 Brown et al., *Preliminary Concordance*, vol. 3, p. 1313.

ל[ג]לים לפניו. While Newsom reads גלים as "waves", the context seems to favor the meaning "heaps".[296] It might have been preceded by a form of היה, as in והיתה בבל לגלים (Jer 51:37). The 3rd masc. sg. pronoun in לפניו refers to God.

ואתם לשׁניה תהלון. It appears that the scroll paraphrases the biblical expression נתן/היה למשל ולשנינה (Deut 28:37; 1 Kgs 9:7; Jer 24:9; 2 Chr 7:20). While שׁניה could be a scribal error for שנינה, "sharp word, taunt",[297] it is more likely that this is a nominal form (pattern קְטָיָה or קְטִילָה) resulting from a fusion of שנ"ן, "to sharpen", and שנ"ה, "to repeat".[298] Compare T^Ps-J,N to Deut 28:37, rendering שנינה as תינוי, "a story", derived from תנ"י.[299] Such an understanding of שנינה is facilitated by the frequent pairing of שנינה with משל.[300] Apparently, שׁניה denotes a story to be told again and again. Note that 11Q19 LIX, 2 reads ולשנניה.

2 א[ין לכם מנוסה בתבל]. The noun מנוסה, usually rendered as "flight",[301] seems to denote here a place of refuge, as does the related noun מנוס (cf. Jer 25:35).[302] Compare the expression אין מנוס in 1QM XIV, 11; 1QH^a XIV, 36.

ראו מֵ[ה] עשׂה לנו. The restoration is that of Qimron.[303]

3 והמים לנׁוׁ. Qimron suggests that this phrase alludes to the expression והמים להם חמה מימינם ומשמאלם from Exod 14:22, 29. If correct, the ensuing traces of letters indicate that the scroll rephrased it. A recollection of the crossing of the Red Sea would be particularly at home in the context of the crossing of the Jordan (as in Josh 4:23).

4 הׁלׁלׁ. While this word could be read as a verbal form of הלל, Newsom's reading of it as a noun הלל, "a praise", is followed here (cf. 4Q403 1 ii 33).[304] Given the possible allusion to Exod 14 in the previous line, this "praise" may refer to the Song of the Sea (Exod 15). If this fragment deals with the crossing of the Jordan, it may suggest that this event was also accompanied by a praise. See frg. 16 and Discussion.

---

296 HALOT, p. 190.
297 Ibid., p. 1606.
298 Ibid., pp. 1598-1599. This interpretation has been suggested to me by Dr. Noam Mizrahi.
299 Sokoloff, *Palestinian Aramaic*, p. 580.
300 LXX to Deut 28:37; 1 Kgs 9:7; 2 Chr 7:20, Vulgate to Deut 28:37; 1 Kgs 9:7; Jer 24:9, and T^O to Deut 28:37 reflect a similar understanding of שנינה.
301 BDB, p. 631.
302 HALOT, p. 600.
303 Private communication.
304 HALOT, p. 249.

Frg. 14

top margin

‏[◦ יֹהוֹֹה וֹגֹם   ] 1

‏וא]ֹין להם מֹסֹפֹֹר   ] 2

‏ברוך הו]אֹ לכל עלמי עד   ] 3

‏מֹ[   ]◦◦[   ] 4

‏[ ]◦◦[5

Notes on Readings

2 מֹסֹפֹֹר. The *DJD* edition reads ◦מֹ◦מֹ. The traces of the third letter may be read both as a medial *mem* and a medial *pe*. The last letter is a *resh* or a *dalet*. The remains of the second letter are illegible. The context suggests a *samech*.

Translation

1. [   ] YHWH and also
2. [and]they [can]not be counted
3. [H]e[is blessed] for all ages of eternity
4. [   ] [   ]
5. [   ]   [   ]

Comments

2 ‏וא]ֹין להם מֹסֹפֹֹר. For the language compare Jer 46:23. Perhaps, this is a praise (cf. Ps 145:3; Job 5:9, 9:10; 4Q392 1 8).

3 ‏ברוך הו]אֹ לכל עלמי עד. The scroll seems to combine two biblical expressions, עד עולמי עד (Isa 45:17; cf. frg. 1 6) and כל עלמים (Ps 145:13). It is proposed to restore here ‏ברוך הו]אֹ לכל עלמי עד (cf. Num 22:12 [with reference to Israel]; Ruth 2:20). Given the remnants of the stitches in the left margin and the presence of the top margin, Newsom suggests that this fragment comes from the top of the column to which frg. 4 belongs. Also, if the proposed reconstruction is correct, it links this fragment with frgs. 15-17, 22 i-ii 1-6 containing blessings and praises.

Frg. 15

‏לעול]ֹם וֹעֹד בכֹל ברכוֹֹת] עד   1

‏[◦]ֹ[ל]   [בֹֹכל ומברֹ]כים   2

‏[כֹֹל טֹוֹב ובֹכֹל] לשון יבֹרֹ]כו   3

‏]◦◦◦◦]◦◦[ ]◦◦[ ]לֹ[ ]◦◦לֹ־בֹֹֹ◦[ ]ֹם במו◦◦◦◦]   4

‏]◦◦◦ יֹרֹ ◦◦[5

Notes on Readings

2 On the photographs (PAM 41.784; 43.218) there is a trace of a letter in the beginning of the line (missing from the *DJD* transcription).

בְּכֹל[. Newsom reads כֹל[. On PAM 43.218 a trace of a base stroke before the medial *kaf* is visible. Perhaps this is a *bet*.

3 יבֹרֹ[כו. The *DJD* edition has]ֹבֹו. There is a trace of a vertical stroke next to the *bet* on PAM 43.218. Strugnell reads יבֹרֹ[כו.[305]

4]∘∘בֹּ∘לֹ[. Newsom reads]∘∘אֹבֹו∘לֹ[, yet the traces of ink next to the *waw* are illegible.

Translation

1. foreve]r and ever with all blessings[of eternity
2.] [   ]in all and (they) are bles[sing
3.]all the best things and with eve[ry] tongue (they) will ble[ss
4.]   [   ]   [ ] [ ]   [
5.   ]   [

Comments

1 עד בֹרכֹוֹתֹ[ן בכֹל וֹעֹדֹ ם[לעוֹלֹ. The language of blessing and praise, particularly the use of the pl. Piel participle of ברך (line 2, reconstructed), links this fragment to frgs. 16-17 (Newsom). The precise occasion of the praise is not made explicit. Tov initially proposed that frgs. 15-16 refer to the ceremony at Mts. Gerizim and Ebal (Josh 8:30-35). Now, following Newsom, he suggests that they deal with the crossing of the Jordan (see Comment to frg. 16 3).[306] The beginning of the line may follow one of the following formulae: ויברכו/ברוך יהוה/שם כבודו/אלהי ישראל לעוֹל[ם וֹעֹד (Ps 72:19, 89:53, 106:48). The reconstruction עד בֹרכֹוֹתֹ[ן בכֹל is based on 1QS IV, 7, yet בכֹל ברכֹוֹתֹ[ן אמת (4Q286 7a i, b-d 4) and בכֹל ברכֹוֹתֹ[ן טוב (Ps 21:4) are equally possible.

2 בֹּכל ומברֹ[כים[. The reconstruction of ומברֹ[כים as a plural participle follows frgs. 16 1 and 17 2. It is supported by the phrase וֹבֹכֹ[ל[לשון in the next line, indicating a communal, rather than an individual, praise. The fragment seems to combine a third person narration about praising God (lines 2-3) and an actual liturgy (line 1).

3 כֹּל טֹוֹב וֹבֹכֹ[ל[לשון יבֹרֹ[כו[. For the language compare Deut 6:11 and 4Q215a 1 ii 7-8.

---

305 Brown et al., *Preliminary Concordance*, vol. 1, p. 526.
306 Tov, "Rewritten Joshua", p. 253; idem, "Literary Development".

Frg. 16

‏[וֹמברכֹ]יֹ[ם המֹהׄ]ׄ	1
‏[מהללֹ]יֹ[ם ומרֹננים]	2
‏[וא][נֹחו עברֹ]יֹ[םֹ]	3
‏[ ]ׄׄׄׄׄׄ[	4

Translation

1.]and they are blessing [
2.]prais[i]ng and rejoicing[
3.] cross[i]ng[

Notes on Readings

3 ‏[וא][נֹחו. The first letter may be read either as a *waw* or a *yod*. There is a short blank space between the *alef* and the base stroke read here (with Newsom) as a *nun*. It is unclear whether this is an interval between two adjacent words or two consecutive letters.

Comments

1 ‏[וֹמברכֹ]יֹ[ם המֹהׄ. The language of this fragment suggests that it may deal with the same episode as frgs. 15 and 17 (see Comment to frg. 15 1). The demonstrative pronoun ‏המֹהׄ may open a new clause (Newsom). Yet, it is also possible that ‏המֹהׄ is the subject of the Piel participle ‏[וֹמברכֹ]יֹ[ם. If the fragment is concerned with the crossing of the Jordan (line 3), "they" may stand either for the priests or/and Levites. See Discussion.

2 ‏[מהללֹ]יֹ[ם ומרֹננים]. Compare the word pair ‏רנה ותהלה in 2 Chr 20:22 (see also 1QS X, 17; 4Q427 7 i 14).

3 ‏[וא][נֹחו עברֹ]יֹ[םֹ]. Newsom (with Strugnell) disregards the lacuna between the *alef* and the *nun* and suggests that ‏[ואנֹחו is either a scribal error for ‏אנחנו or an apocopated form thereof. Such an interpretation would suggest that "they" of line 1 stands for the priests/Levites praising God, while "we" refers to the rest of Israel. Yet, if her reading is accepted, it is also possible that the first word is a form of ‏אנה, "to groan", ‏[ואנֹחֹו.[307] However, if the lacuna is an interval between two adjacent words, then the scroll reads ‏נֹחו, a 3rd masc. pl. of ‏נוח, "to rest" (the reconstructions ‏[כ]יא נֹחו and ‏ל[וא נֹחו seem to be precluded, as 4Q379 consistently reads ‏כי and ‏לא [frgs. 3 i 5, 6 3, 18 5, 6, 22 i 6, 26 3]).

---

307 HALOT, pp. 70-71.

The next word is either עֹבְרִ[י]ם, a masc. pl. Qal participle of עבר (Newsom) or עִבְרִ[י]ם, "Hebrews" (cf. ועברים עברו את הירדן [1 Sam 13:4]).[308] In either case a definite article is expected (yet compare 1 Sam 14:11). The use of עבר might point to the crossing of the Jordan (cf. the use of נוח in Josh 3:13), although the marching around the walls of Jericho (cf. the use of עבר in Josh 6:7) should not be discarded.

Frg. 17

[ ]°[ ]° ° °°[		] 1
[מהללי[י]ֹם ומברכים]		] 2
[יצדק]בְּדבריו ויאמן֯ בתוֹֹרֹתֹ]ו		] 3
° [אברהם יצחק ויעקב וֹמשה		] 4
° ° ° א]לְעָֹזֹר ואיֹתֹמֹר אגילה		[ואהרון 5
[ ]°[ ]לֹ[° ° °[ואכלֹ]ו ° ° ° °[		] 6
תה[		
[		] 7

Notes on Readings

3 ויאמן֯. Newsom reads ויאמֹר. The vertical stroke of the last letter descends below the imaginary base line. While this is also the case with the *resh* in the word ואיֹתֹמֹר (line 5), a reading ויאמן֯ (noted by Newsom with Strugnell[309]) is equally possible and is preferable on contextual grounds.

בתוֹֹרֹתֹ]ו. The *DJD* edition has בת°°°[. Strugnell, as well as García Martínez and Tigchelaar, reads בּתוֹֹרֹתֹ]ו.[310] This reading suits well the traces of the ink on the fragment.

6 ואכלֹ]ו. Newsom reads ° א כלֹ[. On the photographs (PAM 41.778; 43.218) the *alef* is preceded by a vertical stroke with a hook-shaped top, as in a *waw* or a *yod*. All the four letters clearly belong to one word. Thus, Strugnell reads here ואכלֹ].[311]

תה[

7 . The editor reads these two letters as line 7, yet they seem to be written between the lines.

---

308 The latter reading was suggested to me by Dr. Noam Mizrahi.

309 Brown et al., *Preliminary Concordance*, vol. 1, p. 169.

310 Brown et al., ibid.; F. García Martínez & E. Tigchelaar, *The Dead Sea Scrolls: Study Edition* (Leiden: Brill, 1997-98), vol. 2, p. 750.

311 Brown et al., ibid., vol. 1, p. 103.

Translation

2. [are praisin]g and blessing [ ]
3. [he will be found righteous]in his words and trustworthy in [his] teaching[ ]
4. [ ] Abraham, Isaac, and Jacob, and Moses
5. [and Aaron, E]leazar and Ithamar. I will rejoice
6. [ ] [ ] [ ] [ ]
   ] [
7. [ ]

Comments

2 מהללי[ם ומברכים. The context and the language, including the use of the pl. Piel participle of ברך, link this fragment to frgs. 15-16 (see Comment to frg. 15 1). The reconstruction follows Ps 145:2. Alternative restorations are שר[ים ומברכים (with Ps 96:2) and מרנ[נ]ים ומברכים (cf. frg. 16 2). The blank space in the end of the line may mark a beginning of a new section containing the actual wording of the praise.

3 [בדבריו ויאמן בתורת]ו יצדק. From this line on the fragment appears to cite the words of praise. The speaker(s) is unknown. The previous line refers to a group of praisers. At the same time, line 5 contains a 1st person exclamation. The verb ויאמן is to be parsed as a Nifal *wayyiqtol* of אמן, "to prove to be reliable, faithful, trustworthy" (cf. frg. 18 8).[312] The reconstruction follows Ps 51:6; 4Q393 1 ii 2.

4 אברהם יצחק ויעקב ומשה. For the lists of the names of the three patriarchs see Gen 50:24; Exod 6:8. Since Moses' name is preceded by a *waw* conjunctive, Newsom suggests that it opens a new clause. However, this is not a necessary conclusion, as it might also be a continuation of the same list. Tov initially suggested that this fragment alludes to Joshua's farewell speech in Josh 24 vv. 4-5, but now links it (following Newsom) with frgs. 15-16 (see Comment to frg. 15 1).[313]

5 [ואהרון] א[ל]עזר ואיתמר אגילה. Newsom suggests that this line praises God "for the institution of the priesthood".[314] The available space could accommodate the names of Aaron and his other two sons, Nadav and Abihu (cf. Exod 6:23). The reconstructed line would count 40 letter-spaces (frg. 12 4-7 have an average of 39). **אגילה**. For the language compare Hab 3:18; Ps 31:8. The identity of the speaker is not clarified, yet Joshua is a likely candidate.

---

312 HALOT, p. 63.
313 Tov, "Rewritten Joshua", p. 254; idem, "Literary Development".
314 Newsom, "4Q379", p. 275. Cf. m. Middot 5:4: ברוך הוא שבחר באהרן ובניו לעמוד לשרת לפני יי.

Frg. 18

1	‏[עֹל̇ן ∘∘ הֹיֹיתה או א̇שֹׁמֹתי[‏
	‏ו‏
2	‏כי יר]הבו כל [ע]זבי אל ובדברֹי רי]ב‏
3	‏ואלך] לדרךֹי וֹאשענה עליך ואתה]ה‏
4	‏ל]היות לי אדנֹ[ין]וֹ כאב אצֹֹ̇ב̇‏
5	‏אלוה דֹבריך אשמור כי ∘[‏
6	‏ובעדֹו]ת] עליון השכלת כי̇ן‏
7	‏אלהי וֹתֹאמן בכל דברי]ך‏
8	‏ל̇[‏

Notes on Readings

1 ‏א̇שֹׁמֹתי[‏. Newsom reads the first word as ‏יֹׁשֹׁ[ט̇‏. Qimron correctly identifies the last two letters as a *taw* and a *yod* (or a *waw*) and suggests ‏א̇שֹׁמֹתי[‏.

‏או∘‏. The *DJD* edition has ‏הֹ̇איֹׁשֹׁ‏. The first letter is illegible (unnoted in Qimron's transcription). Also, on the photographs (PAM 41.778; 43.217; 43.367) there are no traces of ink after the *waw/yod*.

‏הֹיֹיתה‏. Newsom reads ‏הֹיֹֹ̇תה‏. Qimron suggests ‏ואתה‏, yet the letter before the *taw* is not consistent with an *alef* (PAM 43.367). He also reads the first of the following illegible letters as an *alef*.

2 ‏יר]הבו‏. The *DJD* edition has ‏בי∘[‏. On PAM 41.778 one may see the characteristic upper horizontal stroke of a *he*, as well as its vertical stroke. Qimron reads the traces as ‏יבי[ר‏.

‏כל‏. Newsom reads ‏על‏. Yet the first letter may also be read as a medial *kaf* (Strugnell).[315]

‏ובדברֹי רי]ב‏. Qimron reads correctly thus. Newsom suggests ‏ובר̇ב דֹ[ב]רי]ך‏.

3 ‏לדרֹ̇די‏. The editor reads ‏לדרך ואשענה‏, yet observes that the *waw/yod* of ‏ואשענה‏ stands closer to the final *kaf* of ‏לדרך‏, than to an *alef* of ‏אשענה‏. Thus, it is proposed to read here ‏לדרֹ̇די‏.

‏וֹאשענה‏. Newsom notes that there is a trace of ink before the *alef*. According to the photographs (PAM 41.778; 43.367), this trace of a vertical stroke may well be a *waw*.

4 ‏אצֹֹ̇ב̇‏. The *DJD* edition offers no reading for the last letter in this line. On the photographs (PAM 41.778; 43.217; 43.367) a medial *ṣade* or a *bet* is visible. Qimron reads it as a *bet*.

6 ‏כי̇ן‏. Newsom offers no reading for the vertical stroke visible at the end of the line. Qimron suggests that this is a *yod*.

---

315 Brown et al., *Preliminary Concordance*, vol. 4, p. 1488.

7 וֹתֿאמן. Newsom reads אׄתאמן. On PAM 43.367 a vertical stroke of a *waw/yod* is visible before the *taw*. There is no other trace of ink that may support the reading of an *alef*.

Translation

1.   ] my guilt   was   [
2. for] all those who [ab]andon God will act arrogantly. And with words of qua[rrel
3. and I will go] in my way and I will trust in You and Yo[u
4.   to]be for me, O o[ur] Lord, like a father   [
5.   ]God, Your words I will guard, for [
6.   ]and in the decrees of the Most High You have given understanding for[
7.   ]O my God, and you will prove yourself trustworthy in all [Your] words[
8.   ] [

Comments

1 אׄשֿמֿתי[. The fragment contains a prayer. The identity of the speaker and the occasion are unknown. Perhaps, this is Joshua (Newsom; Berthelot).[316] The reference to the guilt (although the reading is uncertain) and to those who forsake God may point to Achan's sin and the subsequent defeat at Ai (cf. Josh 7:6-9; 4Q378 6 ii). Alternatively, this prayer could suit Joshua as he assumes the role of the leader following Moses' death (cf. 4Q378 13 i).

2 כי ירן]הבו כל [ע]זבי אל ו. The first word seems to be a form of רהב, "to act stormily, arrogantly (Isa 3:5), to be foolish (Sir [Ms A] 13:8)".[317] For the phrase 'עזבי ה see Isa 1:28, 65:11. The scroll uses אל instead of the Tetragrammaton.
ובדברי רינ]ב. For the language, compare Deut 17:8.

3 ואלך] לדרכי ואשענה עליך ואת]ה. The speaker seems to contrast his trust in God to the attitude of those who abandon Him. The reconstruction ואלך] לדרכי follows the recurring biblical phrase (cf. Gen 32:2; 1 Sam 26:25). For the expression לע ועשנ with reference to God see Isa 10:20; Micah 3:11. The last word has been reconstructed as ה[תאו to suit the 2nd person address to God. Qimron suggests ואת]מכה or (reading the last letter as two letters) ואחז]יקה.

4 ל]היות לי אדנ]ינ]וֹ כאב אצֿ]ן. For God as a father see Comment to 4Q378 6 i 8. See also frg. 27 2.

Berthelot, "Joshua", p. 100.
317 BDB, p. 923.

5 אלוה דבריך אשמור כי‬[. For the wording compare Ps 119:17, 101. If Joshua is the speaker, this statement may recall Josh 1:8 (Newsom).

6 ובעדו[ת] עליון השכלת כ‬י‬]. The 2nd masc. sg. *qatal* of שכל in Hifil, "to instruct, to teach", has God as its subject.[318] The phrase עדות עליון alludes to Ps 19:8. The scroll appears to replace the Tetragrammaton with עליון. Thus, this fragments refers to God as אל, אלוה/י, אדונינו, and עליון.

7 אלהי תאמן בכל דברי‬ך‬]. For the language compare frg. 17 3. See also 11QPsᵃ XVII, 2-3(=Ps 145:13): נאמן אלהים בדבריו (Qimron).[319]

Frg. 19

```
]ה‬ י‬[ ]בֹ‬ה‬[ ]ל[ ]ל רשעי‬[ם מֹשׁלם גֹמֹ[ו]‬      1
]בת‬[   ]יֹעֹקֹבֹ לשל‬[   עבדי [י]                       2
]ל ]וֹתכם על שֹׁבֹה[ ] ]ות[ ]ל ה‬[                       3
]ישׁ ל[ ]ן[ ]ל[                                        4
]לו לש‬[ ]ה‬[                                           5
]חֹשׁ אֹ[                                              6
]שיך [                                                7
]ל[                                                  8
```

Notes on Readings

1 גֹמֹ[ו]ל רשעי‬ם‬. Newsom reads]ל‬ ישעי‬[ן. The diagonal stroke of the first letter may be read both as a bottom stroke of a *lamed* and as a left stroke of a *gimel*. The traces of the next letter are consistent with a medial *mem*. The first letter of the second word is certainly a *resh*, as its characteristic upper horizontal stroke is well visible on the photographs (PAM 41.778; 43.217; 43.367).

2 עבדו]. The *DJD* edition has עבדי[. Both readings are possible, as a *waw* and a *yod* are frequently indistinguishable in this scroll.

Translation

1.] paying the rew[ar]d of the wick[ed] ones [   ] [   ] [
2.]My servant [J]acob [   ] [

318 HALOT, p. 1328.

319 On the wording of 11QPsᵃ XVII, 2-3 see R.G. Kratz, "'Blessed be the Lord and Blessed Be His Name Forever': Psalm 145 in the Hebrew Bible and in the Psalms Scroll 11Q5", in J. Penner et al. (eds.), *Prayer and Poetry in the Dead Sea Scrolls and Related Literature* (Leiden: Brill, 2012), p. 235.

Comments

1 [מ]שלם ג̇מ̇ו̇ל̇ רשעי̇ם̇]. The 2nd pl. suffix in line 3 suggests that this is a second person address, apparently by God (cf. עבדי in line 2). The language of this line is reminiscent of Isa 66:6.

2 עבדי י[ע]ק̇ב̇]. This could be a reference to the nation of Israel (cf. e.g., Isa 44:2).

Frg. 20

]ל̇ת̇[	1
]י̇ד[	2

Frg. 21

]∘ ש̇ת̇[	1
]∘[	2

Frg. 22 i

]גבורתיו	2 [
]וא̇י̇ן לי משגב	3 [
]תי והבינותי	4 [זולתו
אי]ן̇ אלוה זולתו ואין	5 [
]∘ות כי אלדעות̇	6 [צור כאלהינו
]∘∘∘∘ן אין עמו	7 [יהוה
]א̇י̇ן̇ כל	8 [

Notes on Readings

3 לי. The *DJD* edition has לו. *Waw* and *yod* are frequently indistinguishable in this scroll. However, contextually לי seems to be a better reading (see Comment).

4 תי[. Newsom reads תו[. Yet, given the similarities between *waw* and *yod* תי[is equally possible.

Translation

2. [   ]His mighty deeds
3. [   ]and I have no refuge
4. [apart from Him   ]I[   ]and I understood
5. [there is n]o God apart from Him. And there is no
6. [rock as our God   ] for a God of knowledge

7. [is YHWH　　　　　　] there is no[　　]with Him
8. [　　　　　　　　　　　　　]not any

Comments

גבורתי 1[. As col. ii, line 7 makes clear, this column contains a praise by Joshua. The occasion seems to be the fall of Jericho (Newsom).

זולתו /]ואִֿין לי משגב 2. The reconstruction follows line 5. Qimron prefers בלתו.

תי והבינותי 4[. Qimron restores כי אין כמוהו /]והבינותי.

אי]ןֿ[אֿלוה זולתו ואין]צור כאלהינו 5. For the language compare 2 Sam 7:22. The reconstruction follows 1 Sam 2:2 (cf. an allusion to Hannah's prayer in line 6). Qimron restores צור מבלעדיו (with Ps 18:32).

כי אלדעות /]יהוה 6. The divine appellation אֿלדעות (1 Sam 2:3) is written as one word (cf. frgs. 22 ii 9, 13; 26 3; see also 4Q368 2 6[אלקנאֿ]; 4Q225 2 ii 10[אֿליהוה]).[320] Qimron restores כֿי אלדעות[ ]הוא.

אין עמו 7. For possible reconstructions see Deut 32:12; 2 Chr 19:7.

Frg. 22 ii

1 הֿאֿדֿם אשֿ]ר
2 לֿ[∘∘∘∘]
3 וֿבֿ ותֿ∘רֿהֿ]
4 שביל ומסֿ[לה
5 ברוך יהוה אלהי יֿ]שראל
6 אל [ ]∘∘ [ ]∘∘∘∘]
7 בעת אשר כֿו]לֿהֿ ישֿ]וֿ[וֿ∘ֿ]ֿןֿ לֿ]הֿ[לֿיל ולהֿ]דֿ[וֿ]ֿת בתהלֿ[ותֿ]יו ויאמר]
8 אֿ]רור האֿ]יֿשֿ אשר יבנֿ]הֿ את [העיֿ]רֿ הזאת בבכוֿ]רו ייסדנה]
9 ובצעיֿ]רֿוֿןֿ]יֿצֿיֿבֿדֿלֿתֿיֿהֿ vacat והֿנֿהֿ]ֿ ארוֿ]רֿ אֿ]חד]
10 עומד להיוֿ]תֿ פח יקוש לעמו ומחתה לכל שכנֿ]יֿ[ו ועמ]ד]
11 [ ]סֿ[להיות שניהם כלי חמס ושבו ובנו אֿ]תֿ]
12 [העיר הֿ]זאת ויציבו לה חומה ומגדלים לעשותֿ] לעוז]
בישראל ושערוריה באפריֿם] וביהודה
13 [רשע וע]ֿשֿ[וֿ]רֿעֿה גדלה{בבני יעקב ושפֿ]כֿ[וֿ]ֿןֿ דֿ]סֿ{ם]
14 [ועשו חנופה בֿ]אֿרץ ונאצה גדלה *כֿמֿיֿ]ם על חל בת ציון]
15 [ובחוק ירושלים] [∘∘∘∘∘]

320 Livneh, "Composition", p. 90.

Notes on Readings

3 ו.ת̊רֹ[ה]. Newsom offers no reading for the second word preserved in this line. Dimant suggests יֹֹ̊̊ר̊ה. According to the photographs (esp. PAM 41.784), the second letter could be a *taw*. It is followed by illegible traces of one or two letters. Next to them a *resh* (or a *dalet*) and a *he* are visible.

4 שביל ומס̊[ל]ה. The *DJD* edition has שׁ̊אֹול ומ[ֹ. Dimant appropriately corrects it to שביל ומס̊[ל]ה.

7 כ̊אשר. Newsom reads אשר. On PAM 41.784 a medial *kaf* before an *alef* is visible.

8 בבכו[רו]. The editor reads בבכֹ̊ו[רו]. Qimron suggests בבכֹ̊ו[רו] (cf. 4Q175 22 בבכורו). The trace of the vertical stroke can be read both as a *waw* and a *resh*.

9 ובצעי[רֹ̊ו]. Newsom reads וֹ̊.ב̊[צ]ע̊י[רו]. I was not able to locate the *waw* and the *bet* on the extant fragments and their photographs. The faint traces of the two letters deciphered by Newsom as *ayin* and *yod* are at a short distance from the following יֹ̊ציבדלתתֹ̊ה. Thus, they are more likely to be the *resh* and the *waw*.
יֹ̊ציבדלתתֹ̊ה. The *DJD* edition reads [י.ציבדלתתֹ̊ה. However, as Dimant observes, a trace of a *yod* is still visible on the fragment.[321]

ו̊הֹ̊נֹ̊ה] ארו]ר̊ אֹ̊[חד]. In the preliminary edition Newsom reads ו̊הֹ̊נֹ̊ה] ארֹ[ור̊ [איש בליעל], yet the final edition has ו̊הֹ̊נֹ̊ה] אר[ור̊ אֹ̊[י]ש בליעל]. Dimant suggests והנה איש ארור [בליעל.[322] Qimron reads ו̊הֹ̊נ̊ה איש ארור בליעל]. Some 4-5 letter-spaces to the left of ו̊הֹ̊נֹ̊ה, there are bottom tips of two letters above the *waw* and the *mem* of ועמ[ד] in line 10 (PAM 43.217; 43.367). Lim reads them as *alef* and *resh*: וֹא̊[נה איש אֹ̊ר̊[ור אֹ̊[חד בליעל.[323] Yet, according to PAM 43.217 the interval between the two letters is too large for them to be two consecutive letters. It is more likely that they belong to two different words.

10 להיו[ן]ת̊. The editor reads [עומד] לֹ̊הֹ̊[י]ות. Yet, as Lim and Dimant (עומד להיות]) observe, there are no traces of *lamed* and *he* on the fragment[324]

11 ם̊[. Abegg & Wacholder, Cross, and Qimron read (correctly) a final *mem*.[325] Lim and Newsom prefer a final *nun*.[326]

---

321 Dimant, "Between Sectarian", p. 122.

322 Dimant, ibid.

323 T.H. Lim, "The 'Psalms of Joshua' (4Q379 22 ii): A Reconsideration of Its Text", *JJS* 44 (1993), p. 312.

324 Lim, "Reconsideration", p. 312; Dimant, "Between Sectarian", p. 122.

325 Wacholder & Abegg, *Preliminary Edition*, vol. 3, p. 185; F.M. Cross, "Testimonia", in J.H. Charlesworth et al. (eds.), *Pesharim, Other Commentaries, and Related Documents* (The Dead Sea Scrolls: Hebrew, Aramaic, and Greek Texts with English Translations 6B; Tübingen: Mohr Siebeck, Louisville: Westminster John Knox Press, 2002), p. 318 note 55.

326 Lim, "Reconsideration", p. 311.

13 וע]שׁורׂעה. Newsom reads [בארץ ר[שׁ]ה{ה}עה]. Yet, Dimant rightly observes that next to a *shin* a *waw* is clearly visible. It is followed by a trace of a *resh* (e.g. PAM 41.778). Thus she reads וע]שׁורׂעה.[327] Apparently, the two words were written without a separating space (cf. יׂציבדלתתׁיׂה [line 9]).

וׂשׁפֿ]כ[וׂן ד]םֿ. Newsom reads וׁשׁפֿ[כו דם]. On the photographs (PAM 42.818; 43.217; 43.367) traces of two (or perhaps) three letters are visible below the cancellation dots. One might be a top of a *waw*, while the second one suits the upper horizontal stroke of a final *mem*.

Translation

1. the man wh[o
2. [   ]
3. in him   [   ]
4. a path and a ro[ad
5. blessed be YHWH, God of I[srael   ]
6. God   [ ]   [   ]
7. When Josh[u]a fin[ish]ed pr[aising and giving] than[ks] with [his] songs of praise [he said:]
8. 'C[ursed be the m]an who rebu[il]ds this [ci]ty. With [his] firstborn [shall he lay its foundations]
9. and with [his yo]ung[est] shall he set up its doors'. *vacat* And behold, an [accur]sed o[ne]
10. [is arising to becom]e a fowler's snare to his people and a terror to all hi[s] neighbours. And he will ari[se]
11. [   ] to become both of them vessels of violence. And they will again build
12. [t]his [city]. And they will establish for it a wall and towers in order to make[(it) a sronghold of]
13a. in Israel and a horrible thing in Ephraim[and in Judah   ]
13. [wickedness. And they made] a great evil {among the sons of Jacob and (they) will po[ur out blo]od}
14. [And they have done ungodliness] in the land and great defamation *like wa[ter upon the rampart of the Daughter of Zion]
15. [and within the boundary of Jerusalem]   [

Comments

שׁביל ומסׂ]לה 2. Lines 1-6 seem to contain Joshua's praises related to the fall of Jericho. The phrase שׁביל ומסׂ]לה is not attested to in the Hebrew Bible (cf. the word

---

327 Dimant, "Between Sectarian", pp. 122-123.

pair דרך and מסלה in Isa 40:3, 49:11). Compare יִמְסלי ... אמת עלמא בשבילי מהלך והוית ארחת קושט in 1QapGen VI, 2-3.[328]

5 יִ[שראל אלהי יהוה ברוך. Lines 5-6 conclude Joshua's praise. A similar closing formula occurs in the concluding section of several psalms (e.g., in Pss 41 and 106 [Newsom]).

7 יו[בתהלות ות[ה[ול[לה וה[ל[ל[ון לה[ל יש[ו[ון כ[ל[ה אשר בעת. This formulation, paraphrasing Josh 6:26a, introduces Joshua's curse. The restoration follows the parallel text from 4Q175 21. Joshua's name is spelled here as ישוע (see Comment to 4Q378 22 i 2). For the construction אשר בעת see 2 Chr 25:27. The verbal pair ולהודות להלל occurs in Neh 12:24; 1 Chr 16:4. For plural בתהלו[ת]יו compare Isa 60:6.

8-9 צי[צ[בדלת[ת]ה[ן] [ובצעי[ר[ון] / יייסדנה] בבכר[ו] הזאת הע[יר]ו את יב[נ]ה[אשר א[רור האِ[י]שׁ אֳ[רור] ויאמר. The scroll cites Josh 6:26 (cf. 4Q175 22-23). Unlike the MT, it lacks the phrases לפני ה', יקום, את יריחו (the latter two are missing also from LXX) and reads יבנה, instead of ובנה. See Discussion.

9-10 שכנ[י]ו לכל ומחתה לעמו יקוש פח לה[יו]ת [עומד / א[ח]ד ארו[ל]ר והٓנٓ[ה. A blank space, some 12 letter-spaces large, intervenes between the curse and its interpretation (4Q175 23 has a two letter-spaces interval). The explication of Josh 6:26 opens with the demonstrative particle והٓנٓה. In Biblical Hebrew it often "functions as a bridge for a logical connection between a preceding clause and the clause it introduces".[329] Thus, this pronoun links Joshua's prophecy to its exposition, which, although formally set apart by a *vacat*, is syntactically presented as a continuation of Joshua's speech. Similarly, 4Q522 9 ii 3 introduces Joshua's prophecy with הנה כי.[330]

א[ח]ד ארו[ל]ר. The restoration follows 4Q175 23-24. Space considerations indicate that the scroll did not contain the words איש and בליעל found in 4Q175 23. For the phrase אחד ארור והנה compare אחד נביא והנה (1 Kgs 20:13).

ת[עומד לחיו]ת. Dimant takes להיו]ת [עומד to be a periphrastic future and renders it as "[is about] to b[e]". Well attested in the Amoraic sources, the construction 'עומד+infinitive' to denote future is rare in the Mishnaic Hebrew (m. Bava Qamma 9:1).[331] It seems more likely that the phrase להיו]ת [עומד should be understood as

---

328 Machiela, *Genesis Apocryphon*, p. 43.

329 B.K. Waltke & M. O'Connor, *An Introduction to Biblical Hebrew Syntax* (Winnona Lake, Indiana: Eisenbrauns, 1990), pp. 627-628.

330 Qimron, "Joshua Cycles", pp. 506-507 note 13; Dimant, "Between Sectarian", p. 126.

331 M. Pérez Fernández, *An Introductory Grammar of Rabbinic Hebrew* (Leiden: Brill, 1997), pp. 147-148, notes (with M. Mishor) that עומד ל- is an Amoraic idiom that was introduced into the text of the Mishnah by later copyists. As to 4Q491 14-15 3, reading להתקרב עומדים הננו ואנו, the participle עומדים does not refer to a future action, but to a standing or rising. See R. Ishay, "Qumran

"is arising to be/become" (for the use of a participle to denote a future action cf. Gen 6:17; Exod 9:17-18; 1 Sam 3:11).[332] Qimron suggests that עומד replaces the biblical יקום ובנה).[333] (אשר יקום) The tendency to use עמד instead of קום in later Biblical and Qumran Hebrew is well known (see Comment to frg. 12 2). As Hurvitz notes, עמד may take the meanings "to rise, appear, take office" (cf. 4Q174 1-2 i 13 paraphrasing Judg 10:1).[334] Qimron proposes that עומד here denotes "to rule" (cf. Dan 8:23; Sir 47:12[Ms B]).

פח יקוש לעמו ומחתה לכל שכנ]יו. The idiom פח יקוש, a "fowler's snare", is borrowed from Hos 9:8 (cf. also Ps 91:3).[335] The phrase מחתה לכל שכניו seems to point to Jer 48:39. Dimant suggests that מחתה, "terror, ruin, corruption", stands here for "terror", rather than for "ruin" (Newsom).[336]

ם] להיות שניהם כלי חמס 10-11 [| / [ועמ]ד |]. The *weqatal* form of עמד presents the accursed one's taking of an office as a future event, as is appropriate for a prophecy. Qimron restores the lacuna (with 4Q175) as ו̊עמ]ד | / [לשים שני בני]ם̊, yet this reconstruction seems to be a little too long. The expression כלי חמס is borrowed from Gen 49:5.

ושבו ובנו 11. This phrase expands the verb יבנה of Joshua's curse (MT has יקום ובנה). ושבו is an auxiliary verb used here in an adverbial sense, "again, further".[337] The reconstruction follows 4Q175 25-26.

ויציבו לה חומה ומגדלים 12. The verb ויציבו points to יציב of Josh 6:26, while the phrase חומה ומגדלים expands the biblical דלתיה (cf. 2 Chr 14:6; see also Isa 26:1).

לעשות] לעוז] / [רשע 12-13. The reconstruction לעוז רשע, following 4Q175 26, seems to be a word-play on Isa 26:1, replacing ישועה ("salvation") with רשע ("wickedness").

** וע]שו̊רעה גדלה 13** בישראל ושערוריה באפרים] וביהודה. The eye of the scribe skipped over the sentence בישראל ... ונאצה גדלה, apparently due to a homoioteleuton (רעה גדלה...ונאצה גדלה). To correct the omission, he marked the phrase ם̊ ד[ו̊]ן וש̊פ̊[כ with dots above the letters and added the missing text between the lines. In line 14, before the word כ̊מ̊]ם, where the deleted phrase ם̊ ד[ו̊]ן בבני יעקב וש̊פ̊[כ belongs, he put

---

Literature Related to the Eschatological War; Manuscipts 4Q491-496: Editions, Commentaries, and Comparisons with the War Scroll (1QM)", Ph.D. diss., University of Haifa 2006, p. 151.
332 Waltke & O'Connor, *Hebrew Syntax*, pp. 627-628.
333 Qimron, "Joshua Cycles", p. 507.
334 Hurvitz, "The Linguistic Status of Ben Sira", p. 79.
335 HALOT, p. 430.
336 Ibid., p. 572.
337 Waltke & O'Connor, *Hebrew Syntax*, pp. 75-76, 656.

a dot to the left of the *kaf*'s upper bar, so that the reader would know where to introduce the misplaced phrase. For the wording see Gen 39:9; Hos 6:10-11.[338]

14 [וְעָשׂוּ חֲנוּפָה] בָּאָרֶץ וּנְאָצָה גְדֹלָה בִּבְנֵי יַעֲקֹב. The beginning of the line is restored with 4Q175 28-29. The nouns חֲנוּפָה, "ungodliness", and נְאָצָה, "defamation, blasphemy", point to Jer 23:15 and Neh 9:18, 26.[339]

14-15 [וּבְחוּק יְרוּשָׁלַיִם] / וַשְׁפ[כ]וּ דָּ[מָּ]ם כַּמַּיִם עַל חֵל בַּת צִיּוֹן]. The restoration follows 4Q175 29-30. The phrase וַשְׁפ[כ]וּ דָּ[מָּ]ם כַּמַּיִם is borrowed from Ps 79:3. The ensuing wording may constitute an elaboration on the phrase סְבִיבוֹת יְרוּשָׁלִם found in this verse. The nouns חֵל, "outer rampart, outwork", and חוּק, "prescribed limit, boundary" (Jer 5:22), may point to Isa 26:1 (alluded to in line 12) and/or to Lam 2:8.[340]

Frg. 23

]∘ב[]∘∘[	1
]∘∘[	2

Frg. 24

]∘ ∘∘∘∘[	1
]וֹ ∘ם שָׁגִיתָ[	2
]∘∘∘∘[	3

Notes on Readings

2]וֹ ∘ם שָׁגִיתָ[. The vertical stroke next to the taw seems to be crossed out and a final *mem*, written half way below this vertical stroke, appears to be a correction (cf. 11QTᵃ XVII, 13).[341] At the end of the line a *waw*, unnoted by the editor, is visible (PAM 42.818; 43.217; 43.367).

Translation

2.]you have made a mistake and[

---

338 H. Eshel, "The Historical Background of the Pesher Interpreting Joshua's Curse on the Rebuilder of Jericho", *RevQ* 15 (1991-92), p. 416, suggests that the names Ephraim and Judah are used here as *pesher* soubriquets, as is the case, for instance, in *Pesher Nahum* (4Q169). Yet, the text offers no support for this claim (Newsom).

339 HALOT, pp. 336, 658.

340 Ibid., p. 312; BDB, p. 349.

341 Tov, *Scribal Practices*, pp. 226-227.

Comments

2 The 2nd masc. pl. from of שגה, "to make a mistake, to do wrong inadvertently, unintentionally", appears to be a part of a 2nd person address. The context is unknown.

Frg. 25

[מחֹתֹ]ה   1

[עֹלִי]ן   2

Translation

1.   ] a terro[r
2.   ] upon [

Comments

1 ה]מחֹתֹ. The reconstruction מחֹתֹ]ה, "terror, ruin, corruption", as in frg. 22 ii 10, suggests that frg. 25 belongs with frg. 22.

Frg. 26

[°ל]°°°[ן התֹאֹ°°°°   1

ובני יש]רֹאֹל שֹבֹוֹ בבֹית אלֹ   2

[°[ ]°°°[בֹירחקו   3

[°°ל]°   4

Notes on Readings

1 Newsom reads the last letter as a final *mem*. The traces of ink are difficult to decipher and do not seem to suit a final *mem*.

2 יש]רֹאֹל. There is a trace of another letter before *alef* (PAM 43.217; 43.367; unnoticed by the editor). Perhaps, this is a *resh*.

שֹבֹוֹ. The *DJD* edition has סֹכֹוֹ.[342] The first letter may also be interpreted as a *shin* (as Newsom observes), while the second letter might be a *bet*, and not a medial *kaf*.

---

342 This reading is endorsed by E. Eshel, "Jubilees 32 and the Bethel Cult Traditions in Second Temple Literature", in E.G. Chazon et al. (eds.), *Things Revealed* (Leiden: Brill, 2004), pp. 28-29, who renders it as "his (God's) abode" and links it to the traditions associating Jacob, the Festival of Booths, and Bethel.

3 בֿיררחקו. Newsom reads כֿי רחקו.

Translation
1.   ]
2. and the sons of Is]rael returned to Bethel
3.   ] [ ]   for they were far off

Comments
2 ובני יש]רֿאֿל שֿבֿוֿ בֿבֿית אֿל. While the first word may be read as a command, שְׁבוּ, "dwell", it is likely that this is a 3rd masc. pl. *qatal* of שוב, "to return". For the construction שוב ב- see 4Q258 VII, 1. Apparently, the fragment deals with the conquest of Ai (Newsom; see Josh 8:12).

3 בֿיררחקו. The Qal *qatal* of רחק, "to be distant", and the conjunction כי have been written as one word (cf. frgs. 22 ii 9, 13; 26 3).[343] Possibly, this is an allusion to Josh 8:16.

Frg. 27

[	ה לֿשֿן] [ ] 1
לֿא]	2 ואבי שחרֿ]תיך
[	3 עזבתנו ולֿ]א
[	4 בֿ]ן

Notes on Readings
2 ואבי. Newsom reads ואבו, yet notes that the *waw* may also be read as a *yod*.

Translation
1. [   ] [   ]
2. and my father. I have search[ed You   ]
3. You have [not] abandoned us and not[   ]
4. [   ]

Comments
2 ואבי שחרֿ]תיך. The fragment contains a prayer. The speaker addresses God as אבי (cf. אבי ואדוני [4Q460 9 i 6]; see also Comment to 4Q378 6 i 8, 7 2). This usage relates this prayer to the one found in frg. 18 (note line 4). The second word seems

---

343 HALOT, p. 1221.

to be a Piel form of שחר, "to be on the look out for".³⁴⁴ The line is reconstructed as שחר]תיך (with Ps 63:2), yet שחר]תי את פניך (Pr 7:15) and שחר]תי אליך (Job 8:5) are also possible.

3 לא]א / עזבתנו ול]א. Newsom suggests that this prayer is related to the defeat at Ai (Josh 7:6-9; cf. Comment to frg. 18 1). Perhaps, one may restore לא] /עזבתנו י (cf. 1QHª XIII 7, 8, 14, 22).

Frg. 28

]∘∘[1

ויתן]אֺת ארצֺוֺתם בידֺין   2

]לֺ[]רֺשע תקוה בארץ וֺ]∘   3

[בצֺוֺר∘∘ עד ∘ש∘הֺ כ]   4

]לֺ[5

Notes on Readings

2 אֺ]. The *DJD* edition offers no reading for the first letter in this line. The vertical stroke descending to the left (PAM 43.367) may well be the left stroke of an *alef*.

2 בידֺן]. Newsom reads ביר∘[. The third letter may also be read as a *dalet*. The shape of the following vertical stroke is consistent with a *waw*.

3]לֺ[. There is a trace of ink to the right of רֺשע (PAM 43.367), which would suit the vertical upper stroke of a *lamed*.

4 בצֺוֺר∘∘ [. There is a trace of a letter added between the lines. The last two letters have been read by Newsom (בצֺוֺרות) as *waw* and *taw*, yet the traces do not seem to match this reading.

Translation

1.] [
2. and He gave] their lands in the hands of [
3.]wicked one a hope in the land and [
4.] until [
5.] [

---

344 HALOT, p. 1465.

Comments

2 [אֵת אֳרְצֹׄתׅׄם בידׄׄן. The missing verb in the beginning of the line is, apparently, a form of נתן. The scroll may refer to the territories of the nations dispossessed by the Israelites (cf. Gen 26:3). If Joshua is the speaker, compare his address to Israel in Josh 3:10.

3 [לׄ] [רׄשע תקוה בארץ. This line seems to deny the wicked ones (perhaps, the Canaanites) of a hope in the land (cf. Pr 10:28; 4Q221 2 i 1[=Jub 22:22]).

Frg. 29

[מׄרׄ כבׄן	1
]°°[	2

Notes on Readings

1 The *DJD* edition reads [נו כמׄ]. The trace of the upper horizontal stroke suggests that the first letter is not a medial *nun*, but a medial *mem* or a *samech*. The second letter is clearly a *resh*, as its long upper horizontal stroke indicates. The last letter is most likely a *bet*, for its base stroke protrudes beyond its vertical one (see PAM 43.367).

Frg. 30

[הׄ]	1
[אׄמת לׄכל תבל]	2
[°° °[ ] [מׄלת וׄ]	3
]°°[	4

Notes on Readings

3 °[ ] [מׄלת. There is a letter-size lacuna before the medial *mem* (unnoticed by the editor).

Translation

1.   ] [
2.]truth to (the) whole world [
3.]   [
4.   ] [

Comments

2 [אׄמת לׄכל תבל. Compare אמת תבל (1QS IV, 6, 19). Note also the wording of 4Q378 12 2: כל תבל בתים [.

Frg. 31 i

$$\begin{array}{lr}
\text{ל}°[& 6 \\
°[& 7
\end{array}$$

Frg. 31 ii

1 [ג]ב̊ו̊ל̊[ן̊
2 [ ]ל̊ב̊ר̊[°ן
3 [ ] עב̊ן [ר]ן
4 [ ]מ̊°° °°[ן
5 גבה ה̊°[ן
6 עמו רב̊ים [ ]
7 עמהם ב°[ן
8 ד̊ברי[ן̊

Notes on Readings

4 °°מ̊[. The *DJD* edition reads °°כ̊[. The first letter is most likely a medial *mem*. A trace of its upper stroke descending to the left is visible on PAM 43.367. The second letter is difficult to decipher.

Translation

1. [b]order[
2. [ ] [
3. [ ] [ ] [
4. [ ]   [
5. was high [
6. with him multitudes [
7. with them [
8. my word[

Comments

1 [ג]ב̊ו̊ל̊[ן̊. This mention of "[b]order" suggests that this fragment deals with either the entrance to the Land of Canaan (cf. frg. 4 1) or with the Israelites' conquest thereof.

5 גבה. It is unclear whether one should read here a noun גֹּבַהּ, "a height" (thus Newsom), an adjective גָּבֹהַ, "high", or a form of a Qal *qatal* of גבה, "to be high".

8 ד̊ברי[ן̊. One may read ד̊ברי[ן̊ as "my word(s)" or as the "words of".

Frg. 32

[וע̊ד̊]	1
א[חד מה̊ם̊]°°	2
[איש הי̊ו̊ מהם ב̊]	3
[לן]° [ ]° אלהינו על כ̊לן]	4
[לע̊ו̊זרו ולש̊°]	5
[ולא̊י̊ש ב°°]	6
[ל ד̊°°]	7
[°] [°]	8

Notes on Readings

3 הי̊ו̊. Newsom reads הו̊א̊. The relatively short vertical stroke of the second letter may indicate that this is a *yod*, and not a *waw*. The shape of the third letter is more consistent with a *waw* than with an *alef*, though the upper diagonal stroke is a little longer than usual for a *waw/yod* in this scroll.

5 לע̊ו̊זרו. Newsom reads ל [° עו̊זרי. The distance between the *lamed* and the *ayin* is similar to that between the *lamed* and the *shin* in the following word. The last letter may be read either as a *waw* or a *yod*.

Translation

1.] and until [
2. o]ne of them   [
3.] men were from them [
4.] [ ]   our God over all[
5.] to help him and to[
6.]and to the man   [
7.]   [

Comments

3 [איש הי̊ו̊ מהם. Most likely, a numeral designating the number of "men" is missing in the beginning of the line.

4 אלהינו. Perhaps, this fragment contains an address to Israel recounting a past event and referring to God as "our God".

Frg. 33

[°אם]	1
[°יום]	2
[או̊ כלמ̊]	3
[°ק̊ מלי°]	4

Frg. 34

]בֿ[מׄ ֯יׄׄן[	1
יׄׄׄם[ ]֯[ ]ל וכֿׄלֿן[	2
הׄ֯ם[ ]֯֯֯[ ]כלו[	3
]֯ אׄהל[	4
]֯[	5

Notes on Readings
3 According to PAM 41.784 the last three letters are medial *kaf*, *lamed*, and *waw*.

Translation
4.]tent [

Frg. 35

]֯תׄ רׄ֯[	1
]֯ ֯וׄ֯֯[	2

Frg. 36

]֯֯הׄ וגדׄולֿה[	1
]֯ נביאים ֯[	2
] ׄׄׄׄׄׄ ׄׄׄ[	3

Translation
1.]   and greatness[
2.]   prophets [

Comments
1 [הׄ֯֯ וגדׄולֿה]. Perhaps, read and restore גב[וׄרׄהׄ וגדולה (with 1 Chr 29:11). Note the use of גדולה in frg. 4 3.

2 נביאים. The context in which "prophets" are mentioned is unclear.

Frg. 37

]רם	1
]ל	2

Frg. 38

]הׄבית[	1

Translation
1.]the house[

Frg. 39

]° ֺוּבשֹׁמֺוֹ[1

Notes on Readings
The *DJD* edition reads יאמֺוֹ. The trace of a base indicates that the second letter is either a *bet* or a medial *kaf*. The traces of *shin*'s lower part are clearly visible on PAM 43.218. On that photograph frg. 39 is placed near the bottom line of frg. 13. This placement seems to be unwarranted.

Translation
1.]and in his name [

Frg. 40

]°°° ם[1
]°°°°°° י'[2
] כל°° °[3

Translation
1.]all[

Frg. 41

]כֹֿלֹ[1

Translation
1.]all[

3.5 Discussion

The extant fragments of 4Q379 elaborate on the biblical account of the crossing of the Jordan and Joshua's curse on the person who will re-build Jericho. A detailed analysis of these passages sheds light on the date and provenance of this composition.

3.5.1 The Crossing of the Jordan

Frg. 12, paraphrasing Josh 3:15-17, contains several exegetical additions. The first one, expanding on Josh 3:17, clarifies the date of the crossing and its significance for the calculation of the jubilean years (lines 3-6). Deriving its chronological data from Josh 4:19 and Deut 1:3; 34:8, frg. 12 dates the crossing to the first month of the forty-first year from Exodus. To these scriptural data, the scroll adds a non-biblical formulation, "this is the year for Jubilees".[345] It suggests that the jubilean computation stipulated in Lev 25 begins in the year of the crossing (Dimant).[346] To further clarify this point, the scroll adds a phrase "from the beginning of their entrance to the land of Canaan". Alluding to Lev 25:2 ("When you enter the land that I assign to you, the land shall observe a Sabbath of the Lord"), this addition modifies the wording of the verse in two ways.

First, it introduces the word לתחלת, "from the beginning". This addition has been taken to indicate that 4Q379 begins the jubilean computation from the month of the crossing, i.e. Nisan (Dimant).[347] Yet, since the clause "from the beginning of their entrance to the land of Canaan" is an apposition to the preceding "this is the year for Jubilees", it explicates the significance of the *year* of the crossing, and not that of the month. According to Lev 25:8-12 the first month of a jubilean year is Tishre. Arriving six months after the crossing, the month of Tishre still falls within the same forty-first year from the Exodus.[348]

---

345 Newsom, "4Q379", p. 271, and (with more detail) Dimant, "Between Sectarian", p. 116, suggest that 4Q379 utilizes a jubilean chronology similar to that of the Book of Jubilees. According to Jub 50:4, the crossing of the Jordan occurred in the Jubilee year, the fiftieth Jubilee since the creation of the world. However, the scroll does not claim that the year of the crossing was a jubilee year. Neither does it provide any evidence that it embraces a Sabbatical/jubilean chronology like that of Jubilees.

346 Dimant, ibid., pp. 115-117, aptly compares the formulation "the year for Jubilees (היא השנה ליובלים)" with m. Rosh Hashana 1:1: "The first day of Tishre is the new year for the reckoning of years (לשנים), for Sabbatical years (ולשמיטין), and for Jubilees (וליובלות)". Cited from J. Neusner, *The Mishnah: A New Translation* (Yale: Yale University Press, 1991), p. 299.

347 Dimant, ibid., believes that, since the Rabbinic tradition places the beginning of the Sabbatical and jubilean years in Tishre, the scroll's wording reflects a polemical stance, perhaps an adherence to the the the solar calendar. Yet, this assumption finds no support in the text.

348 J. Ben-Dov, "Jubilean Chronology and the 364-Day Year", *Meghillot* 5-6 (2007), pp. 49-60 (Hebrew), demonstrates that the ancient sources furnish no evidence for a calendrical system calculating Sabbatical/jubilean years from the 1st of Nisan. Dimant, "Between Sectarian", p. 116, refers to Josh 5:12 as indicating an observance of the *shemiṭṭah* dietary restrictions. However, there is nothing to suggest that this is the intention of the biblical passage or that 4Q379 understood it in this way, for the scroll presents the year of the crossing as the beginning of the Sabbatical/jubilean computation, not as a Sabbatical year.

Second, the scroll rephrases the "land" of Lev 25:2 as "the Land of Canaan". The boundaries of the Land of Canaan, as they are outlined in Numbers 34:2-12 (see also Num 33:51, 35:10; Josh 22:10-11), exclude the territories to the east of Jordan.[349] Accordingly, the wording of the scroll indicates that the Pentateuchal jubilean laws became operative only with the crossing of the Jordan. A similar understanding of the entrance to the Land of Canaan making the jubilean laws effective is found in Jub 50:2.[350]

4Q379's view on the beginning of the jubilean computation, shared by the Samaritan tradition, differs from the rabbinic halakha.[351] The latter postulates that the Sabbatical computation begins fourteen years after the entrance into the Promised Land (Dimant).[352] This view is found already in the Tannaitic sources (t.

---

349 See Z. Kallai, "The Boundaries of Canaan and the Land of Israel in the Bible", *Eretz Israel* 12 (1975), p. 33 (Hebrew); Y. Aharoni, *The Land of the Bible: A Historical Geography* (Philadelphia: The Westminster Press, 1979²), pp. 74, 76.

350 As pointed out by Dimant, "Between Sectarian", p. 116.

351 Compare the 12th century's Tulida: ויהוה הידע כי ראש מחשבון השמטה והיוביל מן ראש חדש השביעי שנת מעברון ארץ כנען: טרם ירשו את הארץ לגבלותיה סביב (M. Florentin, *The Tulida: A Samaritan Chronicle* [Jerusalem: Yad Izhak ben Zvi, 1999], pp. 58-59 [Hebrew]). See also a formulation reminiscent of 4Q379 in the Arabic Book of Joshua (13th century): "And the cloud was lifted up, on the first (day) of the first month, of the first year of the first period of seven years of the Jûbîl (Jubilee), *even from the beginning of the entering in of the children of Isrâîl within the boundaries of the assigned land*" (Crane, *Samaritan Chronicle*, pp. 46-47 [emphasis mine]). As in the case of 4Q379, there is no reason to assume that the phrase "even from the beginning …" implies that the Samaritan jubilean calculation began in Nisan. The Tulida and other Samaritan sources point to Tishre as the first month of a Sabbatical/jubilean year. On dating the crossing to the 1st of Nisan, rather than to the 10th, see T.W.J. Juynboll, *Chronicon Samaritanum, Arabice Conscriptum, cui titulus est Liber Josuae* (Lugduni Batavorum: S&J. Luchtmans, 1848), pp. 230-231. Similar formulations are found in what appears to be Hebrew translations of the 19th century Samaritan work indebted to the Arabic Book of Joshua (Bóid, "Transmission", pp. 16-18). For the texts see F. Niessen, *Eine Samaritanische Version des Buches Yehošuaʿ und die Šobak-Erzählung* (TSO 12; Hildesheim: Georg OlmsVerlag, 2000), p. 76; M. Gaster, "Das Buch Josua in hebräisch-samaritanischer Rezension. Entdeckt und zum ersten Male hereausgegeben", *ZDMG* 62 (1908), p. 243; J. Macdonald, *The Samaritan Chronicle No. II (or: Sepher Ha-Yamim): From Joshua to Nebuchanezzar* (Berlin: Walter de Gruyter & Co, 1969), p. 12 (providing the same Hebrew translation as Gaster). On the Samaritan computation of the Sabbatical/jubilean years see S. Powels, "The Samaritan Calendar", in A.D. Crown (ed.), *The Samaritans* (Tübingen: J.C.B. Mohr, 1989), pp. 712, 717.

352 Dimant, "Between Sectarian", p. 111. The rabbinic chronology postulates that Israel's dwelling in the Promised Land, from the entrance under Joshua to the destruction of the First Temple, lasted 850 years, i.e., 17 Jubilees (b. Arachin 12a-b, 13a). Yet, this calculation presents a difficulty in light of Ezek 40:1. According to the Rabbis, the year when "the beginning of the year" falls on the tenth of the month is a jubilean year, as a Jubilee is announced on the Day of Atonement (10th of Tishre). Yet, if the year mentioned in Ezek 40:1 was a jubilean year and it was the fourteenth year since the fall of Jerusalem, then the destruction of Jerusalem could not have taken place on

Menahot 6:20 [ed. Zuckermandel, p. 521]). If the scroll's reading of the crossing story in light of the Torah jubilean laws betrays a polemic, it could be an argument against a similar tradition positing a later starting point for the jubilean computation.

The second addition to the crossing account in frg. 12 6-7 expands on Josh 3:15. First, it amplifies the biblical description of the Jordan's waters, perhaps, in order to highlight the miraculous aspect of the event: "And the Jordan was full of wat[er] over all its banks and overflowing / [with] its waters". A similar amplification is found in Josephus' account (Dimant):[353]

> "Now since the army was afraid to cross the river, *which had a strong current and could not be crossed by bridges*—for it had not been spanned by any hitherto, and, should they wish to lay them now, the enemy would not, they imagined, afford them the leisure, and they had no ferry boats—God promised to render the stream passable for them by diminishing its volume" (J. Ant. 5:16)[354]

Second, the scroll further expands Josh 3:15 stating that the Jordan overflows with water until the third month, when the wheat harvest takes place. This addition may simply be a clarification of the MT's "throughout the harvest season". Yet, it is more likely that the scroll is familiar with a reading similar to that of 4QJosh[b] 2-3 2 (בימי קציר‏חטים) and LXX (ὡσεὶ ἡμέραι θερισμοῦ πυρῶν),[355] indicating that the harvest of Josh 3:15 is the wheat harvest.[356] The wording of 4Q379 may reflect an attempt to smooth out a difficulty posed by such a reading. The month of Nisan when the Israelites crossed the Jordan is the time of the barley harvest (קציר שערים [2 Sam 21:9; Ruth 1:22, 2:23]), not of the wheat harvest. The latter begins after the barley is gathered and its completion is celebrated during the Festival of Weeks in the third month, the month of Sivan (Exod 34:22).[357] The scroll seems to solve

---

the last year of a Jubilee. In other words, it is impossible to have 17 complete Jubilees from the entrance into the Land to the destruction of the first Temple. To resolve this difficulty and yet to maintain the overall figure of 850 years, it was proposed that the computation of the Sabbatical/jubilean years began fourteen years after the entrance into the Promised Land. These years are said to have been the period when the land was subdued and divided. For an attempt to link this period of fourteen years to Josh 14:7, 10 see b. Zebaḥim 118b.

353 Dimant, "Between Sectarian", p. 113. See further Begg, "Crossing", p. 3 note 3.
354 Thackeray & Marcus, *Josephus*, p. 9.
355 Tov, "4QJosh[b]", pp. 155-157.
356 Both possibilities are noted and discussed by Dimant, "Between Sectarian", p. 114.
357 See O. Borowski, *Agriculture in Iron Age Israel* (Winona Lake, Indiana: Eisenbrauns, 1987), pp. 57, 88-92.

the difficulty by making the month of the wheat harvest the upper time limit of the period when the Jordan overflows with water.[358]

Finally, it is possible that frgs. 15-17 also deal with the crossing of the Jordan. According to one reading, frg. 16 2-3 may juxtapose "blessing" with "crossing". The introduction of liturgy into the biblical account of the crossing may be explained in several ways. First, several biblical episodes describing a transporting of the Ark of the Covenant mention music and songs (2 Sam 6:15; 1 Chr 13:8, 15:16-28 [by Levites]).[359] Second, given possible allusions to the crossing of the Red Sea in frgs. 12 3, 13 2-3, the presence of liturgy may reflect an attempt to model the crossing of the Jordan on the account of the passage through the Red Sea featuring the Song of Moses (Exod 15).[360] In fact, in addition to a communal praise, either by priests or by all of Israel, frg. 17 5 also mentions a first person praise, perhaps, by Joshua. Third, it may reflect a reading of Josh 3-4 in light of the Mosaic commands in Deut 27:1-13.[361] Among other things, this passage includes Moses' instructions pertaining to the pronouncement of blessings and curses at Mts. Gerizim and Ebal, which were to be carried out בעברכם את הירדן (vv. 12-13). According to the MT and LXX, Joshua fulfilled these only after the conquest of Ai (Josh 8:30-35[MT] and 9:2[LXX]).[362] Yet, the scroll 4QJosh[a] seems to interpret the Deuteronomic בעברכם as referring to the crossing itself:

1 [בספר[363] הֹתֹּורה לֹא היה דבר מכל צֹוה מֹשֹהֹ] את יהֹ[וֹשוע אשר לֹא קרא יהשע נגד כל
2 [ישראל בעברו[364]]את הירדֹ[ן]וֹהנשים והטף והג[ר] ההולך בקרבם אחר אשר נתקוֹ[ן
3 [   ] [לֹ]   אֹת ספר התורה אחר אחר בֹן יֹ[עֹ]לֹוֹ[365] נושאי האֹרֹון]
4 [5:2]בעת]הֹהיא אמר יהוה אליהשׁ[ע עֹ]שֹ[ה] לך חרבות צרים]

---

358 Frg. 12 ellaborates on the year and the month of the crossing. Apparently, the day of the event was of no interest to this scroll (Josh 4:19). Dimant's suggestion that its omission allows the scroll to link the beginning of the jubilean computation with the day of the crossing is unnecessary. Dimant, "Between Sectarian", p. 116.

359 Cf. the song accompanying the carrying of the ark in LAB 21:9, influenced, according to Begg, "Ceremonies", p. 79, by 2 Sam 6 and 1 Chr 13-16.

360 Tov, "Literary Development".

361 For a discussion of this passage see M. Fishbane, *Biblical Interpretation in Ancient Israel* (Oxford: Clarendon Press, 1985), pp. 161-162; Tigay, *Deuteronomy*, pp. 486-489.

362 On the difficulties presented by this passage placements in both the MT and LXX, see Rofé, "Editing", p. 77-78; E. Tov, "Some Sequence Differences between the MT and LXX and Their Ramifications for the Literary Criticism of the Bible", in idem, *The Greek and Hebrew Bible: Collected Essays on the Septuagint* (Leiden: Brill, 1999), pp. 411-413.

363 The *DJD* edition reads התורה [בספר]. Yet, there seems to be hardly any blank space before *he* on the parchment.

364 Ulrich restores בעברו with Deut 27:3, 4, 12. The scroll might have also read בעברם.

365 Ulrich reads [ ]לֹ°. Rofé, "Editing", p. 78, suggests [עֹ]לֹו. On the photograph PAM 40.584 a vertical stroke with a hook-shaped top, as in a *waw* or in a *yod*, is visible. As to the last letter,

1. [in the book of]the Law. [8:35]There was not a word of all that Moses had commanded[J]oshua that Joshua failed to read in the presence of the entire
2. [Israel as they were crossing]the Jorda[n] and the women and the children and the strange[rs] who accompanied them after that they stepped[
3. [   ] [   ]the book of the Law. Then c[a]me up the bearers of the Ark[
4. [At]that[time] YHWH said to Joshu[a, "Ma]k[e flint knives]

The first two lines of 4QJosh[a] I correspond to Josh 8:34b-35(MT). Next comes an addition (lines 2-4), followed by Josh 5:2-7.[366] The scholarly publications on 4QJosh[a] frequently assume that it introduces the entire passage found in Josh 8:30-35(MT) prior to Josh 5:2. Yet, as van der Meer demonstrates, followed now by Tov, the scroll seems to duplicate here only the verses dealing with the reading of the Torah (see Chapter 1).[367] By inserting them here, it presents Joshua as carrying out Moses' instructions while the people are still crossing the Jordan. This is made clear by the addition of the phrase בעברו[את הירד]ן ("as they were crossing]the Jorda[n" [line 2]), borrowed from Deut 27 (vv. 2, 4, 12)[368] and the wording of line 3, "then c[a]me up the bearers of the Ark", suggesting that only after the reading was completed, the priests carrying the ark stepped onto the dry ground.[369] What has not been noted until now is that such an interpretation could have been prompted by the wording of Josh 4:10 (RSV):

> "For the priests who bore the ark stood in the midst of the Jordan, until everything was finished that the Lord commanded Joshua *to tell the people, according to all that Moses had commanded Joshua*"[370]

---

although Ulrich notes that its head is too broad for a *waw*, the shape of the hook is clearly that of a *waw* or a *yod*.

366 The text is cited from Ulrich, "4QJosh[a]", p. 147, with several corrections.

367 van der Meer, *Formation*, p. 513, proposes that in addition to vv. 34-35 the scroll duplicates here also verse 32.

368 As is observed, among others, by E. Noort, "4QJosha and the History of Tradition", *JNSL* 24 (1998), p. 133.

369 Rofé, "Editing", p. 78; van der Meer, *Formation*, p. 512. As to the Book of the Law, the scroll may envision it being placed "beside the Ark of the covenant of the Lord your God" (Deut 31:26) after the reading was complete and before the priests emerged from the Jordan. See A. Kempinsky, "'When History Sleeps, Theology Arises': A Note on Joshua 8:30-35 and the Archaeology of the 'Settlement Period'", *Eretz Israel* 24 (1993), p. 178 (Hebrew). Tov, "Literary Development", suggests that the Book of the Law had first to be brought to the dry land. Only then, the bearers of the ark came up.

370 While the phrase "until everything was finished that the Lord commanded Joshua" can be interpreted as referring to God's instructions pertaining to the twelve stones (see S. Aḥituv, *Joshua: Introduction and Commentary* [A Bible Commentary for Israel; Tel Aviv: Am Oved Publishers, Jerusalem: The Magnes Press, 1995], p. 99 [Hebrew]), the wording "according to all that

In fact, the plus את יה[ו]שוע found in line 1 seems to point to this verse. The phrase "commanded Joshua *to tell* the people" also explains why 4QJosh[a] might have included only the reading of the Law, and not the other activities carried out by Joshua in Josh 8:30-35 in fulfilment of Deut 27. The scroll's attempt to bring Josh 3-4 into a closer correspondence with Deut 27 may be compared to Josephus' account envisioning an errection of an altar, as commanded in Deut 27, soon after the crossing (J. Ant. 5. 20)[371] or to the ingenious rabbinic solutions placing the fufillment of Deut 27 right after the crossing.[372]

Given these attempts to read the biblical account of the crossing in light of Deut 27, one wonders whether the "blessing" mentioned in frgs. 15-17 may reflect a similar exegetical move, envisioning the pronouncement of blessings and curses taking place during the crossing. In fact, the discourse in frg. 13, which may also belong here, alludes to the malediction in Deut 28:37.[373]

To be sure, the fragmentary state of 4Q379 makes it difficult to determine which of the aforementioned factors led to the inclusion of liturgy in the scroll's

---

Moses had commanded Joshua" may be construed as referring to Moses' commands from Deut 27. Thus Kimḥi ad loc. See also Rashi ad loc. referring to Joshua's address to the people during the crossing of the Jordan in b. Soṭah 34a.

371 "These, having advanced fifty stades, pitched their camp at a distance of ten stades from Jericho. And Joshua, with the stones which each of the tribal leaders had, by the prophet's order, taken up from the river-bed, erected that altar that was to serve as a token of the stoppage of the stream, and sacrificed thereon to God" (Marcus, *Josephus*, p. 11). Begg, *Antiquities 5-7*, p. 7, notes that Josephus here is apparently influenced by Deut 27:1-8. Yet, he is reluctant to posit a *Vorlage* similar to that of 4QJosh[a] ("Cisjordanian Altar(s)", pp. 201-202), as do Ulrich, "Altar", p. 96, and Rofé, "Editing", p. 79, especially since in J. Ant. 5.69-70 Josephus reproduces the entire passage from Josh 8:30-35.

372 According to one view, the Israelites reached Mts. Ebal and Gerizim on the day of the crossing (t. Soṭa 8:7[ed. Zukermandel, p. 311]; cf. m. Soṭah 7:2). According to another view, they created two artificial mountains near Gilgal, where the ceremony was carried out (j. Soṭah 7.3, 21c). See discussion by Rofé, "Editing", p. 79-80. On the location of Ebal and Gerizim see also E. Noort, "The Traditions of Ebal and Gerizim: Theological Positions in the Book of Joshua", in M. Vervenne & J. Lust (eds.), *Deuteronomy and Deuteronomic Literature* (BETL 133; Leuven: University Press, 1997), pp. 161-180.

373 In light of the recurring use of the verb עבר in 1QS I-II, Brownley proposed that the Covenant Renewal ceremony involved an actual annual crossing of the Jordan. While this seems to be a far-fetched conclusion, one wonders whether the notion of "passing" accompanied by a recital of blessings and curses could have been influenced by an interpretation of the crossing akin to that found in this scroll. W.H. Brownley, "The Ceremony of Crossing the Jordan in the Annual Covenanting at Qumran", in W.C. Delsman (ed.), *Von Kanaan bis Kerala* (Neukirchen-Vluyn: Verlag Butzon & Bercker Kevelaer, 1982), pp. 295-302.

account of the crossing. Yet, it is of interest that the Samaritan accounts of the crossing also include praise by the Levites, the entire people, and Joshua.[374]

3.5.2 Joshua's Curse

Frg. 22 portrays Joshua as praising God, perhaps in relation to the fall of Jericho, and then uttering a curse on the person who will re-build Jericho (Josh 6:26). Introducing the curse, 4Q379 replaces the general biblical formulation "at that time" with a more specific "when Josh[u]a fin[ish]ed pr[aising and giving] than[ks] with [his] songs of praise". The rewritten introductory formula also omits the verb וישבע ("and he laid an oath"), thus presenting Joshua's curse as a prophecy, rather than as an oath.[375] A similar understanding of this malediction is found already in 1 Kgs 16:34, where it is described as "the words that *the Lord* had spoken through Joshua son of Nun".[376] Moreover, the scroll's wording of the curse itself is shorter than that of the MT:

MT:

אַרור האיש לפני ה' אשר יקום ובנה את העיר הזאת את יריחו

4Q379:

אָ[רור הא]יֹשׁ   אשר   יב[נ]הֹ את [העי]רֹ הזאתֹ

---

374 "And when the priests with the ark approached the water of the Urdun, the Liwanites shouted aloud, and the congregation of the children of Israel joined in with them, saying with one voice; "There is no power or strength in the presence of Thy power, O Lord of worlds!" And the water stood still, and rose up in accumulation, by the power of its Creator; He who is almighty over whatever He wills, the Worker of miracles and wonders. And continued to be heaped up, wave upon wave, until it became like unto huge mountains, while the priests stood praising God, and shouting halleluiahs and saying: "Praise be unto Him, in obedience to whom every thing exists." And they stood, with the ark, on the dry ground in the midst of the Urdun, until all the children of Israel, with their large throng, and their cattle, had passed over on the dry ground through the midst of the Urdun, on its bottom, and it was dry like as in the days of harvest. And the Liwanites were praising and shouting halleluiahs, and saying: "Praise be unto Him in obedience to whom every thing exists. Praise be unto Him by whose will this is come to pass ..." Then Yush'a, the son of Nun, and the children of Israel offered up the hymn of praise, which our master Musa the Prophet- peace be upon him- offered up at the sea of el-Qulzum, and they added thereunto praises and halleluiahs, and rendered praise and thanksgiving for what God had generously bestowed upon them". Crane, *Samaritan Chronicle*, pp. 46ff. Similar accounts are found in Niessen, *Samaritanische Version*, pp. 70-73; Gaster, "Das Buch Josua", pp. 240-243; Macdonald, *Chronicle*, p. 11(same text as Gaster's). See also the shorter version of the events in the Chronicle of Abu L'Fath in Stenhouse, *Kitāb*, p. 11. The parallel to Gaster's text is noted also by Tov, "Literary Development".
375 Contrast J. Ant. 5:31. That the author of 4Q379 understood Joshua's curse as a prophecy is noted also by Rofé, "Joshua", p. 342; Dimant, "Exegesis and Time", p. 387.
376 The LXX places the phrase לפני ה' after the word ההיא. Hence, in the LXX Joshua utters his oath in the presence of the Lord.

The replacement of the phrase יקום ובנה with the *yiqtol* יב[נ]ה̊ and the omission of the toponym את יריחו seem to agree with the presumed Hebrew *Vorlage* of the LXX.[377]

A large blank space separates the curse from its actualizing exegesis.[378] While this *vacat* seems to differentiate between the scriptural passage and its interpretation, the following application of the curse to contemporary events can be read as a continuation of Joshua's prophecy.[379] The actualizing exegesis refers to several figures. First, there is the "[accur]sed o[ne]", who is "[arising to becom]e a fowler's snare to his people and a terror to all hi[s] neighbors". This phrase, as well as the following "will ari[se] / [   ] to become both of them vessels of violence", employs a verbal form of עמד. The use of עמד points to the verb יקום found in the MT of Josh 6:26, yet missing in 4Q379. This may suggest that the scroll is aware of the *Vorlage* reading יקום ובנה.[380] Yet, it may also indicate that 4Q379 borrowed the actualizing interpretation of Joshua's curse from elsewhere and juxtaposed it to a shorter text of Josh 6:26.

Second, there are the 'two' who will become "vessels of violence" and "will again build / [t]his [city]". Some understand them to be the accursed one and his brother or son.[381] Yet, both the wording of Josh 6:26 and the phrase "vessels

---

377 See Mazor, "Translation", pp. 191-192, 439-440 notes 5-6 (Hebrew); idem, "The Origin and Evolution of the Curse upon the Rebuilder of Jericho: A Contribution of Textual Criticism to Biblical Historiography", *Textus* 14 (1988), pp. 1-26. As she observes, the phrase לפני ה' is missing from the codex Alexandrinus, yet appears in Vaticanus before the actual curse. She points to a short curse formula lacking the phrase לפני ה' in Deut 27:15, 26; 1 Sam 14:24, 28 and notes that this expression is missing from the rabbinic quotations of Josh 6:26. She concludes that the Greek version reflects a Hebrew text.

378 Since the actualization of prophecy is one of the salient features of *pesher* interpretation, this addition is frequently categorized as a *pesher*. Dimant, "Between Sectarian", pp. 130-131, suggests that the scroll deliberately avoids the term פשר (using instead והנ̊ה̊) in order to present the exposition of the curse as a part of Joshua's pronouncement. Still, since the term *pesher* is absent from frg. 22 ii 9-15, descriptives such as a *pesher*-type interpretation or an actualizing exposition seem to be more appropriate. On the uses and meanings of *pesher* in DSS see G.J. Brooke, "Pesher and Midrash in Qumran Literature: Issues for Lexicography", *RevQ* 24 (2009), pp. 81-87.

379 On the spacing systems in Qumran *pesharim* see Tov, *Scribal Practices*, pp. 323-330. On their implications for considering *pesharim* as a continuation of prophecy see G.J. Brooke, "Aspects of the Physical and Scribal Features of Some Cave 4 "Contunuous" Pesharim", in S. Metso et al. (eds.), *The Dead Sea Scrolls: Transmission of Traditions and Production of Texts* (STDJ 92; Leiden, Boston: Brill, 2010), pp. 144-145, 150.

380 For a similar phenomenon in *pesharim* see 1QpHab IV, 11(to Hab 1:11), XI, 13 (to Hab 2:16). See further B. Nitzan, *Pesher Habakkuk: A Scroll from the Wilderness of Judaea* (Jerusalem: Bialik Institute, 1986), pp. 46-47 (Hebrew).

381 P.W. Skehan, 'Two Books on Qumran Studies", *CBQ* 21 (1959), p. 75; G. Vermes, *The Dead Sea Scrolls: Qumran in Perspective* (London: Collins, 1977), p. 81; Rofé, "Joshua", p. 342.

of violence", borrowed from Jacob's statement regarding Simon and Levi in Gen
49:5, indicate rather that these are his two sons. While in Josh 6:26 the accursed
man re-builds the city, here it is done by his sons, suggesting a reading of the
preposition -ב in בבכר[ו] and ובצעי[ר]ו as denoting the means by which the city
will be rebuilt, and not the cost to be paid for it.[382]

Line 8 citing Josh 6:26 omits the name of Jericho, while lines 14-15 mention
Jerusalem. This led several scholars to conclude that 4Q379 identifies "[t]his
[city]" with Jerusalem.[383] Yet, as in the case of the omission of יקום, the absence
of the phrase את יריחו in line 8 is hardly a decisive factor. It seems that lines 11-13,
describing the construction activity at "[t]his [city]", deal with Jericho.[384] In fact,
the formulation וישבו ובנו (line 11) suggests that this building activity continues
that of Hiel of Ahab's time (1 Kgs 16:34). Still, lines 13-15 make clear that "the two"
also acted wickedly throughout the entire "land". Since the "rampart" and the
"boundary" of Jerusalem mentioned in lines 14-15 ellaborate on דלתיה of Josh 6:26,
it is likely that the scroll interprets the phrase "[t]his [city]" as also applying to
Jerusalem.[385] That actualizing interpretation may include multiple interpretations
of the same biblical word is well known from the Qumran *pesharim*.[386]

Can one identify the historical figures implied in the expanded Joshua's curse?
Scholarly debate on this issue began before the publication of 4Q379. Another
Qumran scroll, 4Q175 (4QTestimonia), published earlier, cites the work preserved
in 4Q379.[387] 4Q175, consisting of a single sheet of leather inscribed by the same

---

382 Noted by Milik, *Ten Years*, p. 63; Skehan, "Two Books", p. 75; Newsom, "Psalms of Joshua",
pp. 70, 72; Qimron, "Joshua Cycles", p. 507. This seems to be the understanding of the LXX,
referring to the younger son as the one who was kept safe, preserved (διασωθέντι). On the LXX
peculiar rendering of Josh 6:26 see Mazor, "Joshua", p. 196-198.
383 Thus, among others, J.M. Allegro, "Further Messianic References in Qumran Literature",
JBL 75 (1956), p. 187 note 109; Milik, *Ten Years*, p. 62; Dimant, "Exegesis and Time", pp. 387-389.
384 For the interpretation of "this city" as applying to Jericho, see Y. Yadin, "Recent Developments in Dead Sea Scrolls Research", in J. Liver (ed.), *Studies in the Dead Sea Scrolls* (Jerusalem:
Kiryat Sefer, 1957), p. 54; F.M. Cross, *The Ancient Library of Qumran* (London: G. Duckworth, 1958),
p. 113 note 84; Newsom, "Psalms of Joshua", pp. 69-70; Eshel, "The Historical Background", p.
414; idem, *The Dead Sea Scrolls and the Hasmonean State* (Grand Rapids, Michigan: Eerdmans,
Jerusalem: Yad Ben-Zvi, 2008), pp. 63-87.
385 Mazor, "Joshua", p. 194, points out that in the Hebrew Bible the phrase העיר הזאת is pre-
dominantly used with reference to Jerusalem.
386 See Nitzan, *Pesher Habakkuk*, pp. 47-51.
387 For the discussion of 4Q175 see G.J. Brooke, "Testimonia", *ABD*, vol. 6, pp. 391-392; A. Steudel,
"Testimonia", *EDSS*, vol. 2, pp. 936-938; J.G. Campbell, *The Exegetical Texts* (Companion to the
Qumran Scrolls; London, New York: T&T Clark International, 2004), pp. 88-99. On 4Q175's dependence on the work preserved in 4Q379 see Strugnell, "Le travail", p. 65; Cross, *Library*, p. 112;
Milik, *Ten Years*, p. 61; Newsom, "Psalms of Joshua", p 59. Eshel's arguments for 4Q175's priority
(Eshel, "The Historical Background", p. 412; ibid., *Dead Sea Scrolls*, pp. 83-86) have been refuted
by Dimant, "Between Sectarian", pp. 130-132, and K. Berthelot, "4QTestimonia as a Polemic against

scribe who penned 1QS, is dated to 100-75 BCE.[388] Classified as an excerpted text, it contains four paragraphs.[389] The first three paragraphs are citations from Exod 20:21 (including, as does Smr, Deut 5:28-29, 18:18-19), Num 24:15-17, and Deut 33:8-11.[390] The fourth paragraph is almost, but not entirely, identical to 4Q379 22 ii 7-15. A comparison between the two passages reveals the following differences:[391]

4Q175	4Q379 22 ii
21 vac[392] בעת אשר כלה ישוע להלל ולהודות בתהלותיהו	7 בעת אשר כ[ל]ﬣ יש[ו]ע[ן] ל[ה]לל ולה[ד]ו[ת] בתהלו[ת]יו ויאמר
22 ויאמר ארור היש אשר יבנה את העיר הזות בבכורו	8 אׄרור הא[יש] אשר יב[נ]ﬣ את [העי]ר הזאﬨ בבכ[ו]רו ייסדנה
23 ייסדנה ובצעירׄו יציב דלתיה ואנﬣ א﬩ ארור (אחׄד) בליעל	9 [ו]בצעי[ר]ון [י]צׄיבדלתיﬨﬣ vacat והׄנﬣ] ארו[ר א]ﬡ[חד]
24 עׄומד להיות פﬡ יקוש לעמו ומחתה לכול שכניו ועמד	10 [עומד להיו]ﬨ פﬡ יקוש לעמו ומחתה לכל שכנ[י]ו ועמ[ד]
25 [לש]ם ש[נ]י בנים[393] להׄ[י]ות שנ·המה כלי חמס ושבו ובנו את	11 [ ] ﬦﬡ להיות שניהם כלי חמס ושבו ובנו אﬡ[ת]
26 [העיר הזואת ויצ]יׄבו לה חומה ומגדלים לעשות לעוד רשע	12 [העיר ה]זאת ויציבו לה חומה ומגדלים לעשות[לעוז]
27 [ועשו ראה גדולה] בישראל ושערוריה באפרים וביהודהׄﬣ	בישראל ושערוריה באפרים[וביהודה
28 [ ] ו[עשו חנופה בארץ ונצה גדולה בבני	13 [רשע וע]שׄוׄﬡﬣ גדלה[בבני יעקב ושפ[כ]וׄﬡ[ן ד]ﬦ
29 [יעקוב ושפכו ד]ﬦ כמים על חל בת ציון ובחוק	14 [ועשו חנופה] בׄארץ ונאצה גדלה *כﬦ[י]ם על חל בת ציון
30 ירׄוׄשלﬦ[394]	15 [ובחוק ירושלים[°°°°°]

the Prophetic Claims of John Hyrcanus", in K. De Troyer & A. Lange (eds.), *Prophecy after the Prophets?* (Leuven-Paris-Walpole, MA: Peeters, 2009), pp. 100-103. The suggestion by P.R. Davies, G.J. Brooke, and P.R Callaway, *The Complete World of the Dead Sea Scrolls* (London: Thames and Hudson, 2002), p. 123, that both 4Q379 and 4Q175 draw on "an older source", perhaps, "an older but superseded edition of the book of Joshua", seems to be unnecessary. While the actualizing interpretation of Josh 6:26 in 4Q379 might have come from elsewhere, the entire passage (the introductory formula, the citation from Josh 6:26, and the actualizing exegesis) seems to have originated in this composition.

388 Allegro, "Messianic References", p. 182; Milik, *Ten Years*, pp. 61-64.

389 Campbell, *Exegetical Texts*, pp. 90-92.

390 P.W. Skehan, "The Period of the Biblical Texts from Khirbet Qumran", *CBQ* 19 (1957), p. 435.

391 4Q175 is quoted from the new edition by Qimron (personal communication).

392 Eshel, "The Historical Background", p. 409 (following J. Strugnell, "Notes en marge du Volume V des 'Discoveries in the Judaean Desert of Jordan'", *RevQ* 1[1969-71], p. 227), suggests that the word בעת is preceded by the word ויהי which has been erased. I was not able to find any traces of ink on the photographs of 4Q175, including the new images prepared by the West Semitic Research Project of the University of Southern California.

393 This is a new reading and reconstruction by Qimron (personal correspondence). Cross, "Testimonia", p. 318, reads וׄע]וׄמדׄ[ים]. Milik, *Ten Years*, p. 61 note 1, suggests [ו]המשׄ]יל את בניו. Strugnell, "Notes en marge", p. 228, doubts Milik's reading, since no traces of *lamed*'s vertical stroke are visible. Yet, Lim, "Psalms of Joshua", p. 311 note 23, points out that it might have been lost in the lacuna under the *taw* of להיות (line 24). Eshel, *Dead Sea Scrolls*, p. 64 note 4, p. 65, follows Milik's reading and restoration.

394 Eshel, "Background", p. 410, following Strugnell ("Notes en marge", p. 227), reads ירשלמ<בת> (בת was erased). However, the photographs (especially, the new ones by the West Semitic Research Project) demonstrate that what Strugnell and Eshel read as a deleted בת is in fact a *yod* of ירושלמ.

1. While 4Q379 22 ii 9 reads ארו[ר א̊[חד], the scribe of 4Q175 crossed out the numeral אחד and added the word איש above the line.[395]
2. 4Q175 contains an apposition בליעל, missing from 4Q379.[396]
3. The lacuna in 4Q175 25, reconstructed by Qimron as ש]ני בנים לה[יות, is larger than the one found in 4Q379 22 ii 11.
4. The lacuna in 4Q175 28 is larger than the corresponding lacuna in 4Q379 22 ii 13.[397]

All these differences are found in the actualizing exegesis, and not in the introductory formula and quotation from Josh 6:26. The latter two are identical in both scrolls, suggesting that 4Q175 indeed quotes the composition preserved in 4Q379 rather than another source containing the actualizing interpretation of the curse. Unless one attributes all of the aforementioned variations to the scribe of 4Q175,[398] it appears that the composition found in 4Q379 was circulated in several versions.

The four quotations in 4Q175 are placed in the order of the biblical books and interlinked by means of catchwords.[399] This suggests that it should be treated as a composition in its own right. Three major theories explaining the relations between the four quotations have been proposed, 1. A collection of Messianic proof-texts,[400] 2. A text addressing current issues within the community,[401] 3. An evaluation of a contemporary ruler(s) implied by the expanded form of Joshua's

---

395 Perhaps, in order to bring the text closer to the wording of Josh 6:26. Eshel, "Background", p. 411.

396 Dimant, "Between Sectarian", p. 127, observes that this addition points to the biblical collocation איש בליעל, and not to the demonic figure, Belial, of the Qumran sectarian literature. She renders the wording of 4Q175 as "a wicked man".

397 One could also include here the size of the lacuna between the quotation from Josh 6:26 and the actualizing exegesis. As noted in Comment ad loc., the lacuna in 4Q175 is shorter than the one found in 4Q379.

398 On this scribe see E. Tigchelaar, "In Search of the Scribe of 1QS", in S.M. Paul et al. (eds.), *Emanuel* (SVT 94; Leiden: Brill, 2003), pp. 439-452.

399 Brooke, *Exegesis*, pp. 311-319; idem, "Testimonia (4Q175)", *EDEJ*, pp. 1297-1298. To the verbal links noted by Brooke, one may add the use of the verb קום (replaced by עמד in the exposition on Josh 6:26) in the four passages.

400 They are taken to refer to three eschatological figures: an eschatological prophet (Exod 20:21[Smr]), a royal Messiah (Num 24:15-17), and a priestly Messiah (Deut 33:8-11). Allegro, "Messianic References", p. 187; Dupont-Sommer, *Essene Writings*, p. 317; J. Carmignac, "Témoignages (4QTestimonia)", in idem et al. (eds.), *Les Textes de Qumran* (Paris: Éditions Letouzey et Ané: 1963), vol. 2, 274; Vermes, *Qumran in Perspective*, pp. 80-81. Cross, *Library*, pp. 112-113, interprets Num 24:15-17 with CD VII, 18-21 as referring to the priestly Messiah and the royal Messiah. He understands the citation from Deut 33:8-11 as pointing to the Teacher of Righteousness.

401 J. Lübbe, "A Reinterpretation of 4QTestimonia", *RevQ* 12 (1985-86), pp. 187-197. His interpretation of 4Q175 as a "self-affirmation by the text and an emphatic condemnation of its opponents" seems to have little support in the text.

curse in light of the three preceding passages depicting ideal figures. Of these four, only the third theory seems to account for all the four citations. The main proponent of this view, Eshel, suggests (with Starcky[402]) that the expanded Joshua's curse refers to John Hyrcanus I and his two sons Antigonus and Aristobulus (on these three see J. Ant. 13.230-319).[403] While other Hasmonean rulers have also been considered (e.g., Mattathias and his sons Simon and Jonathan,[404] Simon and his sons Judas and Mattathias,[405] John Hyrcanus I and his sons Aristobulus I and Alexander Jannaeus,[406] Alexander Jannaeus and his sons Hyrcanus II and Aristobulus II[407]), Eshel adduces Josephus' description of John Hyrcanus I as "the only man to unite in his person three of the highest privileges: the supreme command of the nation, the high priesthood, and the gift of the prophecy" (J. War 1.68; cf. J. Ant. 13.299-300).[408] According to Eshel, he could have been the one criticized by 4Q175 for not living up to what is expected of the ideal prophet, ruler, and priest. Indeed, some of the biblical allusions found in the actualizing interpretation of Josh 6:26 may suggest a critique of a claim for a prophetic inspiration.[409] Furthermore, Eshel points to the recent excavations of the Hasmonean Jericho

---

402 J. Starcky, "Les Maîtres de Justice et la chronologie de Qumrân", in M. Delcor (ed.), *Qumrân: Sa piété, sa théologie et son milieu* (Paris-Gembloux: Duculot, 1978), p. 253.

403 Eshel, "The Historical Background"; idem, *The Dead Sea Scrolls*, pp. 63-87. His interpretation is followed by Berthelot, "4QTestimonia", pp. 99-116. M. Treves, "On the Meaning of the Qumran Testimonia", *RevQ* 2 (1959-60), pp. 569-571, suggests that 4Q175 is a panegyric of John Hyrcanus I. Yet, it is unclear how he explains the negative description of the accursed man in this passage.

404 Milik, *Ten Years*, pp. 61-64.

405 Cross, *Library*, pp. 112-113. Similarly H. Burgman, *Der Sitz im Leben in den Joshuafluch-texten in 4Q379 22ii und 4QTestimonia* (Qumranica Mogilanensia 1; Kraków: "Secesja" Press, 1990), p. 29, identifies the "accursed man" with Simon.

406 O. Betz, "Donnersöhne, Menschenfischer und der Davidische Messias", *RevQ* 3 (1961-62), p. 42 note 4.

407 "Messianic References", pp. 182-187; Yadin, "Recent Developments", p. 54. Yet, the date of 4Q175 seems to rule them out (as argued by Milik, *Ten Years*, p. 64).

408 Thackeray, *Josephus*, p. 35. On Josephus' description of John Hyrcanus I see C. Thoma, "The High Priesthood in the Judgment of Josephus", in L.H. Feldman & G. Hata (eds.), *Josephus, the Bible and History* (Leiden: Brill, 1988), pp. 207-208. For the notion of the "three crowns", royal, priestly and prophetic, and its reflection in this passage see M. Kister, "Metamorphoses of Aggadic Traditions", *Tarbiẓ* 60 (1991), p. 65 (Hebrew).

409 Newsom, "4Q379", pp. 280-281, notes the use of Hosea 9:8 and Jer 23:15, dealing with prophets, in 4Q379 22 ii 10, 14(=4Q175 24, 28). She also points out the allusion to Neh 9:26, where נאצו refers to the killing of the prophets, and relates it to the ensuing description of the bloodshed in 4Q379 22 ii 14-15(=4Q175 29). See further the detailed discussion by Berthelot, "4QTestimonia", pp. 108-111.

revealing extensive building works in the days of John Hyrcanus I.[410] While it is not impossible that 4Q379 applies Joshua's curse to different (perhaps, earlier and otherwise unknown) events than 4Q175,[411] for Eshel both 4Q379 and 4Q175 reflect the same historical circumstances. If correct, this intepretation dates the composition preserved in 4Q379 sometime between 134 and 104 BCE.

3.5.3 The Provenance and the Presumed Authoritative Status of 4Q379

The scholarly opinions regarding the provenance of 4Q379 shifted over the years. Milik takes it to be a sectarian composition as "it deals with sectarian history".[412] A similar view is espoused by Talmon.[413] Tov also tends to classify this scroll with the literature of the *yaḥad*, observing its adherence to the jubilean chronology and its use by 4Q175.[414] Strugnell, Newsom, and Eshel adopt an opposite view, classifying 4Q379 as a non-sectarian work.[415] Finally, Dimant takes a middle course, considering the alleged use of the jubilean chronology and of the *pesher*-type interpretation to be the marks of an intermediate category of Qumran texts, standing between sectarian and non-sectarian works.[416]

The scroll 4Q379 contains no explicit sectarian terminology or worldview. Neither does it deals with the sectarian history, but engages with contemporary events affecting the entire population of the Land of Israel (and even its neighbors). It does not use a jubilean chronology and its actualizing exegesis, presuming that scriptural prophecies (or what is perceived as a prophecy) may have multiple fulfillments, is not peculiar to the sectarian sources.[417] Hence, it seems best to place this scroll within the non-sectarian literature found at Qumran.

---

410 See E. Netzer, "The Hasmonean and Herodian Palaces at Jericho", *IEJ* (1975), p. 92; idem, *Hasmonean and Herodian Palaces at Jericho* (Jerusalem: Israel Exploration Society, Institute of Archaeology, The Hebrew University of Jerusalem, 2001), pp. 1-7.
411 As Newsom, "Psalms of Joshua", pp. 72-73, points out.
412 Milik, *Ten Years*, p. 61.
413 Talmon, "Mas 1039-211", pp. 115-116.
414 Tov, "Rewritten Joshua", pp. 254-255.
415 Newsom, "Psalms of Joshua", p. 59. Strugnell, "Moses-Pseudepigrapha", p. 221, proposes that "Psalms of Joshua" may be presectarian. Eshel, "Note", pp. 92-93, suggests that the actualizing interpretation in 4Q379 22 ii originates in 4Q175, which he believes to be a sectarian work.
416 Dimant, "Between Sectarian", p. 134. Following Dimant, C.A. Evans, "Joshua, Apocryphon of", *EDEJ*, p. 841, suggests that the Apocryphon of Joshua "emanated fom circles that valued the ideology of *Jubilees*".
417 See Dimant, ibid., p. 133. She lists the following examples of actualizing interpretation: Dan 9:2, 24-27 (on Jer 25:11, 29:10); Dan 11:30 (on Num 24:24); Mt 3:2; Mk 1:3; Lk 3:4-6; Jn 1:23 (on Isa 40:3). On the notion of biblical prophecies having multiple fulfillments, see Dimant, "Exegesis and Time".

In addition to affirming its non-sectarian stance, the foregoing analysis notes a few occasions when 4Q379 seems to reflect Levitical/priestly concerns. The list of Jacob's sons in frg. 1 2-4 assigns pride of place to Levi and calls him the "beloved one" of God.[418] The praise of the ancestors in frg. 17 3-4 culminates with Aaron and his sons.[419] The clarification of the starting point of the jubilean computation in frg. 12 4-6 is of importance for the sacred cult and its officials.[420] Still, there seems to be no need to link these Levitical/priestly tendencies with the Qumran community. Similarly, a possible critique of a contemporary Hasmonean ruler(s) in frg. 22 ii 7-15 is not necessarily Qumranic, as it could have been shared by wider Levitical or priestly circles dissastisfied with the Hasmoneans.

Finally, several scholars suggest that the inclusion of a citation from the work preserved in 4Q379 along with the quotations from the Torah in 4Q175 indicates that the author/compiler of the 4QTestimonia viewed it as an authoritative text.[421] If the actualizing interpretation of Joshua's curse in 4Q379 indeed refers to John Hyrcanus I, it will imply that the work found in 4Q379 acquired an authoritative status within a very short time, as 4Q175, quoting it, is dated to 100-75 BCE. While, it is not impossible (given the case of the Book of Daniel), caution is called for as the precise intent of the four passages in 4Q175, as well as the relationships between them, remains somewhat unclear.[422] Perhaps, one could posit that 4QTes-

418 Presented in a negative light in Genesis, Levi is elevated to the lofty status of the ancestor of the priesthood and is depicted as a priest himself in such Second Temple writings as Jubilees and Aramaic Levi Document. See further G.J. Brooke, "Levi and the Levites in the Dead Sea Scrolls and the New Testament", in Z.J. Kapera (ed.), *Papers on the Dead Sea Scrolls Offered in Memory of Jean Carmignac* (Kraków: Enigma, 1993), pp. 105-129; J. Kugel, "Levi's Elevation to the Priesthood in Second Temple Writings", *HTR* 86 (1993), pp. 1-64; J.C. VanderKam, "Jubilees' Exegetical Creation of Levi the Priest", *RevQ* 17 (1996), pp. 359–373.
419 Similarly, Wise, Abegg, Cook, *Dead Sea Scrolls*, p. 428, suggest that the scroll is particularly interested in priesthood. By tracing the lineage of Aaron's sons back to Abraham, 4Q379 recalls the historical survey found in 5Q13 1-2 spanning Enoch, Noah, Abraham, Isaac, Jacob, Levi, and, perhaps, Aaron. See M. Kister, "5Q13 and the "*Avodah*": A Historical Survey and its Significance", *DSD* 8 (2001), pp. 136-148.
420 Compare the arguments adduced for the presumed priestly provenance of Jubilees in M. Segal, *The Book of Jubilees: Rewritten Bible, Redaction, Ideology and Theology* (JSJSup 117; Leiden: Brill, 2007), pp. 10-11.
421 Among the first to observe this was Skehan, "Two Books", p. 73. See further Tigchelaar, "The Dead Sea Scrolls", p. 170; J.J. Collins, "Canon, Canonization", *EDEJ*, p. 462; García Martínez, "The Book of Joshua", p. 107; idem, "Light on Joshua", pp. 146-150. Tigchelaar, "Assessing", pp. 203-204, notes the defective orthography of 4Q379 and suggests that, given the use of this orthography in the biblical mss from Qumran, its use here could reflect a "strategy of authorization".
422 For instance, Tigchelaar, "Scribe", pp. 452, seems to suggest that the scribe of 4Q175, who also produced 1QS, compiled the "scriptural evidence for the motif of the eschatological prophet and messiahs" and used it to compose 1QS IX, 3-11, which is considered to be an interpolation in 1QS.

timonia's citation of Joshua's expanded curse reflects the widely accepted notion of Joshua as a prophet (see Chapter 9), rather than the Torah-like authority of the work preserved in 4Q379.[423]

3.6 Conclusions

The extant fragments of 4Q379 span events from the crossing of the Jordan to the conquest of Ai. Reflecting a concern with the proper observation of the jubilean Pentateuchal laws, this scroll elaborates on the biblical account of the crossing and claims that the year of the crossing constitutes the first year of the jubilean computation. It also amplifies the biblical description of the river Jordan's flow and seems to envision the passage through the Jordan being accompanied by a liturgy. Expanding on the scriptural account of the fall of Jericho, 4Q379 introduces an extensive praise by Joshua and elaborates on his curse of the person who will re-build Jericho, applying it to contemporary circumstances. 4Q175 (4QTestimonia) cites this actualizing interpretation of Joshua's malediction. Its slightly longer text may suggest that several versions of the composition preserved in 4Q379 were in circulation. The recurring interest in priestly/Levitical matters and the presumed critique of a contemporary Hasmonean ruler, apparently, John Hyrcanus I, shed light on the milieu and date of 4Q379.

---

423 Berthelot, "4QTestimonia", p. 115, also objects to this view and notes that this passage was quoted by the compiler of 4Q175 "because it corresponded to what he wanted to say about Hyrcanus and his sons".

4 The Scroll 4Q522

4.1 The Manuscript

The scroll 4Q522, inscribed in a late Hasmonean hand, is dated to the second third of the 1st century BCE.[424] Most of its fragments are small and offer little physical data regarding their relative position in the scroll.[425]

4.2 The Contents of 4Q522

Not unlike the scrolls 4Q378 and 4Q379, the extant fragments of 4Q522 contain diverse materials: a narrative (1-4, 7, 8, 9 i, 10), non-biblical discourses (5[?], 9 ii), a prayer (frg. 6?), and a psalm (frgs. 22-26). The scroll refers to several episodes from the Book of Joshua. Frg. 1 may rework the story of the two spies dispatched to Jericho (Josh 2:23-3:1). Frg. 4 mentions the ceremony at Mts. Gerizim and Ebal (Josh 8:33). The list of the Israelites' conquests in frg. 9 i alludes to the aftermath of the Battle of the Waters of Merom (line 4; Josh 11:8). The non-biblical discourse by Joshua in frg. 9 ii is closely related to the setting of the Tent of Meeting in Shiloh (Josh 18:1). The list of locations that the tribes failed to subdue in frg. 8 (and, perhaps, frgs. 2, 3, and 15) relies on Judg 1. Thus, the extant fragments of 4Q522 span events described in Joshua 2-18 and Judg 1. While the subject matter of frgs. 8 and 9 i suggests that they were positioned in close proximity to each other in the scroll, their precise sequence remains unclear.

4.3 Editions of 4Q522

Assigned to Starcky for publication, 4Q522 was finally edited by Puech as 4QProphétie de Josué (4QapocrJosué[c]?).[426] Qimron and Dimant published improved

---

424 Puech, "4Q522", p. 39.

425 One notable feature of this manuscript is that the letters in it are not suspended from the lines, as is usually the case in the Qumran scrolls, but are inscribed above, below and through the ruled lines. Puech, ibid.

426 Puech, ibid., pp. 39-74. For the preliminary editions see Puech, "Fragment", pp. 547-554; idem, "La Pierre", pp. 676-696.

editions of frg. 9 ii.[427] Qimron is currently preparing a new edition of selected fragments of this scroll.[428]

4.4 Text and Commentary

Frg. 1

וירדו מן ההֿ[ר	1
ויֿשכֿ[ם	2

Notes on Readings
2 ויֿשכֿ[ם. Puech reads וישכֿ[ו. There are no traces of ink next to the *kaf* (PAM 43.606). Still, Qimron reads וישכֿ[ם.

Translation
1. and they came down from the mou[ntain
2. and he wok[e up early

Comments
1 וירדו מן ההֿ[ר. The line may allude to Josh 2:23 (Puech). Qimron restores וירדו מן ההֿ[ר ויבואו אל ישוע.

2 ויֿשכֿ[ם. This verb points to Josh 3:1 (Puech). Qimron reconstructs ויֿשכֿ[ם ישוע בבוקר.

Frg. 2

°[°°°בֿ °[	1
[אֿת יושב]	2
הע[י]ֿר אשר יצאֿו[משם	3
[°וֿ שלוש °[	4

---

427 Qimron, "Joshua Cycles", pp. 503-508; Dimant, "Apocryphon of Joshua", pp. 179-204; idem, "Between Sectarian", pp. 118-121.
428 Qimron, *The Hebrew Writings: Volume Two*.

Notes on Readings

1]ׄ◦◦◦בׄ. Puech, followed by Qimron, reads and restores]ׄבׄיׄתׄוׄ תׄ[א. Of the first letter only a bottom tip of a vertical stroke survives. Next to the *bet* traces of either
ḥet or *waw/yod*, followed by a vertical stroke, appear. The base stroke to the
left is too long to be that of a *taw*. It is also positioned a little lower than one
would expect if it were a *taw*. There is a bottom tip of a vertical stroke next to
it. Qimron's alternative reading,]ׄיׄ בׄ[ושׄ]‍ הׄ, seems to disregard the absence of a
sufficient space between the *bet* and the following letter. Given the uncertainty,
no reading is offered here.

Translation

1.]   [
2.]the inhabitants of [
3. the ci]ty [from where] they went out[
4.]   three   [

Comments

2]ׄאׄת יושב. Apparently, the scroll uses here the formula 'את יושבי + a name of a
locality', with יושב in singular (as in Judg 1:27[Qere: ישבי] Puech). Compare the
use of this formula in frg. 8 3.

3 משם יצאוׄ]ן אשר העׄ]ׄיׄר. The restoration is that of Puech.

4 שלוש. This may be a reference to three (cf. Num 35:14; Deut 4:41) or thirteen
(cf. Josh 19:6) cities.

Frg. 3

[הׄוׄרי]ש	1
[הׄכנעני אשרׄ]	2
צפ[וׄ]ן מעמק עכור]	3
[יׄהׄוׄד]ה	4

Notes on Readings

1 [הׄוׄרי]ש. Puech reads the vertical stroke in the beginning of the line as a *yod* (the
top is missing). The stroke curves slightly to the right at its bottom, as does the
right vertical stroke in the first *he* in the word יהוה (frg. 5 4). Accordingly, Qimron
suggests a *he*, though no trace of its right vertical stroke is visible.

Translation

1.   ]he disposse[ssed
2.   ]the Canaanites who[
3.   nor]th from the Valley of Achor[
4.   ]Juda[h

Comments

1 שׁ[וֹרִֹ֯הֹ]. A Hifil of ירשׁ, "to dispossess, to drive out", is frequent in the Book of Joshua.[429] It may have either God or (more likely) one of the tribes as a subject (cf. the mention of Judah in line 4). Frg. 9 i lists Judah's conquests, while frg. 8 names locations that the individual tribes failed to dispossess. If this fragment belongs with frg. 8 (cf. the reference to the "Canaanites" in line 2), a reconstruction הֹ֯וֹרִשׁ/ו [לֹא(ו)]) is appropriate (cf. Josh 15:63; Judg 1:19).

2 [הכנעני אשׁ֯וֹ]. Most likely a name of a geographical location followed (cf. Josh 5:1).

3 [צפ]וֹן מעמק עכור]. The reconstruction is that of Puech. The Valley of Achor, where Achan and his family were buried (Josh 7:24, 26), is mentioned among the sites marking the northern border of Judah's tribal territory (cf. the mention of Judah in the next line). In Josh 15:7 the Valley of Achor appears in a close proximity to the noun צפון. The scroll might have read something like גבול צפ]וֹן מעמק עכור] (for the language cf. Num 34:7).[430]

4 ה[וֹרִֹ֯הֹ]. See Comment on lines 1 and 3. Also compare frg. 9 i 11.

Frg. 4

[וישתו °[	1
מחציתם מול הר עי]בל ומחציתם מו]ל הר גרזים	2
[°°°[ ] ° [ ] °[את]°	3

Notes on Readings

1 וישתו. Fragment 4 reads ויש°[. Puech places at its top a tiny scrap of leather reading]°תו [(PAM 43.663).

---

429 HALOT, p. 441.

430 The Valley of Achor is frequently identified with the modern El-Buqeah, situated between Hyrcania and Qumran. See C.J. Pressler, "Achor", *ABD*, vol. 1, p. 56. Yet, Ahituv, *Joshua*, p. 244, cautions that the available data is insufficient for a positive identification. He suggests that it might be found in the vicinity of Nebi Musa or further to the north.

2 מון[ל. Puech reads]מ̇ח. Yet, the second letter is clearly a *waw*.

3 There is a trace of a letter in what the *DJD* edition transcribes as a *vacat*. Perhaps, this is a tip of a vertical stroke of a *taw* (cf. a *taw* in ומחציתם).

Translation

1.   ] and they set [
2.   half of them facing Mount Eb]al and half of them fa[cing Mount Gerizim
3.   ] [ ] []   [

Comments

1 וישתו. This is a 3ʳᵈ masc. pl. *wayyiqtol* of either שתה, "to drink" (Puech), or (more plausibly) שית, "to set" (cf. וישתהו [1QS X, 2]).[431] As the next line does, it may refer to the events described in Josh 8:30-35.

2 מחציתם מול הר עי]בל ומחציתהם מון[ל הר גרזים. The fragment seems to paraphrase Josh 8:33, employing the noun מחצית, "half" (cf. Num 31: 30, 42, 47), instead of the biblical חצי.[432] Unlike Josh 8:33, the scroll mentions those facing Mt. Ebal, i.e. those standing on Mt. Gerizim, first. The scroll may be influenced here by Deut 27:12-13 (cf. also 11:29). Thus, it presents Joshua as following very closely the Mosaic command.

Frg. 5

[בש]	1
[ישראל]	2
לכל ה[גוים האל]ה	3
[יהוה אל]והיכם	4
[כ̊א̊ש̊ו]ר	5

Translation

1.   ] [
2.   ] Israel[
3. to all]thes[e] nations[
4.   ] YHWH [your] Go[d
5.   ]whe[n

---

431 HALOT, p. 1484. For the orthography see Qimron, "Dissertation", pp. 200-201.
432 HALOT, p. 571.

Comments

3 לכל ה]גוים האל]ה. The reconstruction follows Josh 23:3, where this phrase occurs in close proximity to the expression יהוה אלהיכם (cf. ל הגוים בכו]ל in 4Q378 3 i+10 9).

4 יהוה אל]והיכם. The line is restored as a 2nd person address (by Joshua?) to Israel (cf. the use of ה' אלוהיך/כם in 4Q378 3 i+12 8, 11 1, 12 3).

Frg. 6

לֹו לֹמֹ] [	1
א]ת עמכה]°	2

Translation

1.   ] to him [
2.   ] your people [

Comments

2 א]ת עמכה. This line is a part of a 2nd person address or a prayer (cf. הו]שֹע את עמי in 4Q378 13 4).

Puech observes that frgs. 5 and 6 seem to belong to the same sheet of leather.

Frg. 7

]°°[	1
צור וצידון]	2
א]ת האֹרֹץֹ לה]ורישה	3
גיבורי ה]חֹיֹלֹ]	4

Translation

1.   ] [
2.   ]Tyre and Sidon[
3.   ] the land to di[spossess it
4.   the valiant]warriors[

Comments

2 צור וצידון]. Josh 19:28-29, outlining the borders of Asher, mentions both cities. Josh 13:6 names Sidon among the unconquered territories (cf. Gen 10:19, where it is mentioned as the northern extremity of the Canaanite territory). Judg 1:31

lists it as one of the cities that the Israelites failed to dispossess.[433] Since Judg 1:31, including the reference to Sidon, is reworked in frg. 8 4, this fragment may either outline tribal borders, or, more likely, the land that yet remains (Josh 13:1-7). Compare also 5Q9 2 1.

3 את הֹאָרֹץ להֹ[ן]ורישה. The restoration לה[ן]ורישה, a Hifil of ירש, "to dispossess", follows Num 3:53. Apparently, a form of נתן is missing in the beginning of the line.

4 גיבורי הֹ[ן]חֹיֹל. The reconstruction is that of Puech (cf. Josh 1:14, 8:3, 10:7). If line 2 describes the land that yet remains (Josh 13:1-7), perhaps this is a reference to the surveyors dispatched by Joshua in Josh 18:4.

Frg. 8

יהוד]הֹ ושמעו]ןֹ [ ] [אֹתֹ]°°	1
כי רכב ברזל]הֹיה להם ודן לוא הכה גם הוא אתֹ]	2
[ויש̇כר את בית שן ואשר א]תֹ] יֹ[ושבי עכו	3
ואת יושבי צ]ידון וֹאֹתֹ אֹחֹלֹ]ב	4
]°[	5

Notes on Readings

1 [°°. The *DJD* edition reads הֹ̇נֹ̇גֹ̇]ב. The traces of the two (or three) letters are difficult to decipher. The first letter may be a *he*. The following base stroke may belong to a *bet*, a medial *nun* or a medial *kaf*. It is unclear whether there is a trace of a third letter on the fragment, as the trace of ink read by Puech as a bottom tip of a *gimel* may belong to the aforementioned base stroke.

3 שן. There are two dots above and below the right stroke of the *shin*.
יֹ[ושבי. Puech reads הֹ[, yet on PAM 41.714 a top of a *waw/yod* is visible.

4 אֹחֹלֹ]ב. The *DJD* edition has כֹבֹ[ו]לֹ]. The top tips of the first two letters may also be read as an *alef* and a *het* (cf. *het* in חדיתא [frg. 9 i 7]).

Translation

1.	Juda]h and Sime[o]n [ ] [
2.	for]they had[iron chariots]. And Dan also did not smite [
3.	]and Issachar Beth-Shean and Asher the i[nhabitants of Acco
4.	and the inhabitants of S]idon and Ahl[ab

---

433 Tyre and Sidon are paired in Jer 47:4; Joel 4:4; Zech 9:2; cf. also Judith 2:28; 2 Esdra 1:11; Mt 11:21; Acts 12:20.

Comments

1 יהוד]ה ושמע]ו[ן. Lines 2-3 suggest that the fragment reworks Judg 1. According to vv. 3ff, Judah and Simeon fought together against the remaining Canaanite population. The reconstruction is that of Puech.

2 היה להם] כי רכב ברזל. The restoration follows Judg 1:19.

ודן לוא הכה גם הוא את]ו. While Judg 1 places the unconquered territory of Dan at the end of the list of the Canaanite enclaves, the scroll seems to mention it after those of Judah and Simeon and before Issachar and Asher (line 3). The preposition אֵ֯ת indicates that a name of a geographical location followed, apparently, one of those listed in Judg 1:34-35.

3 ויישכר את בית שן]. Judg 1:27-28 reports that Manasseh was not able to capture Beth-Shean. Yet, since this city was given to Manasseh by Issachar (cf. Josh 17:11-12), the scroll attributes to him the failure to expel its Canaanite population. See Discussion. The name of ישכר is spelled here phonetically with a single *shin* (MT יששכר). For the spelling בית שן (MT frequently reads בית שאן) see 1 Sam 31:10, 12; 2 Sam 21:12. In the Qumran scrolls two dots placed above and below a single letter usually serve as a cancellation mark.[434] Here the purpose of the dots above and below the right stroke of a *shin* is unclear. Puech suggests that it has to do with the spelling שן, while Qimron proposes that these separate the two components of the toponym, for the scribe began writing בי שן, but corrected himself.

3-4 ואשר א]ת[יֹ]ושבי עכו [/] ואת יושבי צ]ידון וֹאֵת אֹחֹל]ֶב. The fragment depends here on Judg 1:31. 5Q9 2 1 may mention Sidon in a similar context.

The reconstructions produce a line of 45 letter-spaces. The average length of lines in frgs. 22-26 (restored according to the MT) is 55 letter-spaces (varying from 49 to 58 letter-spaces). The reconstructed lines of frg. 9 ii average 54 letter-spaces (varying from 55 to 53). While the length of the lines in different columns may vary, these data suggest that the lacunae in the end of line 3 and the beginning of line 4 might have contained a longer text then that of the MT. Perhaps, the scroll includes the city of Dor prior to Sidon, as does the LXX ad loc. (retroverted into Hebrew): את ישבי עכו ויהיו למס ואת יושבי דו/אר ואת יושבי צידון. See Discussion.

---

434 See Tov, *Scribal Practices*, pp. 191-192.

Frgs. 9 i and 10

]וֹ[	] 1
]ם ואת עין קבֹּֿר בֹּית אֿ °°°°°	] 2
את] בקעֿ ואת בית צפור את	] 3
ו]יכו את כול בקעת מצפֿֿא את	] 4
ו]אֿת היכלים את יעפור ואת	] 5
בא] ואת מנו את עין כובר	] 6
]רֿ גרים את חדיתא ואת עֿושל	] 7
]בֿ°[ ]וֿנֿיֿ°[ ]לֿ[ ]דון אשרֿ	] 8
]וֿרֿ[ ]בא וא°[וא]שקלון [ ]	] 9
ב]גֿליל ושנים שבֿ[ ]ת השרון	] 10
וילכוד י]הודה את באר שבע [וא]ֿת בעלות	] 11
ו]את קעילה את עדולם ואת	] 12
את]גזר ואת תמנו ואת גמזון ואת	] 13
]חקר וקטרֿ]ון[ואפרנים ואת שדֿות	] 14
את]בית חורון התחתֿ]ו[ֿן והעל]יון [אֿת	] 15
א]ֿת גולת עליונה [וא]ֿת התחֿ]תון[ֿה	] 16
עֿ]ד נחלֿ] מצרים [ ]בֿ°[[	] 17
]נמיֿש[[	] 18
]אֿת[[	] 19

Notes on Readings

1 קבֹּֿר ֿרֿית. Puech suggests קבֿוֿצֿות. Qimron reads קבֹּֿר°°. The reading proposed takes the base stroke next to Qimron's *resh* to be a *bet*. If correct, these two words are written close to each other, as is the case with the word next to בֹּֿית.

2 °°°°אֿ. The editor reads אֿת צֿוֿרֿ. On the photographs next to the *alef*, bottom tips of four illegible letters are visible.

3 בקעֿ. The *DJD* edition has בקע{ת}. The third letter is most likely an *ayin*. It is unclear whether there are traces of a deleted letter next to the *ayin*, as Puech suggests.

8]לֿ[. There is a trace of a vertical stroke below the *dalet* of חדיתא in line 7. Apparently, this is a vertical stroke of a *lamed*.
]דון. Puech reads צ]ֿידֿון. It is uncertain whether the two diagonal traces visible on PAM 40.584; 43.606 are ink. In any case, they are not consistent with a *yod*.

9]וֿרֿ[. The *DJD* edition reads thus. The vertical stroke of the second letter is somewhat longer than usual in a *resh* in 4Q522. Therefore, it is possible that the fragment reads]וֿרֿ[.

אב‹[. Puech reads thus. On PAM 40.584 an upper diagonal stroke resembling a hook-shaped top of a *waw/yod* is visible.

ואו‹. Puech reads ק[פֿא. Of the third letter only a base stroke survives. Since it may belong to several letters, no reading is proposed here.

14 שדות. Puech reads שכֿות. The available space seems to be insufficient for a medial *kaf*. Also, no traces of *kaf*'s base stroke are visible on PAM 40.584. The surviving horizontal stroke may belong to a *dalet* or to a *resh*.

17-19 The editor placed at the bottom of frg. 9 i a small fragment found on PAM 43.696.

17 ע[דֿ. Puech offers no reading for the first letter. On PAM 43.696 a left extremity of a *dalet*'s vertical stroke with a characteristic serif is visible (cf. *dalet* in חדיתא [line 7]).

18 [אֿאֿ. The *DJD* edition reads [תֿעֿ]קב. However, the upper tips of the two vertical strokes visible on the fragment may likewise belong to an *alef*.

Translation[435]

2. [   ] and *'yn qvr, byt*
3. [   ] *bq'*, and *byt ṣpwr*, and
4. [and] they [sm]ote the whole Valley of Mizpe/ah
5. [and] *hyklym, 'ypwr*, and
6. [   ] and *mnw*, and *'yn-kwbr*
7. [   ]*r grym*, Haditha, and *'wšl*
8. [   ] [] [and   ]*don* that is
9. [   ]   [and A]shkelon [   ]
10. [in Ga]lilee and *šnym*(?) in[   ] of Sharon
11. [and J]udah[captured] Beersheba an[d] Bealoth
12. [and] Keilah, Adullam, and
13. [   ] Gezer, Timno, Gimzon, and
14. [   ]*ḥqr*, and *qtr*[*wn*], and *'prnym*, and *sdot*
15. [   ] Up[per] and Low[e]r Beth-Horon, and
16. [   ] Upper and Lo[we]r Gullath
17. [t]o the Wadi[of Egypt]   [   ]
18. [   ]we shall remove[   ]
19. [   ]   [   ]

---

435 For the toponyms for which identification is either unknown or doubtful a transcription is provided.

Comments

2 וֹאת עין קֹבֹּ֗ר. This column seems to contain a list of the Israelites' conquests. The *nota accusativi* ואת suggests that a verb, apparently, synonymous to ויכ[ו], "and] they [sm]ote", of line 4, is missing here.

עין קֹבֹּ֗ר. Lines 3-5 seem to be concerned with the northern part of the land of Canaan, yet the toponym עין קֹבֹּ֗ר (if deciphered correctly), is otherwise unknown. This is also the case with the following compound toponym beginning with בֵּ֗ית. It seems to be the only geographical location in this column that is not preceded by את/ו.

3 בקֹעֻ. Puech identifies בקֹעֻ with the city of Baca (el-Buqei'a, modern Peki'in) mentioned by Josephus in J. War 3.39.[436]

בית צפור. Assuming that this line deals with the tribal territory of Zebulun, Puech identifies בית צפור with Sepphoris (ציפורי). Yet the extant ancient sources never refer to Sepphoris as בית צפור.[437] The editor mentions also two other possible identifications: Be Ṣippor-BṢaffur southeast of Zarephath and Bit-Ṣupuri of the Esarhaddon's inscription.[438] The latter is usually identified with the ancient Ornithopolis.[439] Some scholars locate it at Tell al-Burāq, 8 km south of Sidon, while others propose Ain Ṣofar, 21 km east of Beirut.[440]

4 ו]יכו את כול בקעת מצפֹּא. The scroll seems to allude to Josh 11:8 depicting Joshua's pursuit of the King of Hazor and his allies: "The Lord delivered them into the hands of Israel, and they defeated them (ויכום) and pursued them all the way to Great Sidon and Misrephoth-maim, all the way to the Valley of Mizpeh on the east". The scroll adds an emphatic כול בקעת, "the entire valley of". While the Masoretic Text reads מצפה, the scroll's מצפֹּא may be vocalized either as מצפָּא (cf. 3Q15 VI, 2; 4Q225 2 i 5) or מצפֶּא.[441] The latter vocalization finds some support in Josh 11:3 (MT) referring to ארץ המצפה and the LXX[A, mss] of Josh 11:3, 8. Scholars assume that

436 S. Mason, *Flavius Josephus: Judean War 2* (Flavius Josephus Translation and Commentary 1B; Leiden, Boston: Brill, 2008), p. 182.

437 Y. Elitzur, *Ancient Place Names in the Holy Land: Preservation and History* (Jerusalem: The Magnes Press: 2004), pp. 79-82.

438 The inscription refers to Bit-Ṣupuri as one of the "cities in Sidon's environment". D.D. Luckenbill, *Ancient Records of Assyria and Babylonia* (New York: Greenwood Press Publishers, 1968), vol. 2, p. 205 (#512).

439 On Ornithopolis see R. Dussaud, *Topographie historique de la Syrie antique et médiévale* (Bibliothèque Archéologique et historique; Paris: Librarie orientaliste Paul Geuthner, 1927), pp. 39-41.

440 E. Ebeling & B. Messier, *Reallexicon der Assyriologie* (Berlin: Walter de Gruyter, 1978), vol. 2, p. 52; E. Lipínski, *Itineraria Phoenicia* (Orientalia Lovaniensia Analecta; Leuven: Peters, 2004), pp. 18, 294.

441 For the scrolls' use of an *alef* to mark 'a' and 'e' vowels see Qimron, *Hebrew*, pp. 23-24.

both the valley and the land of Mizpe/ah refer to the same area, which should be sought at the foot of Mt. Hermon. Marj 'Ayyun is one likely candidate.[442]

5 היכלים. Elitzur suggests that היכלים is Haikālim, a city in northern Canaan mentioned in the Egyptian sources.[443]

יעפור. Puech identifies it with Ya'afur situated 20 km to the west of Damascus.

6 בא]. Puech suggests כפר סבא (Χαβαρσαβα [J. Ant. 13.390]; כפר סבא [b. Nidda 61a]; כפר סבה [Rehob inscription, line 26]).[444]

מנו. The editor suggests Menin, 15 km north of Damascus,[445] yet, since line 7 mentions חדיתא, it is likely that this line is no more concerned with the conquests in the north.

עין כובר. Puech suggests Kiboreia (Deir el-'Ashair) found several kilometers northwest of Ya'afur. More plausible is Elitzur's identification with the modern village of Kubar, situated some 20 km east of the ancient Haditha, in the tribal territory of Ephraim.[446]

7 גרים ר̇]. The editor restores אש]ר̇ גרים את חדיתא and renders it as "qui habitent Haditha". However, the construction לגור את is difficult. Perhaps, גרים ר̇] is a toponym.

חדיתא. This is the biblical חדיד of the tribe of Benjamin, modern el-Hadithe, 6 km east of Lydda (Ezra 2:33; Neh 7:37, 11:34). While the Hebrew Bible and the Tannaitic sources name it חדיד, Eusebius, Jerome, the Madaba map, as well as the aforementioned Arabic name of the site, reflect the spelling Haditha.[447]

עושל. This toponym is unknown from other sources.

8 אשר̇]דון. Puech, reading a *yod* before the *dalet*, suggests that the scroll mentions here צידון, Sidon. Yet, assuming that the more cautious reading דון[is correct,

---

442 Aharoni, *Land*, p. 217; Ahituv, *Joshua*, p. 182. On the Valley of Mizpeh as the northern extremity of the conquered territory see further Kallai, "Boundaries", p. 32.

443 Elitzur, *Names*, p. 259 note 9 (Hebrew edition); S. Ahituv, *Canaanite Toponyms in Ancient Egyptian Documents* (Jerusalem: Magnes Press, 1984), pp. 104-105.

444 A. Kasher, *Jews and Hellenistic Cities in Eretz Israel* (TSAJ 21; Tübingen: J.C.B. Mohr Paul Siebeck, 1990), p. 207, places it to the north of Antipatris, modern Rosh HaAyin, in the tribal territory of Ephraim. Y. Sussmann, "A Halakhic Inscription from the Beth-Shean Valley", *Tarbiz* 43 (1974), p. 135 (Hebrew), points to Kefar Sib, 4 km northwest of Tul-Karem.

445 Puech's other proposal, בקעת פני מנון in Galilee, is based on a difficult reading in Exodus Rabbah 52, as cited in A. Neubauer, *La géographie du Talmud* (Hildesheim: G. Olms, 1967), p. 274. The printed editions of Exod. Rab. have בקעה אחת של פגי מדון, which might be a corruption of בקעה אחת שלפני מרון.

446 Personal communication. Note also the mention of Kbr in the list of the geographical localities in Medinet Habu. See W.F. Edgerton & J.A. Wilson, *Historical Records of Ramses III: The Texts in Medinet Habu: Volumes 1 and II* (Chicago: University of Chicago, 1936), p. 100 (#23).

447 Elitzur, *Names*, p. 140.

it is far from clear which toponym is mentioned here (especially, in light of the tendency to add a *nun* after 'o' in the last syllable, as in גמזון in line 13). אֲשֶׁר is apparently a relative particle "that", explicating the location of this city.

9]וֹרֹ[. One possible reconstruction is דור (cf. Josh 12:23; Judg 1:27).

וא[שקלון. The available space seems to be insufficient for the particle (ו)את. Josh 13:3 places Ashkelon within "the land that yet remains". Judg 1:18(MT) states that it was captured by Judah. See Discussion.

10 את השרון] שבֹן ושנים ב[גֹליל. The reconstruction ב[גֹליל (Puech) assumes that the scroll names here a locality in Galilee (cf. קדש בגליל [Josh 20:7]). ושנים could be either a cardinal number, "and two" (cf. שלשת נפת of Josh 17:11), or a top-onym.[448] Puech restores שבֹ[שפל]ת השרון. The term שפלה conveys a meaning of lowness and usually applies to a region adjacent to the highlands of Judah.[449] While compound toponyms 'שפלת + a name of a locality' occur in the Rabbinic literature (cf. שפלת לוד and שפלת הדרום in m. Sheviit 9:2), the phrase שפלת השרון is unattested in the ancient sources.[450] The editor also proposes two alternative restorations שבֹ[שדו]ת השרון (cf. בשד שרנ from the inscription of Eshmunazar II [line 19]) and שבֹ[נפ]ת השרון.[451]

11 וילכוד י]הודה את באר שבע [וא]ת בעלות. From this line onwards the fragment seems to list the locations captured by the tribe of Judah. Tov restores (with Judg 1:18): וילכוד י]הודה.[452]

באר שבע [וא]ת בעלות. Both Beersheba and Bealoth (unidentified) are found in the tribal territory of Judah, though Beersheba is allocated to Simeon (Josh 15:24, 28).

---

448 The Bible mentions the city of Shunem (שונם [Josh 19:18, 1 Sam 28:4; 2 Kgs 4:8]). However, its location at the foot of the Hill of Moreh in Issachar's territory (Josh 19:18) does not match the ensuing mention of "Sharon", unless one assumes that it does not stand for the Plain of Sharon. Eusebius mentions in his Onomasticon that in his days the territory from Mount Tabor to Lake Tiberias was called Σαρωνᾶς (ed. Klostermann, p. 162). See comments by R.S. Notley & Z. Safrai, *Eusebius, Onomasticon: A Triglot Edition with Notes and Commentary* (Leiden, Boston: Brill, 2005), p. 152. Eusebius mentions also Σωναμ, "from whence came the the Shunammite (1 Kgs 1:3)", which Notley & Safrai, ibid., p. 150, identify with Sasim in the Beit Dagan valley, to the east of Neapolis.
449 In Josh 11:2, 16 שפלה refers to a region in the north of Canaan. Ahituv, *Joshua*, pp. 182, 188, suggests that it designates the hills of the Lower Galilee.
450 The Rabbinic sources referring to Sharon are collected and analyzed in Y. Waitz, "Was the Sharon on the Sea Coast", *BJES* 6 (1940), pp. 132-141 (Hebrew); A.Y. Brawer, "The Sharon on the Coast", *BJES* 7 (1940), pp. 34-38 (Hebrew).
451 According to M. Ben-Dov, "נפה—A Geographical Term of Possible 'Sea People' Origin", *Tel-Aviv* 3 (1976), pp. 70-73, נפה is derived from the Greek νάπη designating forest in a plain.
452 Tov, "Rewritten Joshua", p. 244.

12 קעילה. Keilah, about 13.5 km northwest of Hebron, is a city in Judah (Josh 15:44). עדולם. Adullam, at the midpoint of a line running from Bethlehem to Gath, was captured by Joshua (Josh 12:15) and allocated to Judah (Josh 15:35).

13 גזר. While Joshua is reported to have defeated the king of Gezer (Josh 10:33, 12:12), the Ephraimites, in whose territory this (Levitical) city is situated (21:21), were not able to dispossess it (Josh 16:10; Judg 1:29).

תמנו. Timno (MT תמנה) is a Danite town (Josh 19:43 reads תמנתה) found on the northern border of the tribal allotment of Judah, between Beth-Shemesh and Ekron (Josh 15:10).[453]

גמזון. Gimzon (MT גמזו[454]), situated 4.5 km southeast of Lydda, is mentioned alongside with Timna in 2 Chr 28:18 (in the same order). It belongs in Judah's tribal territory.

14 חקר] חקר. is otherwise unknown. The Egyptian sources mention Aqar.[455]

וקטר[ון]. The reconstruction [וקטר[ון (Puech) may be slightly long for the lacuna. According to Judg 1:30, the tribe of Zebulon failed to dispossess Kitron.[456] Yet a Zebulonite city would hardly fit this section of the list concerned with Judah's conquest. Perhaps, the scroll refers to Kedron (Κεδρων [1 Mac 15:39]) identified with the village of Qatra, southwest of the biblical Gezer (Puech).[457]

ואפרנים. This toponym is unattested in other sources.

ואת שדות. שדות could be a compound toponym, 'שְׂדוֹת + name of a locality', as in שדות גבע (Neh 12:29), where Geba is a Levitical city in the tribal territory of Benjamin (Josh 18:24, 21:17).[458]

15 בית חורון התחת[ו]ן והעל[י]ון. Assigned to the tribe of Levi, the Upper and the Lower Beth-Horon are situated in the tribal territory of Ephraim (Josh 16:3, 5, 18:13, 14, 21:22).

16 א[ו]ת גולת עליונה [וא]ת התתת[ו]תונ[ו]ת. This location, 3 km northeast of the ancient Debir-Kiryath Sepher, is in the tribal territory of Judah. Judg 1:15 reads גֻלֹת עלית and גֻלֹת תחתית, whereas Josh 15:19 has גֻלֹת עליות and גֻלֹת תחתיות. The scroll seems to read Gullath, i.e. a sg. form, a reading suggested by the wording of Judg 1:15

---

[453] A different city bearing the same name occurs in Josh 15:57. See W.R. Kotter, "Timnah", *ABD*, vol. 6, pp. 556-557.

[454] For the addition of *nun* see Elitzur, *Names*, pp. 314-316.

[455] Ahituv, *Toponyms*, p. 63.

[456] Kitron has not yet been identified. See Aharoni, *Land*, p. 214.

[457] J. Goldstein, *1 Maccabees*, p. 520. As Puech notes, the LXX of Judg 1:30 reads Κεδρων.

[458] Puech reads שׂכֹות, namely the biblical סכות (spelled with a *sin*, instead of a *samech*). Yet, it is difficult to explain how this Transjordanian location (in the tribal territory of Gad [Josh 13:27]) fits frg. 9 i listing cities to the east of Jordan only.

(with the fem. sg. adjectives עלית and תחתית) and reflected in LXX (codex Alex. for Josh 15:19), S, T, V to Josh 15:19 and Judg 1:15. Note also the absence of the definite article before עליונה.

17 מצרים נחל[ן]ע. The reconstruction follows Josh 15:4, 47, where עד נחל מצרים stands for Judah's southern border. In Num 34:5 is designates the southern boundary of the Promised Land, while in 1 Kgs 8:65 it is the southern extremity of Solomon's kingdom (cf. 2 Chr 7:8). Usually, it is identified with Wadi el-Arish.[459]

18 [נמיש]. Perhaps, this is a 1st pl. Hifil *yiqtol* of מוש, "to remove" (cf. [Micah 2:3]). The reading [נמוש], a 1st pl. Qal *yiqtol* of מוש, "to withdraw", is equally possible. The use of the 1st pl. reminds one of ועתה נ[ש]כינה found in 9 ii 12. Perhaps, this line is already concerned with the events of frg. 9 ii.

Frg. 9 ii

```
[                    ]∘∘∘∘[                    ] 1
[ לוֹא[ ] ]∘[ ]∘[ לצי]וֹן להשכין שם את אהלֹ מו[עד עד אשר יעברו ] 2
[העתים כי הנה בן נולד לישי בן פרץ בן יה]ודה הוא אשר ילכוד] 3
[את סלע ציון ויורש משם את כל האמורי מיר]ושלם ויהי עם לבבו] 4
[לבנות אΧ הבית ליהוה אלוהי ישראל זהב וכסף] נחושת וברזל יכין] 5
[ארזים וברושים יביא] מ]לבנון לבנותו ובנו הקטֹן] יבננו        [ 6
[יכהן שם ראישוֹן מֹ]   [חסדֹ]   [ ואותוֹן יר]צֹה יֹ[הוה ויברכהו] 7
[[מן] [המ]עֹֹון מן השמי]ם כי] ידיד יהֹו]ה י]שכון לבטח יֹ]   כול] 8
[[ה]יֹמים ו]עֹמו ישכון לֹעֹד ועתה האמוֹרי שם והכנענ]י בקרבנו] 9
יושב אשר החטיוֹנֹי אשר לוא דרשתי אֹ[ת מ]שפטֹ הֹ[אורים והתומים] 10
מאתכה והשלוני וה]נֹ]ה נתתיו עבד עֹ[בדים ליש]רֹא]ל        [ 11
ועתה נ[ש]כינה את א]הל מֹ]וֹעד רחוק מן הֹ]אמורי והכנעני וישאו] 12
אלעזרֹ] ויישוֹ]ע את אֹ]הל מוֹ]עד מבית [אל לשילה              [ 13
ישוע]         שֹ]רֹ צבא מעֹ]רכות ישראל                       [ 14
שֹ∘[ש                         לֹ] [לֹ]                        [ 15
```

---

459 See Ahituv, *Joshua*, p. 243. N. Na'aman, "The Brook of Egypt and Assyrian Policy on the Border of Egypt", *Tel Aviv* 6 (1979), pp. 74-90, identifies it with Nahal HaBesor. His interpretation of the data is criticized by A. Rainey, "Toponymic Problems", *Tel Aviv* 9 (1982), pp. 131-132, supporting the identification of the Brook of Egypt with Wadi el-Arish. P.K. Hooker, "The Location of the Brook of Egypt", in M.P. Graham et al. (eds.), *History and Interpretation* (JSOTSS 173; Sheffield: JSOT Press, 1993), pp. 203-214, agrees with Na'aman that in the early Assyrian inscriptions the Brook of Egypt is Nahal HaBesor, yet suggests that sometime "between the early stages of the reign of Sargon II and the middle of the reign of Esarhaddon" it became associated with Wadi el-Arish.

Notes on Readings

The left side of the column is missing. The length of the reconstructions varies from one scholar to another.[460] Restored according to the MT, frgs. 22-26, containing Ps 122, produce lines with an average length of 55 letter-spaces (varying from 49 to 58 letter-spaces). Hence, here the reconstructed lines average 54 letter-spaces (varying from 53 to 55).

1 Bottom tips of three or four letters are preserved in this line (Qimron and Tov). Puech proposes ‏.[נֹתַתֹּנ‏. Dimant suggests ‏.[נֹתֹתֹ‏.[461] Yet, the traces are illegible and therefore no reading is offered here.

2 Three letter-spaces to the left of ‏לֹוֹא‏ a bottom tip of a vertical stroke appears (PAM 41.948). Further to the left there is a diagonal vertical stroke descending from left to right, as in *alef*. Qimron ignores these traces and reads ‏לֹוֹא[נוכל לבוא‏. Tov notes the first one, yet ignores the second: ‏לֹוֹא.[462 נו[כֹ]ל לבוא‏ Puech reads ‏לֹוֹא[יכל‏[נֹ]נו לבו[אֹ‏. However, the lacuna is not large enough to contain the restoration ‏לֹוֹא[יכל‏[נֹ]נו‏. Dimant's reading, ‏לֹוֹא ‏[בוא]‏ יֹ[‏], is also difficult. The distance between ‏לֹוֹא‏ and the trace of ink read by her as a *yod* is too large to be an interval between two adjacent words. Also, the lacuna between the two aforementioned traces of ink is larger than the restoration ‏יֹ[בוא]וֹ‏.

7 ‏.[הֹסֹד‏]. Qimron reads thus in his revised text of 4Q522.[463] On the photographs PAM 41.948; 43.606 there is a faint trace of a vertical stroke that may belong to a *dalet*. The *DJD* edition reads (with Qimron's first edition of the fragment[464]) ‏.פֹי[נֹ הֹסֹ]‏. ‏יֹ.[הוה]. Puech reads ‏בֹ.[כול‏. The very faint trace of ink visible on the photographs seems to be that of a vertical stroke. Thus Qimron suggests ‏וֹ.[יברכהו‏. Alternatively, it may also be read as a *yod*.

8 | ‏.[מן]. The *DJD* edition has ‏לֹ[בכו]‏. Dimant suggests ‏לֹ[עֹמ]‏. It is unclear whether the faint trace visible on the photographs is ink. Qimron disregards it.

10 ‏החטיונֹי‏. Puech reads ‏החטיוֹם‏, yet, as Qimron observes, the traces of ink are consistent with a medial *nun* and a *yod*, ‏.החטיונֹי‏[465] Eshel, Tov, and Dimant also read thus.[466]

---

460 Qimron's reconstructions are usually shorter than those proposed by Puech and Dimant.

461 Dimant, "Apocryphon of Joshua", p. 183.

462 Tov, "Rewritten Joshua", p. 237.

463 Qimron, *The Hebrew Writings: Volume Two*.

464 Qimron, "Joshua Cycles", p. 504.

465 Qimron, ibid..

466 Eshel, "Note", p. 90; Tov, "Rewritten Joshua", p. 237; Dimant, "Apocryphon of Joshua", p. 183.

12 ﯾ̇|. The editor reads and restores ל[ון. Yet, according to the photograph PAM 41.948, the surviving vertical stroke better suits a *he* (thus Qimron, Tov, and Dimant).

14 מ̇ע̇|רכות. Puech reads מש̇[מרות. Yet, as Qimron (followed by Tov and Dimant) notes, the vertical stroke next to a medial *mem* belongs to an *ayin*.

Translation

1.]   [
2. not[ ] [ ] [to Zi]on, to set up there the Tent of Mee[ting until] the times [will pass.]
3. For, look, a son is born to Jesse son of Perez son of Ju[dah. He will seize]
4. the rock of Zion and drive out from there <all> the Amorites, from Jeru[salem. And it will be his will]
5. to build the temple for YHWH, God of Israel. Gold and silver, [copper and iron he will prepare.]
6. Cedar and pine will he bring [from] Lebanon to build it. And his younger son [will build it   ]
7. will minister there first from[   ]piety[   ]. And [YHWH will fa]vor him [and bless him]
8. [from the ab]ode, from heave[n. For] the beloved of YH[WH]will dwell securely [all]
9. [the]days [and]with him He will dwell forever. But now, the Amorites are there, and the Canaan[ites] are dwelling
10. [in our midst], who made me sin, for I have not sought the [ju]dgement of the [Urim and Thummim]
11. from you. And they have misled me. And lo[o]k, I have made him slave [of slaves for Is]rae[l   ]
12. Now, let us s[e]t up the T[ent of Mee]ting far from the [Amorites   And]
13. Eleazar [and Joshu]a [carried] the T[ent of Mee]ting from Beth[el to Shiloh   ]
14. Joshua[the comman]der of the army of the batt[le arrays of Israel   ]

Comments

2 עד|מו אהל את שם להשכין לצי|ון]∘[   ]∘[   ]∘[**ל̇ו̇א**. Lines 2-12 appear to be Joshua's address to the High Priest Eleazar. He explains why the Tent of Meeting has to be established in Shiloh, as reported in Josh 18:1, rather than in Jerusalem. Paraphrasing Josh 18:1, the scroll adds a negation ל̇וא, making clear that the Tent is not taken to Zion. Puech's restoration, עדות/הברית ארון ואת מו|עד אהל את, is superfluous and creates an unnecessarily long line.

עד אשר יעברו] / העתים 2-3. The restoration follows 1 Chr 29:30 (Dimant). Puech and Qimron restore העתים [קץ/עד סוף] (cf. Dan 11:13). Eshel suggests עד בוא] העתים.

כי הנה בן נולד לישי בן פרץ בן יה]ודה 3. Joshua foretells the birth of David. The masc. sg. Nifal participle of ילד denotes a future event (Qimron; for the formula הנה בן נולד ל- see 1 Chr 22:9-10; 1 Kgs 13:2).[467] He traces David's genealogy back to Phares and Judah (cf. Ruth 4:18-22; 1 Chr 2:4-15; Mt 1:3-5; Lk 3:31-33).[468] Puech's restoration, בן יעקוב, creates a longer line.

הוא אשר ילכוד] / את סלע ציון 4. The reconstruction follows 2 Sam 5:6-7 (Dimant; Qimron has והוא ילכוד). The scroll replaces the biblical מצודה, "mountain strong-hold", with סלע, "rock" (Qimron).[469] The nouns סלע and מצודה are frequently paired (e.g., 2 Sam 22:2; Job 39:28; Dimant). See Discussion.

ויורש משם את כל האמורי מיר]ושלם. Joshua envisions David dispossessing all the Amorites from Zion. The wording is reminiscent of Num 21:32 with an addition of the emphatic כל. The verb ויורש, a Hifil *yiqtol* of ירש with a *waw* conjunctive, denotes a future action (Qimron).[470] Josh 10:1, 5 refers to the inhabitants of Jerusalem as Amorites.[471] The reconstructed word מיר]ושלם (for the orthography see frg. 22-26 2) stands in an apposition to משם. Puech reconstructs מיר]ושלם ועד הים. Yet, this restoration hardly fits the circumstances implied by the scroll, namely, that Jerusalem has not yet been fully dispossessed. Qimron restores (with Ezra 4:4) מיר]אה פן יבהלוהו. See Discussion.

ויהיה עם לבבו] / לבנות אֵת הבית ליהוה אלוהי ישראל 4-5. The scroll follows 1 Kgs 8:17 or 1 Chr 22:7.

זהב וכסף] נחושת וברזל יכין / ארזים וברושים יביא] מ]לבנון לבנותו 5-6. The reconstructions (Puech) follow the description of David's preparations in 1Chr 22:16, 29:2. The phrase עצי ארזים ועצי ברושים occurs in 1 Kgs 5:22, 24; 2 Chr 2:7 reporting the construction of the Temple by Solomon (Dimant).

ובנו הקטון] יבננו. Joshua foresees the construction of the Temple by Solomon (cf. the reference to him as נער ורך in 1Chr 22:5). The reconstruction follows 2 Chr 6:9 (Qimron).

467 *Contra* Milik and Puech who parse it as a *qatal* form. Milik, "5Q9", p. 179.
468 On Phares in the Rabbinic sources see R. Bloch, "Juda engendra Pharès et Zara, de Thamar", *Mélanges bibliques, rédigés en l'honneur de André Robert* (Travaux de l'institut catholique de Paris 4; Paris: Bloud & Gay, 1957), pp. 381-389.
469 HALOT, pp. 622, 758.
470 Qimron, "Joshua Cycles", p. 505.
471 Puech, "4Q522", pp. 58, 73, argues unconvincingly that by describing the inhabitants of Jerusalem as Amorites, this scroll reflects an interpretation of ארץ/הר המוריה (Gen 22:2; 2 Chr 3:1), identified with Mt. Zion, as the 'land/mount of Amorites'.

6-7 [‏[הٌסד]‏ ‏מٌ ראישٌוֿٌן‏‏ ‏יכהן שם‏. The use of the verb ‏יכהן‏ suggests a priestly figure
(Tov), apparently, Zadok (Qimron; Dimant),[472] rather than Solomon (Puech [pre-
liminary edition]; Eshel).[473] Qimron restores ‏[הٌסד אל ‏[לפני ‏מٌ ראישٌוֿٌן‏‏ ‏/ יכהן שם ובנכה‏
‏[יהוה]‏. Dimant prefers ‏[וצדוק]‏ / ‏יכהן‏, yet neither of the other two future figures
(David and Solomon) are referred to by their names. Given the allusions to Deut
32 in the ensuing text, ‏[הٌסד]‏ "piety" (cf. discussion of Sir 46:1-8 in Chapter 1), may
point to Moses' blessing of Levi in Deut 33:8: ‏תמיך ואוריך לאיש חסידך‏.

7-8 ‏[והם]‏ ‏[ון]‏ מן השמٌי[ם]‏ / ‏[מן]‏ ‏[והٌוٌן]‏ ‏יٌהוה ויברכהו‏ ‏יٌרٌ[צֶֿה]‏ ‏ואותוٌ‏. The combination of ‏רצה‏ and
‏ברך‏ is found in the Mosaic blessing of Levi in Deut 33:11 (Qimron). The rest of this
phrase alludes to Deut 26:15: ‏השקיפה ממעון קדשך מן השמים וברך את עמך‏. Puech,
Qimron, and Tov suggest that the object of the blessing is Solomon, while Dimant
proposes that this is still Zadok mentioned in the preceding clause. She restores
‏יٌ. יהוה ויברכהו‏. Qimron suggests a shorter ‏וٌ. יٌברכהו‏. The reconstruction ‏[הٌמٌ]‏עٌון‏ might
be a little too long for the lacuna. Still, Qimron's ‏שוכן‏ (‏[עٌון‏ ‏מٌ]שוכן‏) is certainly too
long for the short lacuna (two letter-spaces) in the beginning of the line.

8 ‏[וٌ]שכון לבטח‏ ‏יהוٌ[ה]‏ ‏ידיד‏ ‏כٌיٌ‏. The scroll may apply the language of the Mosaic blessing of Benjamin (Deut 33:12) to Zadok (cf. 4Q379 1 2; ALD 13:2; Dimant). This may
imply that the establishment of the Temple with a Zadokite priest officiating in
it constitutes a fulfilment of Moses' blessing to Benjamin, in whose territory Jerusalem was situated. If ‏ואותוٌ‏ of line 6 refers to Solomon, then he is the referent
here (Puech, Qimron, Tov). Solomon's other name ‏ידידה‏ (2 Sam 12:25), and the
description of his peaceful rule (‏וישב ... לבטח‏ [1 Kgs 5:4-5, 18]; cf. Sir 47:12) lend
some support to this interpretation.

8-9 ‏לعٌד‏ ‏ועٌמו ישכון‏ / ‏[ה]ٌימים]‏ / ‏כולٌ[ן]‏ ‏יٌ. The scroll seems to paraphrase Deut 33:12b.
The restoration ‏[ה]ٌימٌים‏ / ‏כٌולٌ‏ is supported by ‏כל היום‏ of Deut 33:12 (thus read the
LXX and T[Ps.-J.,Necf.,Fr.]). It is unclear whether the scroll reads ‏[ו]עٌמו‏ (Dimant) or ‏וٌעֶٿמו‏
(Puech). The reconstruction of the *waw* is also uncertain. Still, since both the
biblical verse and lines 7-8 are concerned with an individual, the reading ‏ועٌמו‏
(paraphrasing ‏ובין כתפיו‏?) seems to be preferable. If the referent is Zadok, then
the scroll echoes here the promise of the eternal priesthood to Phineas (Num
25:13; cf. Sir 45:24[Ms. B]; Dimant).[474] If this is Solomon, it may allude to the divine

---

472 Qimron, "Joshua Cycles", p. 504. He initially proposed ‏[וצדוק]‏, yet his new edition has ‏[ובנכה]‏.
473 Puech, "La pierre", pp. 683-686; Eshel, "Note", pp. 91-92. Tov, "Rewritten Joshua", p. 239,
takes a middle-course suggesting that the scroll refers to Zadok "and by extension also David,
who sacrificed offerings at the altar of Aravna in 2 Sam 24:25, and Solomon".
474 The phrase ‏[ה]ٌימים‏ / ‏[כול]‏, paraphrasing Deut 33:12, occurs in the divine address to Eli in 1
Sam 2:35: "And I will raise for Myself a faithful priest ...and he shall walk before my anointed
evermore (‏והתהלך לפני משיחי כל הימים‏)".

promise to David in 2 Sam 7:13 (cf. 1 Chr 23:25). Dimant restores (with Tg⁰ to Deut 33:12): מִים עמו ישכון לְעֻד[ה] / [ה]ימִים[ה] / [ובאחרית]. Qimron proposes יִשכון לבטח ו[יהוה מגינו כול] / [ובאחרית].

9-10 יושב /]ועתה האמֹרי שם והכנענ[י בקרבנו הוא[. ועתה. ועתה signals that Joshua turns his attention to the present (Qimron). האמֹרי apparently stands for Jebusites (cf. line 4), while שם refers to Jerusalem. As the ensuing text indicates, והכנענ[י refers to the Gibeonites. Although elsewhere they are called Hivites and Amorites (Josh 9:7; 2 Sam 21:2), the scroll seems to emphasize their being descendants of Canaan (cf. Comment to line 11).[475] The restoration follows Dimant and Qimron (revised edition; cf. Josh 9:7, 16, 22). Puech proposes והכנענ[י את (בכול) הארץ] / יושב.

10-11]אשר החטיונֹי אשר לוא דרשתי אֹ[ת מ]שפט הֹ[אורים והתומים] / מאתכה והשלוני. Joshua declares that the Gibeonites "made him sin". Alluding to Josh 9:14, he blames himself with failing to inquire of the Lord in the case of the treaty with the Gibeonites. The scroll replaces the verb שאל of this biblical verse with דרש, reflecting a later usage (Dimant). The collocation דרש משפט occurs elsewhere with reference to seeking justice (Isa 1:17, 16:5). Here this phrase stands for ascertaining the divine decree (cf. 1QS VI, 7).[476] Following Num 27:21, Qimron (with Kister) restores [אורים הֹ[אורים] מֹ[שפט. Here the longer מֹ[שפט הֹ[אורים והתומים] is adopted (Puech; Dimant; cf. 11QTᵃ LVIII, 18). The pronoun מאתכה in the present context leaves no doubt that the addressee is the High Priest Eleazar.

החטיונֹי. The quiescent *alef* in this Hifil *qatal* of חטא, "to sin", has been dropped.

והשלוני. Josh 9:22 employs the verb רמה, "to betray", to describe the Gibeonites' ruse, yet the scroll prefers a Hifil of שלה. In 2 Kgs 4:28 it denotes "to set at ease, lead to a false hope".[477] Indeed, the Gibeonites pretended to come from far away, so that they might be treated in accordance with the law of Deut 20:10-15.

11 והֹ[נ]וֹה נתתיו עבד ע[בדים ליש]רֹא[ל. The scroll reworks Joshua's decree regarding the Gibeonites from Josh 9:23, 27. ליש]רֹא[ל replaces the biblical לעדה (the LXX has "for the whole community"). The restoration follows Gen 9:25 (Dimant; Qimron [revised edition]). Dimant further restores (with Josh 9:27): ליש[רֹא[ל ולמזבח יהוה].

---

475 On the Gibeonites in the Hebrew Bible see, for instance, J. Day, "Gibeon and the Gibeonites in the Old Testament", in R. Rezetko et al. (eds.), *Reflection and Refraction* (Leiden: Brill, 2007), pp. 113-138..

476 On this shift in the meaning in דרש see A. Hurvitz, "Continuity and Innovation in Biblical Hebrew—the Case of "Semantic Change" in Post-Exilic Writings", in T. Muraoka (ed.), *Studies in Ancient Hebrew Semantics* (Louvain: Peeters Press, 1995), pp. 7-9.

477 HALOT, p. 1504. Qimron, "Joshua Cycles", p. 506, notes that שלה is better attested in Aramaic than in Hebrew.

12 ועתה נ[ש]כינה את א[הל מ][ועד רחוק מן ה][אמורי והכנעני. This line echoes Josh 18:1 (cf. line 2). The reconstruction is that of Dimant. Qimron offers a shorter רחוק מן ה[כנעני.

12-13 וישאו[/ אלעזר[ן וישו][ע את א[הל מו][הל מו][עד מבית [אל לשילה. The restorations are those of Qimron. He (following Kister) proposes that since Bethel is situated at the crossroads on the way from Gilgal to Jerusalem, the scroll places Joshua's address to Eleazar there.[478] The reconstruction לשילה is suggested by Josh 18:1 (cf. line 2). According to this passage, the transfer of the Tent of Meeting to Shiloh took place when "the land was … under their control", which seems to match the catalogue of the cities conquered by the Israelites in frg. 9 i. Joshua is mentioned after Elea-zar, as is always the case in the Hebrew Bible and the DSS (CD V, 3; 1Q22 I, 11-12).

14 ישוע. For the short form ישוע (MT יהושע) see Comment to 4Q378 22 i 2.

ש]ר צבא מע[ר]כות ישראל. The restoration, a combination of the phrases שר צבא (Gen 21:22) and מערכות ישראל (1 Sam 17:8, 10), is that of Qimron. It may refer to Joshua (for Joshua as στρατηγός see J. Ant 4.13, 165). Dimant suggests that the scroll alludes here to Josh 5:14.

Frg. 11

[יˊˆם נעדר א]	1
[אותם ולוא ˆ]	2
[ל ˊ הואה מˆראˆם]	3
[הˆוˆא]ה	4

Translation

1.   ] lacking   [
2.   ] them and not   [
3.   ] He is their fear[
4.   ]h[e

Comments

1 נעדר. The context of this 3ʳᵈ masc. sg. Nifal *qatal* of עדר, "to be missing", is unclear.[479]

3 הואה מˆראˆם. The editor takes מˆראˆם as a masc. sg. Hifil participle of ראה, "to show", with a 3ʳᵈ masc. pl. suffix. Yet, it may also be read as a noun מורא, "fear", spelled

---

478 Qimron, "Joshua Cycles", p. 507.
479 HALOT, p. 793.

defectively (as in Deut 26:8).[480] Compare והוא מוראכם (Isa 8:13). Apparently, the 3rd masc. sg. pronoun refers to God.

Frg. 12

]יום[	1
]∘[	2

Translation
1.]day[
2.] [

Frg. 13

]אׄדמהׄ[	1
]∘∘[	2

Notes on Readings
1 Puech reads]אׄדמהׄ[. The first and the last letter are represented each by a bottom tip of a vertical stroke.

Translation
1.   ]ground[
2.   ] [

Frg. 14

]וייר שׄ[ו	1
]∘[	2

Translation
1]and [they] dispossess[ed
2   ] [

Comments
1]וייר שׄ[ו. Forms of ירש, "to dispossess", are frequently attested in the Book of Joshua (1:15, 12:1, 13:12). Compare frg. 3 1.

---

480 HALOT, p. 560.

Frg. 15[481]

ה[   ]1

אנ[תֹדון   ]2

Translation
1. [   ]
2. [An]thedon

Comments

2 אנ[תֹדון. Apparently, this is the name of a city near Gaza, Anthedon (Ἀνθηδόν; J. Ant. 13.357, 395, 14.88; J. War 1.87, 164).[482] The editor notes that this fragment may belong with frg. 9 i. Frg. 9 i 9 mentions Ashkelon situated to the north of Gaza.

Puech observes that it is uncertain whether frgs. 16-20 belong with the scroll 4Q522.

Frg. 16

[ער]

Comments

Perhaps, read [ער]ים, "cities".

Frg. 17

[שים   ]   1

[ימין מי]ן   2

Comments

1 שים[. This may be a form of שׂים.

2 [ימין מי]ן. Puech proposes to restore the first word as בנ]ימין, "Ben]jamin".

---

481 I was not able to locate this fragment on the PAM photographs. The editor does not indicate on which image it appears.
482 G.M. Cohen, *The Hellenistic Settlements in Syria, the Red Sea Basin, and North Africa* (Berkeley: University of California Press, 2006), pp. 225-226, identifies Anthedon with Khirbet Teda, 3 km north of Gaza.

Frg. 18

]◦ מׄ[

Frg. 19

]לׄמׄ[

Frg. 20

]ימת[

Frg. 21

]◦המ	1
א]מרו	2

Translation

1. [   ]
2. [s]aid

Frgs. 22-26(=Ps 122)[483]

1 [שיר המעלות לדויד שׄמחתי ב]אומרים [לי ב]ית יהוה נלך עומדות היו[

2 [רגלינו   בשעריך י]ׄרושלם ירו[של]ׄם הבנוי[ה כעיר שחוברה לה יחדיו ששם]

3 [עלו שבטים] שבטי יה עדות לישראל להוד[ות לשם יה]וׄה כי שם [ישבו]

4 [כסאות למ]שׄפט כסאות לבית דויד שאל[ו שלום י]ׄרושלם ישליו

5 [אוהביך יהי שלום] בׄחׄ[י]ׄלׄךׄ [ש]ׄל[ו]ׄם בארׄמׄוׄ[נותיך למען]אׄחי ורעי אדׄ[ברה]

6 [נא שלום בך למען בית יהוׄ]הׄ [אלוהינו אבקשה] שלום ל[ך

7]   vac   [

Notes on Readings

---

483 Puech's *DJD* edition of Ps 122 is reproduced in E. Ulrich et al. (eds.), *Qumran Cave 4.XI: Psalms to Chronicles* (DJD 16; Oxford: Clarendon Press, 2000), pp. 169-170.

בשעריך] ירושלם 2. Puech reads בשערי[ך ירושלם. However, there are no traces of the final *kaf* on the photographs. In fact, even the *yod* of the following ירושלם has only partially survived. The copy of the text drawn by Puech in the preliminary edition shows clearly that the *kaf* of שעריך is not extant.[484]

באר[מ]ונותיך 4. Qimron reads a *waw*, instead of a *nun* (Puech), next to the medial *mem*.

Translation

1. [A song of ascents. Of Davi]d. I rejoiced when[they said to me, "We are going to the House of YHWH". Our feet stood]
2. [inside your gates,]O Jerusalem, Jeru[sale]m buil[t up, a city knit together, to which]
3. [tribes would make pilgrimage,] the tribes of YHWH,—as was enjoined upon Israel—to pra[ise the name of YH]WH. There
4. [the thrones of jud]gement [stood], thrones of the house of David. Pra[y for the well-being of Je]rusalem;
5. [May those who love you be at peace. May there be peace] within your ram[pa]rts, [p]e[a]ce in your ci[tadels". For the sake] of my kin and friends I pr[ay]
6. [for your well-being; for the sake of the house of YHW]H [our God, I seek] yo[ur] peace.
7. [   ]   [   ]

Variants

122:1 (1)	לדוי[ד M 11QPsᵃ III, 7 α' σ' V] > G S T	
122:4 (3)	עדת ישראל M G V S T] עדת ישראל 11QPsᵃ III,10[485] σ'	
122:5 (4)	כסאות M G V S T] 11QPsᵃ III, 11 כסא	
122:6 (4)	ישליו M α' σ' V S T] καὶ εὐθηνία (=ושלוה) G	
122:7 (5)	ש[לל[ו]ם] [ש]לוה M σ' T] ושלוה 11QPsᵃ III, 12 G V S	
122:9 (6)	שלום] M טוב 11QPsᵃ III, 14 (טובה) G V S T	

---

484 Puech, "Fragment", p. 551.
485 On this reading see further A. Rofé, "The Scribal Concern for the Torah as Evidenced by the Textual Witnesses of the Hebrew Bible", in N.S. Fox et al. (eds.), *Mishneh Todah* (Winona Lake, Indiana: Eisenbrauns, 2009), pp. 236-237.

4.5 Discussion

The foregoing analysis suggests two topics deserving a more detailed study. These are the geographical data found in the scroll and Joshua's prophetic discourse.

4.5.1 The Geographical Data

The extant fragments of 4Q522 contain a considerable number of toponyms (frgs. 3, 7, 8, 9, 15).[486] Most of these geographical data are either places that Israelites subdued (frg. 9 i) or left unconquered (frg. 8 and, perhaps, frgs. 2-3, 7, 8, 15).[487]

Frg. 9 i appears to list the Israelites' conquests. The book of Joshua contains similar lists (e.g., ch. 12), yet the one found in frg. 9 i differs in both form and contents.

As to the form, with a few exceptions (lines 2[?], 8-10, 14) the names of the localities in frg. 9 i are preceded by a *nota accusativi* (את), assuming a presence of a verb.[488] One such verb, "and] they [sm]ote", is still extant in line 4. Sometimes the particle את appears with a *waw* conjunctive. Its presence may indicate that these toponyms are grouped together.[489] It remains unclear whether they are grouped in pairs (באר שבע [וא]ת בעלות את [line 4], את יעפור ואת [line 7], את חדיתא ואת עושל) [line 11], את עדולם ואת [line 12]) or in longer chains with a *waw* attached to the last את. In one case, the construction ואת is used repeatedly (line 13), yet in another instance three toponyms are grouped by means of a *waw* conjunctive without a *nota accusativi* (line 14). The logic behind these groupings is elusive. Thus, in line 13, where all the listed toponyms are known (את [גזר ואת תמנו ואת גמזון ואת), their sequence reveals no obvious geographical pattern. Also, in at least two cases a toponym is followed by an explanatory remark (beginning with conjunctions אשר and -ש) clarifying its location (lines 8 and 10).

As to the contents, the list includes toponyms that are mentioned in the Hebrew Bible (Valley of Mizpe/ah, Haditha, Ashkelon, Galilee, Sharon, Beersheba, Bealoth, Keilah, Adullam, Gezer, Timno, Gimzon, Kitron(?), Upper and Lower Beth-Horon,

---

486 4Q522 is missing from P.K. McCarter, Jr., "Geography in the Documents", *EDSS*, vol. 1, pp. 306-308.
487 Frg. 3 3 may contain a third type of data, namely, a description of a tribal border.
488 The formula 'nota accusativi + toponym' is found in Josh 21 (cf. 1 Chr 6:39-66) listing the cities given by the tribes to the Levites, where the names of the cities are preceded by את, as required by the verb נתן. Yet frg. 9 i is clearly not a list of the Levitical cities.
489 As observed by Tov, "Rewritten Joshua", pp. 242-243.

Upper and Lower Gullath, Wadi[of Egypt), as well as non-biblical geographical locations (אפרנים, חקר, עׄושל, עין כובר, מנו, יעפור, היכלים, בית צפור, בקעׄ, ציּן קׄבׄרׄ).[490]

Among the biblical toponyms, there are places reported to be conquered by Joshua (Valley of Mizpe/ah, Adullam, Gezer), toponyms found in the description of the tribal allotments (Beersheba, Bealoth, Keilah, Adullam, Gezer, Timno, Gimzon, Upper and Lower Beth-Horon, Upper and Lower Gullath, Wadi[of Egypt), a city that is said to be conquered after Joshua's death (Ashkelon), and a city that is not mentioned in the Books of Joshua and Judges (Haditha). All these geographical data are used by 4Q522 to depict the extent of the Israelites' conquests.

The list in frg. 9 ii proceeds from the north of the land of Canaan to the south. Since line 11 mentions Judah, Puech assumes that the scroll groups the locations according to the tribal allotments. However, the following table indicates that the toponyms in lines 2-10 resist a neat division along these lines:

Locality	Tribe
בקעׄ	Naphtali?
בית צפור	"the land that yet remains"?
Valley of Mizpe/ah	Naphtali?[491]
יעפור	"the land that yet remains"?
עין כובר	Ephraim?
Haditha	Benjamin
Ashkelon	"the land that yet remains"/Judah
a city in Galilee	Asher? Zebulon? Naphtali?
a location(s) in Sharon	Manasseh

The description of the conquests in the north of Canaan (lines 2-5), alluding to Josh 11:8 (line 4), includes several locations (היכלים, בית צפור בקעׄ, and יעפור) that are not attested to in the Hebrew Bible. Although their identification remains tentative, it seems that at least two of them (בית צפור and יעפור) are situated within the "land that yet remains" (Josh 13 2). יעפור appears to be found in the vicinity of Damascus, which is reported to come under the Israelite control only in the days of David (2 Sam 8:3–8[=1 Chr 18:3–8]; 1 Kgs 11:23–25), while בית צפור, if indeed Ornithopolis, lies even further to the north of David and Solomon's northern border.

As the list moves south, it mentions the city of Haditha (line 7). According to the Rabbinic tradition its walls were fortified in the days of Joshua (m. Arachin

---

490 Only the well-preserved names are listed here.
491 Kallai, "Boundaries", p. 32, considers the Valley of Mizpeh to be the northern boundary of the land that was conquered with the "land that yet remains" laying further to the north.

9:6 [Puech]). Yet, in the biblical sources Hadid/Haditha emerges for the first time in the days of Ezra and Nehemiah (Ezra 2:33; Neh 7:37, 11:34). Later on, it appears as a strategically important location during the Hasmonean wars (1 Macc 12:38, 13:13; cf. J. Ant. 13.203, 392). Ashkelon, mentioned in line 9, is located further to the south. One of the cities of the Philistine Pentapolis, it is named in Josh 13:3 as one of the localities situated within the "land that yet remains". According to Judg 1:18(MT), relating the events that took place after Joshua's demise (1:1), Judah captured Ashkelon.[492] Still, in frg. 9 i Ashkelon appears before the section dealing with Judah's conquests.[493]

One indication that the list in frg. 9 i might not have proceeded consistently from north to south is found in line 10 referring to a location in Galilee. It seems to be out of place here, as line 9 lists Ashkelon, whereas line 11 mentions Beersheba. One possible explanation is that the reference to Galilee is somehow linked to the locality in the coastal Plain of Sharon mentioned further on in the same line.

Line 11 mentions Judah, the only tribal name in the extant text of frg. 9 i. Apparently, the locations listed in lines 11-17 were subdued by this tribe. The Book of Joshua says nothing of Judah's military activities. Yet Judges 1, presenting an account of the tribes' successes and failures in dispossessing the allocated land, gives particular attention to Judah's campaigns (1:1-19). Perhaps this account served as a model for the scroll's description of Judah's conquests.

This section of the list begins with Beersheba and concludes, as far as one can tell, with the Wadi of Egypt. It includes not only cities allocated to Judah (Bealoth, Keilah, Adullam, Gimzon, Upper and Lower Gullath), but also cities situated in its territory (Beersheba and Timno), yet given to other tribes (Simeon and Dan respectively).[494] Moreover, there are two Ephraimite cities, Gezer and Beth-Horon. Given the description of Judah's campaigns outside of their tribal

---

492 The LXX of Judg 1:18 states that Judah did not dispossess Ashkelon. Still, Josephus assigns it to Judah's tribal territory (J. Ant. 5.81). On the status of Ashkelon in the Rabbinic literature, see m. Gittin 1:2; t. Sheviit 4:11; Sif. Deut. 51. For discussion see B.-Z. Rosenfeld, "Flavius Josephus and His Portrayal of the Cost (Paralia) of Contemporary Roman Palestine: Geography and Ideology", *JQR* 91 (2000), p. 152; M. Avi-Yonah, "Ashkelon", *Encyclopaedia Judaica* (Detroit: Macmillan, 2007²), vol. 2, p. 568.
493 On Ashkelon's peaceful relations with the Hasmoneans see 1 Macc 10:86, 11:60, 12:33; J. Ant. 13.149, 180. See further G. Fuks, "Antagonistic Neighbours: Ashkelon, Judaea, and the Jews", *JJS* 51 (2000), pp. 42-47.
494 On the inclusion of Dan's tribal territory in Judah's allotment in the Rabbinic sources see Z. Safrai, *Boundaries and Administration in Eretz-Israel in the Mishnah-Talmud Period* (Tel-Aviv: Ha-Kibutz Ha-Meuhad, 1980), pp. 182-183 (Hebrew). On the historical questions related to Dan's allotment see Z. Kallai, *Historical Geography of the Bible: The Tribal Territories of Israel* (Jerusalem-Leiden: The Magnes Press, 1986), pp. 361-371.

territories in Judges 1, it is possible that the scroll envisions this tribe campaigning in Ephraim's territory. Gezer presents yet another difficulty. While Josh 10:33 and 12:12 report that Joshua defeated the king of Gezer, Josh 16:10 and Judg 1:29 state that the Ephraimites were unable to dispossess its Canaanite population.[495] Only much later, in the days of Solomon, Pharaoh is said to have captured Gezer and presented it as a gift to the king (1 Kgs 9:16) who fortified it together with Beth-Horon (1 Kgs 9:17; 2 Chr 8:5). One possible explanation for its inclusion here is that the scroll is interested here in the conquests alone (cf. the case of Ashkelon mentioned above). Alternatively, the inclusion of both Gezer and Beth-Horon under Judah's conquests may reflect contemporary Judea. The First Book of Maccabees reports the important role played by the city of Beth-Horon during the Maccabean revolt (3:16, 24, 7:39). It also tells of Simon's capture of the Hellenistic Gezer (Gazara) in 142 BCE (13:43-48, 53), which later became the headquarters of John Hyrcanus (13:53).[496] The mention of Haditha could be similarly explained. Indeed, the references to various non-biblical locations, including the Hellenistic city of Anthedon (frg. 15),[497] suggest that, like Josephus, the author of 4Q522 reads biblical geographical data with an eye on the contemporary map.[498] Among other factors at play, such a reading could have been prompted by an analogy between the Hasmonean struggle for the control over Eretz Israel and Joshua's conquest of the Promised Land (cf. 2 Macc 12:13-16 discussed in Chapter 1).[499]

The list of conquests in frg. 9 i spans territory from Beth-Zippor (Ornithopolis) in the north to the Wadi of Egypt in the south.[500] By introducing locations that are not mentioned in the biblical account, especially in the north of Canaan, the scroll aggrandizes Joshua's conquests. Foreshadowing David's expansion, the scroll may aim at the boundaries of the Promised Land as outlined in Num 34:1-2

---

495 The LXX of Josh 16:10 adds: "until Pharao, king of Egypt, went up and took it (Gezer), and he burned it with fire, and they massacred the Chananites and the Pherezites and those living in Gazer, and Pharao gave it as a dowry to his daughter" (NETS).

496 See further Kasher, *Jews*, pp. 108-110.

497 It is unclear whether Anthedon belongs with the list of the conquests or, more likely, with the unconquered territories.

498 See Z. Kallai, "Biblical Geography in Josephus", *Eretz Israel* 8 (1967), pp. 269-272 (Hebrew). Compare also the "modernization" of the biblical geographical terminology in 1QapGen XXII, 13-14.

499 On the various views on the Land in Second Temple sources see D. Mendels, *The Land of Israel as a Political Concept in Hasmonean Literature* (TSAJ 15; Tübingen: Mohr Siebeck, 1987); idem., *The Rise and Fall of Jewish Nationalism* (New York: Doubleday, 1992), pp. 81-105.

500 Gen 15:18 sets the southern border of the land promised to Abraham at נהר מצרים, i.e. Nile. This is also the understanding of 1QapGen XXI, 11, 15. T [N,Ps.J,Fr] to Num 34:5 identify נחל מצרים, mentioned in frg. 9 ii 17, with Nile (thus also Rashi and Radak to Josh 13:3).

(cf. Gen 15:18).[501] Be that as it may, the explicit mention of Judah and the amount of space allocated to his conquests indicate, that 4Q522 is particularly interested in this tribe's allotment.

In addition to the conquests, 4Q522 also records the locations which the Israelites failed to dispossess (frg. 8 and, perhaps, frgs. 2-3). Some of these are named in the Book of Joshua. Yet, frg. 8, where this list is found, relies on the roster of the Canaanite enclaves in Judges 1.[502] Judges 1 claims to describe the events that took place after Joshua's death (1:1). Perhaps, 4Q522 assumes that some of the data provided in Judges 1, especially those details that have parallels in the Book of Joshua, date prior to his death.[503]

As it reworks Judges 1, 4Q522 introduces several alterations in the order of the tribes:

Judges 1	4Q522 8
Judah and Simeon	Judah and Simeon
Benjamin	Dan
Manasseh	Issachar
Ephraim	Asher
Zebulon	
Asher	
Naphtali	
Dan	

The comparison between the two lists is hindered by the fragmentary state of lines 1-3. Still, it is clear that, unlike Judges 1, which places Dan last, 4Q522 mentions him next (or, at least, close) to Judah and Simeon.[504] Also, while Judges 1

---

501 For Eupolemus' aggrandizing David and Solomon's conquests see E.S. Gruen, *Heritage and Hellenism* (Berkeley: University of California Press, 1988), p. 141. Other contemporary works, particularly, Jubilees and Genesis Apocryphon, reflect an attempt to claim the rights for the Promised Land. See further P.S. Alexander, "Notes on the Imago Mundi in the Book of Jubilees", *JJS* 33 (1982), pp. 197-213; idem., "Jerusalem as the Omphalos of the World: On the History of a Geographical Concept", in L.I. Levine (ed.), *Jerusalem: Its Sanctity and Centrality to Judaism, Christianity, and Islam* (New York: Continuum, 1999), pp. 104-119; J.C. VanderKam, "Putting Them in Their Place: Geography as an Evaluative Tool", in J.C. Reeves & J. Kampen (eds.), *Pursuing the Text* (JSOTSS 184; Sheffield: JSOT Press, 1994), pp. 46-69.

502 As noted by Tov, "Rewritten Joshua", pp. 243-244.

503 Note that in Judg 2:6 Joshua is still reported to be alive.

504 This placement might have been suggested by the close proximity of Dan's tribal territory to that of Judah (Josh 19:40-48). In fact, some of the cities allocated to Dan (Josh 19:40-46) are also listed as belonging to Judah (e.g., Zorah and Eshtaol in 15:33). See further Kallai, *Historical*

does not mention the tribe of Issachar, the scroll states that he was not able to dispossess Beth-Shean (line 2).[505] According to Judg 1:27 it was Manasseh who left Beth-Shean unconquered. As Tov notes, the scroll relies here on Josh 17:11-12 reporting that Beth-Shean, Ibleam, Dor, En-Dor, Taanach, and Megiddo were taken from Issachar and Asher and given to Manasseh, who was not able to dispossess them (cf. J. Ant. 5.83). Perhaps by attributing Beth-Shean to Issachar the author of 4Q522 attempts to introduce the "missing" tribe into the list of the Canaanite enclaves (cf. the inclusion of Simeon in 4Q379 1-2).

Of all the cities listed in Josh 17:11-12 as given by Issachar to Manasseh (i.e., Beth Shean, Ibleam, En-Dor, Taanach, and Megiddo), the scroll names Beth-Shean alone. The scroll might be influenced here by Josh 12:21, reporting that Joshua defeated the kings of Taanach and Megiddo. Yet this would still leave unexplained the omission of Ibleam and En-Dor. Perhaps, the mention of Beth-Shean reflects its contemporary status as a Hellenistic city, Scythopolis. The Hasmoneans subdued it in 107 BCE, but it regained independence in 63 BCE.[506] If the inclusion of Gezer among Judah's conquests is taken as a reflection of Gazara's conquest in 142 BCE and the listing of Beth-Shean among the unconquered cities is interpreted as an indication of its independence prior to 107 or after 63 BCE, then we have two sets of dates for dating the composition preserved in 4Q522: between 142 BCE and 107 BCE or between 63 BCE and sometime around 50 BCE (the paleographic dating of 4Q522).[507]

In addition to shortening the list of the unconquered cities (Issachar), the scroll also seems to expand it. This appears to be the case with Asher in lines 3-4, where the lengths of the lacunae suggests a longer catalogue than that in Judg 1:31(MT). Perhaps, as in the case of Beth-Shean, re-attributed to Issachar,

---

Geography, pp. 361-371; Ahituv, *Joshua*, pp. 321-324. At the same time, the mention of Dan together with Issachar and Asher, situated in the north, may indicate that the author of the scroll was influenced by the story of Dan's migration to the north in Judg 18.

505 The tribal territories of Reuben and Gad are also missing from the list found in Judg 1. Their absence might be due to the fact that their tribal territories were situated in Transjordan.

506 See G. Fuks, "The Jews of Hellenistic and Roman Scythopolis", *JJS* 33 (1982), pp. 407-409; Z. Safrai, "The Gentile Cities of Judea: Between the Hasmonean Occupation and the Roman Liberation", in G. Galil & M. Weinfeld (eds.), *Studies in Historical Geography and Biblical Historiography* (SVT 81; Leiden: Brill, 2000), pp. 72-73.

507 It seems appropriate to mention here a caveat pointed out by Crown, observing that "it is always dangerous to strive to prove dating from city lists or border delineations, since these divisions may merely be ideal divisions which were never achieved ..." A. Crown, "The Date and Authority of the Samaritan Hebrew Book of Joshua as Seen in Its Territorial Allotments", *PEQ* 96 (1964), p. 79.

4Q522 includes here the city of Dor, given by Asher to Manasseh (Josh 17:11-12; Judg 1:27), as does also the LXX ad loc.

The sequence of frgs. 8 and 9 ii, and thus of these two lists, remains unclear. The discourse found in frg. 9 ii presupposes the fact that the Canaanite population of Jerusalem and its vicinities was not completely dispossessed by Joshua. Thus, thematically frg. 8 would fit rather nicely at the bottom of frg. 9 i (Tov).[508] However, the 1st pl. verb in frg. 9 i 18 may suggest that this section of the column is already concerned with the same topic on which frg. 9 ii focuses. Hence, the list of the unconquered territories could either precede or follow frg. 9.

4.5.2 Joshua's Address to Eleazar

Frg. 9 ii contains Joshua's address to the High Priest Eleazar. In this discourse he foretells the birth of David, the expulsion of the Amorites from Jerusalem, David's preparations for the construction of the Temple, and the actual building of the Temple by Solomon. Joshua seems to announce to Eleazar that his descendant will officiate in the newly built Temple. Finally, he confesses his sin in establishing a covenant with the Gibeonites.

While this discourse depicts Joshua as uttering a remarkable prophecy, its immediate purpose seems to be not so much to aggrandize Joshua, as to solve an exegetical difficulty: Why was the Tent of Meeting established in Shiloh (Josh 18:1), rather than in Jerusalem? This difficulty is absent from the Book of Joshua, as it assumes that God has not yet revealed "the place that He would choose" (Josh 9:27). Still, the author of 4Q522, who is familiar with the subsequent biblical history, wishes to clarify what may seem to a reader as an inconsistency. Hence, he makes Joshua aware of the divine plan and has him to explain why Jerusalem is not an appropriate place for the Tent now and how this will be rectified in the future.

The time and place of Joshua's speech are not spelled out, yet the scroll offers several hints. First, the discourse is framed by two references to Josh 18:1. Line 2 indicates that the Tent cannot be taken to Jerusalem, while line 13 depicts it being taken from Bethel (partially reconstructed) elsewhere, apparently, to Shiloh. Second, the preceding column contains the list of the Israelites' conquests in the Promised Land. This suits well Josh 18:1, where the people are reported

---

508 Tov, "Rewritten Joshua", p. 244, notes that the list of the cities allocated to Judah in Josh 15 concludes with the report of their failure to dispossess Jerusalem (15:63). He suggests that the scroll might have followed the biblical lead, describing first Judah's conquest of the cities (frg. 9 i 11-17) and then dealing with Jerusalem.

to have established the Tent of Meeting in Shiloh after the land was subdued.[509] Apparently, the scroll envisions the discourse to take place after the conquests on the way from Gilgal, where the camp and the Tent were located during the military campaigns (Josh 4:19, 5:10, 9:6, 10:6, 7, 9, 15, 43, 14:6).[510] Bethel, situated at the crossroads leading to Jerusalem and Shiloh (Qimron), lends itself easily as a geographical location at which the future site of the Tent could have been determined.[511] Besides the geographical considerations, Bethel is a fitting place for Joshua's prophecy regarding Jerusalem and its Temple. Here Jacob received his vision (Gen 28:11-19), interpreted by the later sources as pertaining to the priesthood and the eschatological Temple.[512]

While for Josephus the reason for the choice of Shiloh is aesthetic, "its beauty" (J. Ant. 5.68), for 4Q522 Shiloh is chosen because of its being "far" from the Canaanites (9 ii 12).[513] In fact, this concern with the non-Jewish presence in Jerusalem and its vicinities, defying the explicit commandments of the Torah, underlies both Joshua's prophecy and confession.

Having said that at the present time the Tent cannot be taken to Zion (line 2), Joshua foretells that David will capture Zion and "drive out from there <all> the Amorites". To be sure, Torah commands annihilating the Canaanite nations (e.g., Deut 20:17) and condemns their practices as defiling the land (Lev 18:24-30; Deut 20:16-18) and the Temple (2 Chr 36:14).[514] Yet biblical sources (2 Sam 5; 1 Chr 11) do not mention David's driving out the Jebusites from the subdued Jerusalem. On the contrary, later on David is said to purchase the land that would become the site of the future Temple from a Jebusite (2 Sam 24:18–24; cf. Solomon's enslaving of the remaining Jebusites in 1 Kgs 9:20-21). The attribution of this act to David and the emphasis on its completeness, "<all> the Amorites", present him as a model of scrupulously fulfilling the divine commandment regarding the Canaanite

509 In a similar fashion, Josephus, J. Ant 5.68, dates the transfer of the camp (together with the Tent) after Joshua's victorious northern campaign (Josh 11).
510 Dimant, "Apocryphon of Joshua", pp. 199-200, comments that by tracing the Tent's journey from Gilgal to Shiloh via Bethel the scroll fills a gap in the information provided in the Book of Joshua regarding the Tent's whereabouts.
511 See Comment ad loc. Note also the wording of Judg 1:22, which might be understood as taking the Ark (with or without the Tent) to Bethel. In fact, Tov, "Rewritten Joshua", pp. 246-247, notes that the LXX of Judg 2:1, 5 suggests that the Ark of the Covenant was situated at Bethel. However, Dimant, "Apocryphon of Joshua", p. 197 note 35, aptly observes that one should distinguish between the whereabouts of the Tent of Meeting and of the Ark of the Covenant.
512 See Jub 32; ALD 5:2-5; 11QTª XXIX, 8-10 (cf. Abram's visions in Bethel in 1QapGen XIX, 8; XXI, 7-8). See further Eshel, "Jubilees 32", pp. 21-36.
513 Shiloh is situated some 40 km north of Jerusalem.
514 On the moral impurity attributed to the idols and idolatry see Hayes, *Gentile Impurities*, pp. 40-43. Compare also Josh 22:19.

population. It also reflects 4Q522's reading of the events through the lens of the Deuteronomic legislation, an interpretation shared (although without presuming a total expulsion) by Josephus (J. War 6.439; J. Ant. 7.65, 67).

The phrase "(will) drive out from there <all> the Amorites" also contrasts David with Joshua.[515] The biblical account reports that Joshua defeated the king of Jerusalem, yet Judah failed to dispossess it (Josh 10:23, 12:10, 15:63). A similar description of Judah's victory and the Benjaminites' failure is found in Judg 1:8, 21.[516] The wording "<all> the Amorites" may indicate a recognition that Joshua expelled some of the Jebusites, while David completed the task (2 Sam 5:6-9; 1 Chr 11:4-7). If correct, this betrays a harmonization of the conflicting biblical data on the fate of Jerusalem in the days of the conquest.

Another indication of such a harmonistic reading might be found in the scroll's reference to David's future capture of סלע ציון, "the rock of Zion" (9 ii 4; cf. the use of Zion, rather than Jerusalem, in line 2).[517] In attempt to reconcile the biblical data, Josephus in his rewritten version of Judg 1:8 suggests that Jerusalem comprises of a lower city and an upper city.[518] During Judah's attack on the city only the lower city was captured, while David was able to seize both cities (J. Ant 5.124, 7.62-63). Such an interpretation could have been prompted by the fact that 2 Sam 5:6-9(=1 Chr 11:4-7) mentions both Jerusalem (or Jebus) and the "stronghold of Zion (מצדת ציון)". Perhaps, 4Q522's choice of the phrase סלע ציון, "rock of Zion", in its description of David's future campaign against Jerusalem suggests a similar exegesis.

The scroll's view of the Canaanite presence is made clear also in the second part of Joshua's speech. As if the presence of the Amorites(=Jebusites) in Jerusalem was not sufficient for justifying the decision to take the Tent to Shiloh, 4Q522 also links this decision to the presence of the Gibeonites. Since the Gibeonites dwelt at some distance from the city of Jerusalem, 4Q522 appears to preclude the Canaanite presence not only in Jerusalem itself, but also in its vicinities.[519] Moreover, given the Gibeonites' status as "slave [of slaves for Is]rae[l" (9 ii 11),

---

515 Dimant, "Apocryphon of Joshua", p. 188.
516 I. Kalimi, "The Capture of Jerusalem in the Chronistic History", *VT* 52 (2002), pp. 66-68, remarks that in Jud 19:11-12 Jebus is depicted as a city populated by non-Israelites.
517 Tov, "Rewritten Joshua", p. 238, suggests that the phrase סלע ציון points to David's acquisition of Araunah/Ornan's threshing floor (2 Sam 24:18-24; 1 Chr 21:18-22:1). Yet the scroll seems to be concerned here with the conquest of the city, and not with the purchase of the land for the construction of the Temple.
518 C.T. Begg, "David's Capture of Jebus and its Sequels according to Josephus", *ETL* 74 (1998), pp. 96-97.
519 Gibeon is situated 13 km northwest of Jerusalem. Of the other Gibeonites' cities, Chephirah is found 8 km west of Gibeon, Kiriat-jearim—13 km northwest of Jerusalem, while the location

which is in accord with the stipulations of Deut 29:9-10, the scroll seems to object even to the presence of those Canaanites who threw in their fate with Israel.[520] Perhaps, this is why 4Q522 emphasizes the Canaanite pedigree of the Gibeonites, referring to them as "the Canaan[ite" (line 9), a designation that is never applied to them in the Hebrew Bible.[521] Paraphrasing Joshua's verdict from Josh 9:23, 27, it also proclaims them as "slave of s[laves", an allusion to the curse of Canaan from Gen 9:25. Thus, the scroll leaves no doubt that the Canaanite Gibeonites had to be dispossessed and their presence in the vicinities of Jerusalem is just as detrimental to the setting of the Tent in Jerusalem as that of the Jebusites in the city itself.

One could suggest that such a negative view of the Gibeonites reflects a belief that they continued practicing idolatry even after the covenant with Israel.[522] Yet it is also possible that it is based on a halakhic view ruling out the presence of any Gentile, even a proselyte, in or even in a close proximity to the Tent/Temple and the Temple City. One may recall Ezekiel's condemnation of the admission of aliens (בני נכר) to the sanctuary (Ezek 44:6-9) and the foreigner's lament "The Lord will keep me apart from his people" from Isa 56:3.[523] More to the point, the Temple Scroll seems to forbid the proselytes from entering the middle court of the Temple until the fourth generation (11QTª XXXIX, 5-7, XL, 6).[524] Moreover, 4QFlo-

---

of Beeroth is disputed. Compare Josephus's observation: "Now the Gabaonites, who lived quite close to Jerusalem ..." (J. Ant. 5.49; Thackeray & Marcus, *Josephus*, pp. 23-24).

520 For a recent discussion of Josh 9 and Deut 29:9-10 see S. Hultgren, *From the Damascus Covenant to the Covenant of the Community* (STDJ 66; Leiden: Brill, 2007), pp. 163-182 (and the bibliography cited there). The Rabbinic sources identify Gibeonites with the Nethinim of Ezra and Nehemiah (e.g., b. Yeb. 78b-79a), but this identification is disputed. See M. Haran, "The Gibeonites, the Nethinim and the Sons of Solomon's Servants", *VT* 11 (1961), pp. 159-69; B.A. Levine, "The Netinim", *JBL* 82 (1963), pp. 207-212; idem, "Later Sources on the Nethinîm", in H.A Hoffner (ed.), *Orient and Occident* (Neukirchen-Vluyn: Neukirchener Verlag, 1973), pp. 101-107; Hultgren, ibid. On the presumed epigraphic evidence for the presence of the Nethinim in late Second Temple times see É. Puech, "The Tell el-Fûl Jar Inscription and the 'Nĕtînîm'", *BASOR* 261 (1986), pp. 69-72. Also, note 4Q340 (4QList of Netinim), which its editors interpret (in light of the Rabbinic restrictions on the marriage imposed on the Nethinim) as "a list of blemished people unfit for marriage". See M. Broshi & A. Yardeni, "On Netinim and False Prophets", in Z. Zevit (ed.), *Solving Riddles and Untying Knots* (Winona Lake, Indiana: Eisenbrauns, 1995), pp. 32-33; idem, in M. Broshi et al. (eds.), *Qumran Cave 4. XIV: Parabiblical Texts, Part 2* (DJD 19; Oxford: Clarendon Press, 1995), p. 83.

521 Josephus in J. Ant. 5.56 also says that the Gibeonites "were of the stock of the Canaanites". In j. Qiddushin 4.65b.1 David declares Gibeonites to be non-Israelites.

522 This appears to be Dimant's opinion in "Apocryphon of Joshua", p. 201.

523 Haran, "Gibeonites", p. 159, notes that the Gibeonites as Hivites were apparently non-circumcised (cf. Gen 34:2), while Ezekiel refers to the aliens uncircumcised of heart and flesh.

524 Compare the apparent prohibition on the Gentile sacrifices in 4QMMT (B 8-9; cf. J. War 2.409). See E. Qimron & J. Strugnell, *Qumran Cave 4. V: Miqṣat Ma'ase Ha-Torah* (DJD 10; Oxford:

rilegium bans a "foreigner" (בן נכר, apparently, a non-Israelite Temple servant) and a "proselyte" from entering the sanctuary "forever" (4Q174 1-2 3-4).[525]

Whether the author of 4Q522 espouses similar views or not, his negative stance towards Gibeonites helps elucidate his take on Joshua's treaty with them. This covenant is also criticized in the Hebrew Bible, as is indicated by the phrase "the men took [their word] because of their provisions, and did not inquire of the Lord" (Josh 9:14).[526] Yet, 4Q522 denounces it in much stronger terms: Joshua confesses that the Gibeonites "made him sin" (line 10). As Dimant notes, two divine regulations were breached in this case. First, the Torah prohibits establishing a covenant with Canaanite nations (Exod 23:32; 34:12). In fact, the use of the verb החטיוני points to the Torah's warning on this matter from Exod 23:33.[527] Second,

---

Clarendon Press, 1994), pp. 149-150; I. Knohl, "The Acceptance of Sacrifices from Gentiles", *Tarbiẓ* 48 (1979), pp. 341-347 (Hebrew); Y. Gilat, "A Comment to 'The Acceptance of Sacrifices from Gentiles'", *Tarbiẓ* 49 (1980), pp. 422-423 (Hebrew). On the prohibition of the Gentiles' entrance to the Herodian Temple, see E. Bickerman, "The Warning Inscriptions of Herod's Temple", *JQR* 37 (1946-47), pp. 387-45.

525 Note also the Rabbinic regulation prohibiting גר תושב from dwelling permanently in Jerusalem (t. Negaim 6:2 [ed. Zukermandel p. 625]), as noted by G. Blidstein, "4Q Florilegium and Rabbinic Sources on Bastard and Proselyte", *RevQ* 8 (1974), p. 433. For the discussion of these sources see J.M. Baumgarten, "The Exclusion of Nethinim and Proselytes in 4QFlorilegium", in idem, *Studies in Qumran Law* (Leiden: Brill, 1977), pp. 75-87; idem, "Exclusions from the Temple: Proselytes and Agrippa I", *JJS* 33 (1982), pp. 215-225; K. Berthelot, "La notion de גר dans les textes de Qumrân", *RevQ* 19 (1999), pp. 195-198; L.H. Schiffman, "Exclusion from the Sanctuary and the City of the Sanctuary in the Temple Scroll", in idem, *The Courtyards of the House of the Lord* (STDJ 75; Leiden: Brill, 2008), pp. 384-386; idem, "Non-Jews in the Dead Sea Scrolls", in idem, *Qumran and Jerusalem* (Grand Rapids, Michigan, Cambridge, UK, Eerdmans, 2010), p. 372; Y. Moynihan Gillihan, "The גר Who Wasn't There: Fictional Aliens in the Damascus Rule", *RevQ* 25 (2011), pp. 282-295. On the negative attitude towards proselytes as originating in priestly circles, see D.R. Schwartz, "On Two Aspects of a Priestly View of Descent at Qumran", in L.H. Schiffman (ed.), *Archaeology and History in the Dead Sea Scrolls* (JSOT/ASOR Monographs 2; Sheffield: JSOT Press, 1990), pp. 157-179. For the discussion of the notion of Gentile impurity in Second Temple sources see J. Klawans, "Notions of Gentile Impurity in Ancient Judaism", *AJSReview* 20 (1995), pp. 285-312; Hayes, *Gentile Impurities*, pp. 45-67; H. Harrington, "Keeping Outsiders Out: Impurity at Qumran", in F. García Martínez & M. Popović (eds.), *Defining Identities: We, You, and the Other in the Dead Sea Scrolls* (STDJ 70; Leiden: Brill, 2008), pp. 187-203; V. Noam, *From Qumran to the Rabbinic Revolution: Conceptions of Impurity* (Jerusalem: Yad Ben Zvi Press, 2010), pp. 294-296 (Hebrew).

526 On Joshua's role in this episode see S. Lebhar Hall, *Conquering Character: The Characterization of Joshua in Joshua 1-11* (New York, London: T&T Clark, 2010), pp. 156-160.

527 The formulations "made me sin" and "they have misled me" (lines 10-11) suggest an unintentional sin. See further G.A. Anderson, "Intentional and Unintentional Sin in the Dead Sea Scrolls", in D.P. Wright et al. (eds.), *Pomegranates and Golden Bells* (Winona Lake, Ind.: Eisenbrauns, 1995), pp. 49-64.

as the scroll makes clear, Joshua failed to consult God by means of Urim and Thummim as required in Num 27:21.

Undoubtedly, 4Q522's interpretation of the events was prompted by the critical remark from Josh 9:14. Also, Num 27:21 offers itself for such an interpretation, for the phrase "by such instruction they shall go out and by such instruction they shall come in" is used in the Hebrew Bible with reference to military activities (Josh 14:11; 1 Sam 18:13, 16). In fact, the Temple Scroll applies Num 27:21 to those situations where a king considered declaring a voluntary war (11QTª LVIII, 18-21).[528] The question of whether to sign a treaty with the Gibeonites or to declare a war against them falls within the range of issues where the regulation from Num 27:21 applies. Apparently, since in Num 27 this directive is given to Joshua, in 4Q522 he assumes the full responsibility for failing to do so, while in the biblical story "the chieftains of the community" are also involved (Josh 9:55).[529] Thus, while David is depicted as fulfilling the divine Law regarding the Canaanites, Joshua, even if unwillingly, fails to do so. Once again, the scroll reads the biblical story in light of the Torah stipulations.[530]

This passage poses a question: May this expansion of the biblical story mirror contemporary historical circumstances? Berthelot suggests, following Puech, that the emphatic description of Joshua's failure as a military leader to inquire of the High Priest may reflect a critical stance towards the Hasmoneans who occupied both offices.[531] She points particularly to John Hyrcanus I, who, according to Josephus' report, was endowed with a gift of prophecy (see Chapter 3). By depicting Joshua as a prophet and yet criticizing him for ignoring God's commandment, 4Q4522 might have wished to demonstrate that prophetic gift does not exempt one from obeying God's arrangements.[532] Indeed, Joshua, the military commander who also acted as a ruler of Israel, could be associated with the Hasmonean rulers.[533] If Berthelot's proposal is correct, one may further speculate that 4Q522's critique

---

528 See further L. Goldman, "The Rules Regarding Fighting a Permitted War in 4Q376", *Meghillot* 8-9 (2010), pp. 319-342 (Hebrew).

529 Compare Josephus' version of the events in J. Ant. 5.55-56, where Eleazar and the council of elders swear to Gibeonites, whereas the entire people ratify the oaths.

530 Dimant, "Apocryphon of Joshua", p. 202.

531 Puech, "4Q522", p. 71.

532 Berthelot, "Joshua", p. 102.

533 Dimant, "Apocryphon of Joshua", pp. 203-204; idem, "Between Sectarian", pp. 120-121, suggests that since 11QTª LVIII, 18-21 applies the injunction from Num 27:21 to a king (in a case of a voluntary war), it may be that the author of 4Q522 perceived Joshua's role as analogous to that of a king. While this suggestion must remain hypothetical, one may observe that Philo compares Joshua's position to that of a king (On the Virtues 54, 66). LAB 20:5 refers to Joshua as a "ruler in Israel". The Samaritan sources frequently refer to Joshua as a king. On the royal

could have also been particularly directed against the Hasmonean policy of judaizing the non-Jewish population of the land of Israel.[534] The author of the scroll might have taken the conversion of the Idumaeans and the Ituraeans in the days of John Hyrcanus and Arystobulus (J. Ant. 13.257, 258, 318) as a violation of God's law, similar to that of the preservation of the Gibeonites.[535]

4.5.3 The Place of Psalm 122 in 4Q522

Attributed to David and featuring Jerusalem as a seat of the House of YHWH (vv. 1, 9), Psalm 122, also preserved in 11Q5 III, 7-14,[536] can be thematically linked to the frg. 9 ii, foreseeing David's birth, his conquest of Jerusalem, and the preparations for the construction of the Temple (Puech). Still, it remains unclear as to how this Davidic psalm fits into the reality described in 4Q522 9 ii, where David is yet to be born, Jerusalem is in the Canaanite hands, and the Tent of Meeting is set in Shiloh.[537]

The text of the psalm is close to the MT, with two notable exceptions. Whereas the MT reads in lines 7 and 9 שלוה and טוב (אבקשה טוב לך; cf. Ezek 7:25; Ps 34:15), the scroll has in both instances שלום. With the three occurrences of שלום in the MT, the scroll's text of Psalm 122 seems to have used this noun five times. It is unknown whether the emphasis on "peace" to Jerusalem reflects any contemporary events.

The amplification of the biblical stories with prayers and praises is a part and parcel of the Rewritten Bible literature. Still, an inclusion of an entire psalm in a Rewritten Bible composition is rather unusual.[538]

---

features of the biblical Joshua, see Chapman, "Joshua son of Nun", pp. 18-20 (and the pertinent bibliography there).

534 L.H. Schiffman, "Political Leadership and Organization in the Dead Sea Scrolls Community", in idem, *Qumran and Jerusalem* (Grand Rapids, Michigan, Cambridge, UK, Eerdmans, 2010), p. 100, finds a polemic against Hasmoneans' occupying the offices of the High Priest and ruler/king in the "Law of the King" in the Temple Scroll.

535 See S. Cohen, *The Beginning of Jewishness: Boundaries, Varieties, Uncertainties* (Berkeley: University of California Press, 1999), pp. 110-119. On the surprisingly little evidence regarding controversies on the Hasmonean judaizing policy, see S. Schwartz, *Imperialism and Jewish Society, 200 BCE to 640 CE* (Princeton: Princeton University Press, 2001), p. 42.

536 Tov, "Rewritten Joshua", pp. 249-250, cautiously notes that although frgs. 22-25 display a similar script and a tendency to inscribe the letters in disregard of the ruled lines as the rest of 4Q522, they may still derive from another composition.

537 A similar caveat is raised by Puech, "4Q522", p. 71.

538 García Martínez, "Book of Joshua", pp. 107-108, notes two additional examples: the inclusion of Ps 91 in 11Q11 VI, 3-14 and the poem attested in Sir 51:13-30 and 11Q5 XXI, 11-XXII, 1. However, these are not Rewritten Bible works.

4.5.4 The Provenance of 4Q522

As with 4Q379, several features of 4Q522 may suggest a Levitical/priestly milieu. First, the very attempt to explain the setting of the Tent of Meeting in Shiloh, instead of Jerusalem, may betray Levitical/priestly concerns.[539] Second, the motivation for taking the Tent to Shiloh, i.e. the avoidance of the Canaanite presence, reflects a concern for the Tent/Temple purity, which would be at home not only, but, particularly, in the Levitical/priestly circles. Third, the possible mention of Zadok as the first High Priest to officiate in the Solomonic Temple and the application of Deut 33:12 to him and his descendants, standing in sharp contrast to the reality of the Hasmonean times, may locate the putative author either within the Zadokite priesthood or among its supporters. The priestly background of the author would also tally well with an emphatic description of Joshua as subordinate to the High Priest possessing the Urim and Thummim. While these features of 4Q522 remind one of the views espoused by the Qumran community,[540] they could have been shared by wider Levitical/priestly circles (cf. Sir 51:29). Thus while Puech considers a possibility of 4Q522 being an Essene work,[541] Tov suggests a Qumran copyist,[542] and Dimant places it within the intermediate category of scrolls, between sectarian and non-sectarian,[543] Still, Eshel rightly highlights the absence of the sectarian terminology in 4Q522.[544]

4.6 Conclusions

The extant fragments of 4Q522 refer to several episodes from the Book of Joshua, paraphrase the first chapter of the Book of Judges, and cite Psalm 122. In its present form, this scroll shows a significant interest in the extent of the Israelites' conquests in the Promised Land. Utilizing both biblical and non-biblical data, it provides a list of locations subdued by Israel. This list expands on the biblical record of Joshua's campaign in northern Canaan by including several non-biblical

---

539 As is observed by Tov, "Rewritten Joshua", p. 246.
540 Dimant, "Apocryphon of Joshua", pp. 203-204; idem, "Between Sectarian", pp. 120-121, proposes that 4Q522's depiction of Joshua's subordination to Eleazar implies an ascendancy of the priesthood over the kingship, a notion espoused by the Qumran sectarians. Of course, here it is based on Num 27:21, where Joshua is required to consult the High Priest.
541 Puech, "La pierre", p. 691.
542 Tov, "Rewritten Joshua", p. 255; idem, *Scribal Practices*, p. 343, finds in 4Q522 several features of Qumran scribal practices, indicating that it might have been copied at Qumran.
543 Dimant, "Between Sectarian", pp. 118-121
544 Eshel, "Note", pp. 92-93.

locations that place the northern limits of the Israelites' conquests beyond those of David's kingdom, closer to the northern boundaries of the Promised Land as outlined in Num 34. The scroll also names locations that the Israelites failed to conquer. Particular attention is given to the case of Zion/Jerusalem. Reading the scriptural report on the establishment of the Tent of Meeting in Shiloh in light of later biblical history, 4Q522 claims that Joshua and Eleazar were unable to set the Tent in Zion because of the presence of a non-Jewish population, including the Gibeonites, in Jerusalem and its vicinities. The scroll's negative stance toward the Gentile presence in the Promised Land is further made clear by its presentation of Joshua's treaty with the Gibeonites as a sin. The concern with the boundaries of the Promised Land and the purity of Jerusalem as the seat of the Tent/Temple may suggest a Levitical/priestly milieu. The inclusion/exclusion of certain geographical locations, along with a possible implied critique of the Hasmonean judaizing policy, may place this composition sometime during the rule of John Hyrcanus I.

5 The Scroll 4Q123

5.1 The Manuscript

The scroll 4Q123 is extant in four fragments written in a paleo-Hebrew script.[545] McLean dates its handwriting to the last half of the second century BCE, prior to 100 BCE.[546]

5.2 The Contents of 4Q123

The extant fragments of 4Q123 are concerned with Josh 21. Frgs. 1 and 2 allude to vv. 2, 5 (frg. 2) and vv. 9, 11 (frg. 1). Since it is likely that the scroll follows the order of the verses as found in the MT and other textual witnesses, frg. 2 should be placed before frg. 1.

5.3 Editions of 4Q123

Assigned initially to Skehan for publication, this scroll was finally published by Ulrich and Sanderson under the title 4QpaleoParaJoshua.[547]

5.4 Text and Commentary

Frg. 1[548]

מִגְרשֵׁיֹן [	1
ערי]הֺֻם·ומגר]שיהם	2
ויתנו·ממטה·בני·יהו]דֻה·וממֹ]טה·בני·שמעון	3
מגרשין] [°°] [	4
ויתנו·להם·קר]יֹתֹ·]]ארבע·א]בי·העֻנוק·היא·חברון	5
יֹהֹ[ ]°[	6

---

545 Skehan et al., "4Q123", pp. 201-203.
546 M.D. McLean, "The Use and Development of Palaeo-Hebrew in the Hellenistic and Roman Periods", Ph.D. diss., Harvard University, 1982, p. 65. He designates 4Q123 as 4QpaleoSn44ᵃ (pp. 44, 63-66 and plate 3). Tov, "Rewritten Joshua", p. 252, dates it to the last half of the first century BCE.
547 Skehan et al., "4Q123", pp. 201-203.
548 The paleo-Hebrew script does not distinguish between medial and final forms of the letters. The final forms are used here to facilitate reading.

Notes on Readings

Since the paleo-Hebrew Qumran scrolls frequently split words at the end of the lines, it is not impossible that the blank space at the end of line 2 (next to the *resh* of ומגר) does not result from a damage to the leather, but represents the left intercolumnar margin (cf. blank spaces at the end of lines 1 and 4; on the use of word-dividers see Notes on Readings to frg. 2). In this case the text would be transcribed as following:

מֹגֹרשִֹׁי [	1 [
ערי]הֹםֹ·ומגר	2 [הם
ויתנו·ממטה·בני·יהו]דֹה·ומֹמֹ	3 [שיהם
מגרשי[ ]°°[	4 [טה·בני·שמעון
ויתנו·להם·קר]יתֹ[·]ארבע·א	5 [הם
]°[הֹן]יֹ[	6 [בי··העננוק·היא·חברון

1 מֹגֹרשִֹׁי[. The editors read]°°°°מ[. Yet, they observe that this line might have read]°מֹגֹרשֹׁ[. Indeed, the surviving traces of the letters are consistent with this reading. The trace of the last letter may belong to a *yod*. Such a reading seems to be supported by the context. There appears to be a blank space before the *mem*.

2 ומגר|שיהם. The *DJD* edition has]ומגרשֹׁ. Yet on the photographs (PAM 41.387; 43.033; IAA 225.836) no traces of a *shin* are visible.

3 ומֹמֹ|טה. The editors read]ומֹנ. The upper horizontal stroke of the third letter has been only partially preserved and may be read either as a *nun* or as a *mem*. The reading ומֹמֹ]טה is preferable on contextual grounds (see Comment).

4 The editors suggest that the traces of the second letter may belong to a *samech* or a supralinear *yod*.

ו.|מגרשי. It is not entirely clear whether the short blank space next to the *yod* is an interval between two adjacent words or between two adjacent letters (cf. the space next to the *resh* in ומגר]שיהן [line 2]).

Translation

1.   ] pasture lands of[
2.   ] their [cities] and [their] pasture]lands
3.   and they assigned from the tribe of the sons of Ju]dah and from the tri[be of the sons of Simeon
4.   ] [ ] pasture lands of[
5.   and they assigned to them Kir]iath[-]Arba the fa[ther of the Anak, that is Hebron
6.

Comments

1 מִגְרָשׁן. The allusions to Josh 21:9 and 11 in lines 3 and 5, as well as the recurring use of the noun מגרש, standing for a city's outskirts and pasture lands, indicate that this fragment is concerned with the allocation of cities to priests and Levites.[549] Here, as well as in the next line, the scroll seems to use a variation on the phrase 'city(ies) and (its/their) pasture lands', which occurs in several forms in Josh 21 (cf. את הערים האלה ואת מגרשיהן [21:3, 8]), as well as in other biblical passages concerned with Levitical cities (Lev 25:34; Num 35:2-7; Josh 14:4; 1 Chr 6:39-66). Hence such reconstructions as ואת ·[מִגְרָשִׁי]הן (with frg. 2 2), ואת ·[מִגְרָשִׁי]הם, ואת ·[מִגְרָשִׁי]ה (with frg. 4 1) or מִגְרָשִׁן· הערים (with Num 35:4, 5) are appropriate.

2 ערי·[הֹם·ומגר]שיהם. Perhaps, this line alludes to Josh 21:8: ויתנו בני ישראל ללוים את הערים האלה ואת מגרשיהן. If correct, the 3rd masc. pl. possessive suffix in ערי·[הֹם re-fers to the tribes allocating the cities. The scroll might have read ערי·[הֹם· ומגר]שיהן (with a 3rd fem. pl. possessive suffix pointing to cities, as is the case in Josh 21:3, 8) or (with frg. 2 2) ערי·[הֹם·ומגר]שיהם (with a 3rd masc. pl. possessive suffix pointing to the Israelites or the Levites). See Comment to frg. 2 2.

3 ויתנו·ממטה·בני·יהו]דה·ומֹ[טה·בני·שמעון. Given the mention of Kiriath-Arba in line 5, the scroll may allude here to Josh 21:9.

4 מגרשי]. This line seems to paraphrase Josh 21:10. As noted above (see Notes on Readings), it remains unclear whether another letter appeared next to the *yod*. Hence, one may restore here מגרשי]ה/הן/הם or ו]·הערים·[מגרשין (with Num 35:4, 5).

5 ויתנו·להם·קרן·ית]·[ארבע·א]בי·הענוק·היא·חברון. This phrase is borrowed from Josh 21:11.

Frg. 2

] 1	כאשר·צוה·י]הוה·ביד·מֹשה·עבד
יהוה] 2	את·העריֹ[ם·ואֹת·מגרשיהֹם·
] 3	ממשפחת·מטה·א]פֹרים·ומֹמֹטה· *vac*
דן] 4	[·הֹ·]

Notes on Readings

The blank spaces at the ends of lines 1-3 may belong with the left intercolumnar margin. The editors note this possibility, yet discard it for two reasons. First, a

---

549 HALOT, p. 546.

word-divider appears after the words מגרשיהֹם (line 2) and וֹמֹמֹטֹה (line 3). Second, lines 1-2 reach beyond the *vacat* in line 3. Both arguments can be contested. First, while most of the paleo-Hebrew Qumran scrolls have no word-dividers at the end of the lines, 2QpaleoLev does.[550] If correct, this scribe is not consistent in his use of the word-dividers, omitting one in the end of line 1, while using them in the end of lines 2-3. Second, given the fragment's state of preservation, it is uncertain whether lines 1-2 actually continued beyond the *vacat* in line 3.

1 יהוה[י. The *DJD* edition reads הֹ∘[. The editors observe that the first letter may be read as a *he* or as a medial *ṣade*. The traces of three horizontal strokes visible on the photographs (PAM 41.387; 43.033) are consistent with a *he* (cf. the shape of *he* in line 3), yet not with a medial *ṣade*.
] עבֹד. The editors read]עבֹד. According to the photographs (PAM 41.387; 43.033) there is a blank space next to the *dalet*. As the editors note, there are no traces of a word-divider after עבֹד.

3 אֹ]פֹרִים. The *DJD* edition reads גֹֹרֹ∘[. It is proposed with some hesitancy to read the hook-shaped remains of the second letter as a *resh*, although the top of *resh* usually has a triangular loop form. Compare the shape of *resh* in אר[(frg. 3 2) As to the first letter, the upper horizontal stroke descending to the left may well belong to a *pe*.
וֹמֹמֹטֹה. The editors read הֹ∘∘טֹה. Still, they note that the word in question may be read as ומטה. In fact, according to PAM 41.387 the first letter may well be a *waw*. Its upper horizontal and vertical strokes have been preserved. The curving upper horizontal stroke of the next letter is consistent with a *mem*. As to the third letter, the shape of its upper horizontal stroke is similar to that of a *mem* in the preceding word.

Translation
1. [as Y]HWH[has commanded] through Moses the servant of
2. [YHWH   the citie]s and their pasture lands
3. [from the clans of the tribe of E]phraim and from the tribe of
4. [Dan   ]   [   ]

Comments
1 יהוה / עבֹד. כאשר·צוה·י]הוה·ביד·משה·עבד. Since line 3 seems to allude to Josh 21:5, it is likely that this line paraphrases the Levitical chieftains' request in 21:2, yet uses the wording of 21:8, describing the carrying out of their demand. Neither v. 2 or

---

550 Tov, *Scribal Practices*, pp. 132-133.

v. 8 refers to Moses as עבד ה',[551] a Deuteronomic phrase (Deut 34:5) frequently applied by the Book of Joshua to Moses (see Josh 1:1, 13, 15, 8:31, 33, 11:12, 13:8, 14:7, 18:7, 22:2, 4, 5; cf. also 4Q378 22 i 2).[552] Notably, it is repeatedly used in Joshua with the verb צוה: אשר/כאשר צוה משה עבד ה' (1:7, 13, 8:31, 33, 9:24, 11:12, 15, 22:2, 5).

2]את הערי[ם°ו̊°את·מגרשיה̊ם̊. This line may paraphrase Josh 21:3. Since עיר is a feminine noun, it is somewhat unclear whether the 3rd masc. pl. suffix in מגרשיהם̊ points to the cities, to the tribes allocating them, or to the Levites (cf. frg. 1 2). For a similar ambiguity compare the phrases הערים להם לשבת ומגרשיהם (Num 35:3 [thus also 4QNum^b XXX, 24; Smr has ומגרשיהן]) and ערים לשבת ומגרשיהם (Josh 14:4). While one could restore here with fr. 1 2: את עריה[ם̊, it is proposed to reconstruct the line with a related passage that reflects the same ambiguity, 1 Chr 6:49: את הערים ואת מגרשיהם.

As the editors observe, the trace of ink before ו̊את seems to be a slip of the pen.

3]דן / ממשפחת·מטה·א[פ̊ר̊ים̊·ו̊מ̊מ̊ט̊ה̊. The scroll alludes here to Josh 21:5. Either line 2 or this line could have mentioned the number of the cities allocated by Judah and Benjamin (Josh 21:4).

Frg. 3

ו]א̊ת·מ̊]גרשיה   1

[ערים·אר]בע   2

b]ottom mar[gin

Notes on Readings
1 ו]א̊ת. The *DJD* edition has ת°[. However, the editors note that "the leather favours aleph", though *shin* and *ṣade* are also possible. According to the photographs (PAM 42.718; 43.033) the shape of the letter is consistent with an *alef* (cf. *alef* in line 2).

Translation
1. and its] p[asture lands
2.]cities fo[ur

---

551 The editors propose to restore the noun עבד as עבד[ו. However, as was noted above (Notes on Readings), there is a blank space next to the *dalet*.
552 Aḥituv, *Joshua*, p. 10.

Comments

1 וֹ[את·מֹ|גרשיה. The wording of line 2 suggests that this fragment also deals with Josh 21. The second word may be a toponym preceded by a *nota accusativi*, as is frequently the case in Josh 21. Yet, it is more likely that this is a noun מגרש with a possessive suffix. In Josh 21 the lists of the cities allocated by various tribes to the Levites conclude with the total number of the given cities. This seems to be the case with line 2. Therefore, it is probable that this line contained the names of the cities. Hence, it is proposed to restore the line with another phrase that recurs in Josh 21, את ... ואת מגרשֶׁהָ. For the orthography מגרשיה (with a *yod* after a *shin*) compare frg. 4, line 1, וֹמגר[שיה.[553] The name of the city has not survived.

2 ערים·אר|בע. As the editors note, the surviving text may be restored as]ערים·אר|בע (thus Josh 21:18, 22, 24, 29, 31, 35, 37, 39) or as]ערים·אר|בעים ושמנה (as in Num 35:7 and Josh 21:41).

Frg. 4

ואת·מגר[שיה·אתֹ]	1
]וֹ [ ] ֯ [ ]עֹ[	2

Translation

1. and]its[pasture la]nds [
2.] [ ] [ ] [

Comments

1 ואת·מגר|שיה·אתֹ. The noun מגר[שיה identifies this fragment as another piece of the scroll's paraphrase of Josh 21. On the spelling מגרשיה see Comments to frg. 3 2.

5.5 Discussion

The foregoing analysis demonstrates that 4Q123 does not follow Josh 21 word for word, but reworks it employing techniques common to the Rewritten Bible compositions.

---

553 In light of the consistent spelling מגרשה (without a *yod*) in Josh 21, J. Barr, "Migraš in the Old Testament", *JSS* 29 (1984), pp. 15-31, suggests that this orthography reflects a reading מגרֶשָׁה, where מגרש is a collective noun denoting "a demarcated area extending outside the walls and actual inhabited region of a city" (p. 25). According to Barr, this original meaning was forgotten already when 1 Chr 6:40ff was composed, for it reads מגרשיה (in plural), as does also 4Q123.

Sometimes the scroll seems to paraphrase its base text (frg. 1 4). To that end it employs phraseology borrowed from parallel biblical passages (e.g., frg. 2 2). 4Q123 (or its *Vorlage*) also omits/summarizes (frg. 2 1-3) and expands the biblical account, as in the case of frg. 2 1 expanding Josh 21:2 with the phrase עבד / [יהוה (frg. 2 1). Referring to Moses as the servant of the Lord, it emphasizes the fact that the allocation of the cities to priests and Levites was sanctioned by God.

Still, two concerns have been raised regarding the classification of 4Q123 as a Rewritten Bible text. First, it has been suggested that 4Q123 may be "a variant edition of the biblical book of Joshua".[554] While this possibility should not be ruled out, the aforementioned deviations from the ancient textual witnesses, as well as the presence of other Qumran scrolls rewriting the Book of Joshua (4Q378, 4Q379), including its geographical sections (4Q522, 5Q9), seem to support the classification of 4Q123 with the Rewritten Bible literature.

Second, the identification of 4Q123 as a Rewritten Bible composition was questioned "because the palaeo-Hebrew script in which it is written suggests the Biblical character of this manuscript".[555] Indeed, the majority of the Qumran paleo-Hebrew scrolls contains biblical books.[556] Still, given 4Q123's treatment of Josh 21 and the fact that there are other paleo-Hebrew scrolls containing non-biblical compositions (three unidentified works 4Q124-125, 11Q22; cf. also an unidentified text from Masada [Mas 1039-320, also designated Mas 1o]),[557] it seems appropriate to retain the grouping of 4Q123 with the Rewritten Bible works.

---

554 Skehan et al., "4Q123", p. 201.
555 A. Lange & U. Mittmann-Richert, "Annotated List of the Texts from the Judaean Desert Classified", in E. Tov (ed.), *The Texts from the Judaean Desert: Indices and an Introduction to the Discoveries in the Judaean Desert Series* (DJD 39; Oxford: Clarendon Press, 2002), p. 126 note 8. In his recent *Handbuch*, p. 189, Lange refined his position on 4Q123 suggesting that it resists a definite classification.
556 Since these include the Pentateuch and Job, a suggestion was made that the use of the paleo-Hebrew script reflects an understanding that these books were authored by Moses (on the attribution of Job to Moses see b. Bava Bathra 14b-15a). Ulrich takes this further proposing that the use of the paleo-Hebrew script in 4Q123 indicates that it was not reserved to the writings ascribed to Moses, but also to his contemporaries. While these conjectures are intriguing, they should be treated with caution given the accidental nature of the Qumran findings. E. Ulrich, "The Palaeo-Biblical Biblical Texts from Qumran Cave 4", in D. Dimant & L.H. Schiffman (eds.), *Time to Prepare the Way in the Wilderness* (STDJ 16; Leiden: EJ. Brill, 1994), p. 105.
557 See Sh. Talmon, "A Papyrus Fragment Inscribed in Palaeo-Hebrew Script", in idem et al. (eds.), *Masada VI: Yigael Yadin Excavations 1963-65 Final Reports* (Jerusalem: Israel Exploration Society, The Hebrew University of Jerusalem, 1999), pp. 138-147; Tov, *Scribal Practices*, pp. 246-247.

Due to the scroll's fragmentary state, we do not know whether it rewrote the entire list of the Levitical cities, as found in Josh 21, and whether it also dealt with other sections of the Book of Joshua.[558] The extant text betrays an interest in Levitical matters, which may suggest a Levitical/priestly milieu.[559]

---

[558] The allocation of Levitical cities is not featured extensively in other Second Temple sources. In addition to Josephus, J. Ant. 5.90-92, there is a possible, admittedly a midrashic, use of Num 35:4-5 to establish the distance of the Sabbath journey in CD X, 21(cf. also 4Q264a I, 1), XI, 5-6 and the distance between the camp or the Temple City and the latrines in 1QM VII, 7 and 11QTᵃ XLVI, 13-16 (respectively). See Schiffman, *Halakha*, p. 91; Y. Yadin, *The Temple Scroll* (Jerusalem: The Israel Exploration Society: 1983), vol. 1, pp. 298f.

[559] Tov, *Scribal Practices*, p. 248, suggests a Sadducean origin of the Qumran paleo-Hebrew scrolls.

6 The Scroll 5Q9

The scroll 5Q9 is written in a mid-late Herodian hand.[560] Milik's edition, entitled
Ouvrage avec Toponymes, remains the only edition of this scroll.[561] A selective
new edition of 5Q9 is being prepared by Qimron.[562]

6.1 Text and Commentary

Frg. 1

Milik joined three scraps of leather to obtain the following text:

[ ]והיה ישוע[	1
[ ]וֹאת קדֹה אתֹ[	2
[ ]עֹוֹלֹ[	3

However, it is unclear whether the three scraps belong together. The shapes of the
edges, as well as the traces of ink (particularly, in the second *he* of והיה, but also
in the *yod* of]ישוע) do not match. Therefore, they are presented here separately
as 1a, 1b, and 1c (from right to left):

1a

[ ]והיהֹ[	1
[ ]וֹאת ק[	2

Translation
1.   ] and was[
2.   ] and   [

Comments
The fragment may belong with the same section of the scroll as frg. 1a, as line 2
apparently contains another toponym (opening with *qof*).

---

560 Milik, "5Q9", pp. 179-180. The editor does not date the manuscript. The dating quoted above
is from *DJD* 39, p. 374.
561 Milik, ibid.
562 Qimron, *The Hebrew Writings: Volume Two*.

1b

]°ה[1
]°°[2

Notes on Readings
2 The shape of the second letter suits a *waw* or a *yod*.

1c

]ישוע[1
]את מק[דֹה אתֹ 2
]עֹוֹלֹ[3

Translation
1.   ]Joshua[
2.   Mak]keda and[
3.   ]burden (?)[

Comments
1]**ישוע**[. For the spelling ישוע (MT יהושע) see Comment to 4Q378 22 i 2.

2 **את מק]דֹה אתֹ**. This line may read]אתֹ דֹה[מק את (cf. the use of *nota accusativi* in frg. 2 2 and 4Q522 9 ii). Makkeda, situated near Azekah (Josh 10:10) and Lachish (Josh 15:41), is mentioned in Joshua 10 (vv. 10, 16, 17, 21, 28, 29). Its king is included in the list of the Canaanite kings defeated by Joshua in Josh 12:16. Makkeda was allocated to the tribe of Judah (Josh 15:41).

Frg. 2

] אֹת צידוֹן[1
]° וֹא ואת[° 2
]°[3

Translation
1.   ] Sidon [
2.   ]   and [
3.   ] [

Comments

1 אֵת צִידֹן[. On Sidon see Comments to 4Q522 7 2 and 8 4. It is unclear whether the scroll refers here to Joshua's conquest or, more likely, to the Israelites' failure to conquer Sidon.

Frg. 3

```
                              ]∘∘[        1
              א[ת בֵ֗ית תפֻ֗]וח         2
                              ]∘[         3
```

Translation

1.   ]   [
2.   ] Beth-Tap[puah
3.   ]   [

Comments

2 א[ת בֵּית תפֻ]וח. Beth-Tappuah (Milik) is mentioned among the cities allocated to Judah (Josh 15:53). It is identified with Taffuḥ, 5 km west of Hebron.[563]

Frg. 4

```
                          א[ת עין צידֹֿן ]        1
                              ]∘∘ דֹֿדֹ∘[          2
```

Translation

1.   ] 'yn ṣydwn [
2.   ]   [

Comments

1 א[ת עין צידֹֿן. The toponym עין צידֹֿן is otherwise unknown.

---

563 Aharoni, *Land*, p. 300.

Frg. 5

1   א[ת כוכבֹה ואתֹ]

2   [ואת שרדיֹ ואתֹ]

3   [ ]◦[ ] [על מי דן וֹ◦]

Translation

1.   ] *kwkbh* and [
2.   ] and *srdy* and [
3.   ] [   ]upon the waters of Dan and   [

Comments

1 א[ת כוכבֹה ואתֹ. The phrase "waters of Dan" in line 3 indicates that the scroll deals here with the northern part of the land of Canaan (cf. 4Q522 9 i 2-5). Milik suggests that כוכבֹה is the village of Κωχαβα mentioned by Eusebius along with Nazareth as the place where the relatives of Jesus lived (Ecclesiastical History 1.7.14).[564] It has been identified with Kaukab in the Valley of Beth Netophah near Nazareth.[565] Perhaps, this is the town of כוכבה where R. Dosethai (Pesiqta Rabbati 16) lived (Milik).[566] In addition to this Κωχαβα/כוכבה there are several other localities bearing a similar name (from north to south):[567]

a. Kokeba northwest of Rashaya in Beqa'a.[568]

b. Kaukab near Artouz in the vicinity of Damascus.[569]

c. Kaukeba east of Hassbeya in the vicinity of Mt. Hermon.[570]

d. Cocabe in the region of Bashan mentioned by Epiphanius (Panarion 30.2.18) as a place where Ebionites lived. It has been identified with the village of Kaukab situated to the east of the modern Haspin in the southern Golan Heights.[571]

2 ואת שרדיֹ]. Milik suggests that שרדיֹ refers to the inhabitants of the biblical שריד situated in the tribal territory of Zebulon (Josh 19:10, 12). Yet in light of lines 1 and 3 it may also be another toponym. Finally, the possibility of a scribal mistake (שרדי instead of שריד) should be considered.

---

564 K. Lake, *Eusebius: The Ecclesiastical History* (London: Heinemann, New York: G.P. Putnam's Sons, 1926), p. 63.

565 Dussaud, *Topographie Historique*, map I, B3.

566 Neubauer, *La géographie du Talmud*, p. 269.

567 See the entry Kaukab in Dussaud, *Topographie Historique*, pp. 600-601.

568 Dussaud, ibid., p. 393 and map III, C3.

569 Ibid., p. 321.

570 Ibid., map III, B3.

571 Ibid., p. 336, map I, D3.

3 עַל מֵי דָן[. The scroll mentions here a locality situated near River Dan. Milik points to a similar phrase in 1 En 13:7.

Frg. 6

1	[וֹאת קטֹנֹת]
	[°]
2	[וֹד ואת צרדֹהֹ]
3	[ויבאו כול]

Notes on Readings

2 Above the *he* of צרדֹה a bottom tip of a vertical stroke is visible. Perhaps this is a letter added above the line or a final letter from the preceding line.

Translation

1.]and *qṭnt*[
2.] and Zeredah[
3.] And all [ ] came [

Comments

1 [וֹאת קטֹנֹת. Milik (followed by Qimron) suggests that a vertical stroke next to a medial *nun* belongs to a *taw*, קטֹנֹת. The city of קטת in the tribal territory of Zebulon (Josh 19:15) appears as Καταναθ in the LXX. Rabbi Yossi in j. Meg. 1.70a.1 refers to it as קטונית.[572] Kattath might have been located at the northwestern edge of the Jezreel Valley.[573]

2 [וֹד ואת צרדֹה. Milik points to Zereda of 1 Kgs 11:26 identified with ʿAin Serida, 20 km southwest of Shechem.[574]

3 ויבאו כול. The word כול may refer to the entire nation of Israel, as in Exod 16:1 (cf. Josh 18:1).

Frg. 7

1	[אנשׁ]י
2	[° °]

---

572 Aharoni, *Land*, p. 115.
573 Ibid., p. 212.
574 Ibid., pp. 112, 281.

Translation
1.   ]me[n of
2.   ]   [

6.2 Discussion

The extant fragments of the scroll 5Q9 preserve names of geographical localities preceded by a *nota accusativi* and interspersed with narrative remarks (frg. 1a 1, 6 3). Given the explicit reference to Joshua (frg. 1c 1) and the formal similarities with 4Q522 8 and 9 i, it seems probable that these are localities that were conquered or left unconquered by the Israelites. Both 4Q522 and 5Q9 mention the city of Sidon (צ]ידי[ו]ן את [4Q522 8 4]; אֵת צידוֹן [5Q9 2 1]). Yet, this is the only toponym they have in common. If the scroll indeed deals with the Israelites' conquests, it seems to expand the biblical records of such with several types of toponyms: 1. Locations mentioned in the descriptions of the tribal allotments (Beth-Tappuah, קטנֹת), 2. Toponyms mentioned elsewhere in the Hebrew Bible (Zereda), and 3. Non-biblical toponyms (Ein Sidon, כוכבֹה, שרדי[?]). While the precise purpose of the inclusion of these locations remains unknown, the analogy with 4Q522 may suggest an attempt to aggraindize Joshua's conquests.

7 The Scroll Mas 1039-211

7.1 The Manuscript

The scroll Mas 1039-211 (Mas 1l) is written in an early Herodian hand.[575] It is represented by two fragments.[576]

The editor assumes that the small fragment (frg. b) should be placed above the large fragment (frg. a). It is impossible to determine how many lines, if any, are missing between the second line of frg. b and the first line of frg. a.

7.2 Editions of Mas 1039-211

The only edition of this scroll is that of Talmon, who published it under the title MasapocrJosh.[577]

7.3 Text and Commentary

Upper margin

1(b)	א[שׁ̇ר בעבר הי̇ר̇דֹ[ן
2	וי[שׁ̇פלם לפֹנ̇[י
1(a)	[אֹמ̇רֹו]∘
2	[ם יד יום]
3	ה]ראה ויפחדוֹ]
4	ויודו כו]ל̇ם לשם עליון כי ראֹו אֹ[ת כול אשר עשה
5	ו]י̇לחם לעמו באויביהם ולואֹ]
6	∘[ולוא יראו] מפניהֹ̇ם̇ כי אל עמהם ויברכם ויֹושֹׁיעֹ̇ם̇]
7	וכול̇ אשר] דבר עֹ̇ל̇י̇הֹם בא להם ולואֹ[ן נפ]ל̇ דבר ארצה
8	וכ]בֹ̇וֹד הרבה להם מואדה ג̇[ד]וֹ̇ל̇ אדוני

Bottom margin

575 Talmon, "Mas 1039-211", pp. 105-116.

576 Mrs. Noga Zeevi of the Israel Antiquities Authority informs me that these fragments are now catalogued as IAA 2008-7139. I wish to thank Mrs. Zeevi for providing me with a new digital image of this scroll, B-182651.

577 Ibid. For the preliminary editions see Talmon, "Fragment", pp. 147-157; idem, "Fragments of a Joshua Apocryphon", pp. 128-139.

Notes on Readings

1(b) וי|שֶׁפלם. Talmon reads וֹ|פלם. However, the upper tip of the vertical stroke visible on the fragment lacks the characteristic hook shape of a *waw*. It seems to curve to the right, as in the left stroke of a *shin*.

1(a) אָמרֹו|. The editor suggests פֿנֹיו|. On the new photograph B-182651 traces of an *alef* are visible in the beginning of the line. The base and the vertical strokes that appear next to the *alef* may belong either to a medial *pe* or to a medial *mem*. The shape of the upper horizontal stroke of the third letter indicates that this is either a *dalet* or a *resh*.

2 יום|. Talmon reads thus in the preliminary edition of the scroll.[578] The traces of the last letter make clear that a final *mem* is the only possible reading. Still, in the final edition Talmon corrected his reading to יונ|, chiefly because "the resulting word combination יד יום does not make any sense".[579]

4 כו|לֿם. The editor suggests מ◦[. The curving bottom tip of a vertical stroke seems to suit a *lamed*.

5 ללֿחם|. Talmon reads ללֿח◦[. On the photograph, a tiny trace of an upper tip consistent with a *waw* or a *yod* is visible.
ולוֹא| [. On the new photograph B-182651 there is a blank space next to an *alef*.

6 ◦[וֹיֿשֿמֿם|. The editor reads וֹיֿ◦עֿ◦[. The final letter is clearly a final *mem*. Its bottom part is well visible on the photograph B-182651. The fourth letter has been read as a *shin*, though the reading of a surviving trace of ink is admittedly difficult. Two letter-spaces to the left of the *shin*, a trace of ink is visible.

7 ולוֹא|. Talmon has ולוֹ◦[. The vertical stroke of the fourth letter suits an *alef*.

8 וכ|בֹֿד. The editor reads ם[. According to the photograph B-182651, the last letter is clearly a *dalet*. The second letter is most likely a *waw* (cf. a *waw* in עליון [line 4]). A trace of a base stroke may belong to a *bet* (cf. the base stroke of a *bet* in דבר [line 7]).
גֿ|ד|וֹלֿ. Talmon suggests לֿ◦   מואדה. The diagonal stroke before the lacuna (omitted in Talmon's transcription) is consistent with the right stroke of a *gimel*, while the vertical stroke preceding the *lamed* may well be a *waw*. Tov also reads thus.[580]

---

578 Talmon, "Fragment", p. 152.
579 Idem, "Mas 1039-211", p. 107.
580 Tov, "Rewritten Joshua", p. 252.

Translation

1(b).   ]which is (who are) on the other side of the Jordan[

2.   and He]brought them low befor[e

1(a).   ]they said [

2.   ] a hand day[

3.   H]e and they were afraid[

4.   and al]l[of]them [thanked] the name of the Most High because they saw [all that He has done

5.   and]He fought on behalf of his people against their enemies and they were (He was) not

6.   and they did not fear] them, for God (was) with them and He blessed them and saved them[ ]

7.   and all that] He promised them came true for them and not a single word f[ell] to the ground

8.   and] He heaped [ho]nor upon them. Great is the Lord

Comments

1b א]שֶׁר בעבר הֹיֹרֹדֹן. This phrase is likely to refer to the Land of Canaan (e.g., Deut 3:25), though elsewhere it also designates the Transjordan (Deut 3:8; Josh 2:10).

2 וַי]שֶׁפלם לפנֹי. The first word is restored as a *wayyiqtol* Hifil of שפל, "to bring low, humiliate" (spelled defectively) with a 3rd masc. pl. objective suffix.[581] Apparently, it refers to God's humiliation of the Canaanite nations before Israel (cf. Ps 75:8, 147:6).

1a אָֹמֹרוּ[. It is unknown how many lines (if any) are missing between this and the preceding lines. Similarly, it is unclear who is the subject of the verb אָֹמֹרוּ[(or אָֹמֹרוּ[י/ו) and whether the following line(s) contain(s) direct speech.

2 ם] יד יום[. One possible reconstruction is ויר]ם יד with Exod 17:11-12 (cf. Josh 8:18, 26). If this is indeed an allusion to Moses' lifted hands during the war with Amalek, one might consider restoring ויר]ם יד יום] תמים (cf. Josh 10:13) or ויר]ם יד יום] אחד (Sir 46:4:]הלא בידו עמד השמש יום אחד). Alternatively, the scroll might have read ויתן בה]ם יד (cf. Exod 7:4).

3 ה]ֹוֹאה ויפחדוֹ. Perhaps, one could restore וידעו כי אלהים ה]ֹוֹאה (for the language cf. 1 Kgs 18:27).

4 ויודו כו]נֹלֹם לשם עליון כי ראֹו אָ]ת כל אשר עשה. The reconstructions follow Ps 92:2 and Josh 23:3. The precise occasion implied by the scroll is unclear.

---

581 BDB, p. 1050.

5 | ‏ו[‏יּלחם לעמו באויביהם ולוֹאֹ. This line may allude to Deut 20:4 (cf. also Josh 23:3).

6 | ‏ולוא יראו[ן מפניהֹם כי אל עמהם ויברכם ויוֹשֹׁעֹםֹ. The reconstruction is that of Talmon. The verb ‏ויוֹשֹׁעֹם may point to Deut 20:4 (alluded to in the previous line 5). For the word pair ‏ישע and ‏ברך see Ps 28:9.

7 ארצה ‏וכל אשר[ן דבר עֹלֹיֹהֹם בא להם ולוֹאֹן נפ[ל דבר ארצה. The scroll paraphrases Josh 23:14. The addition of the noun ‏ארצה seems to have been influenced by the parallel formulations from 1 Sam 3:19 and 2 Kgs 10:10 (Talmon).

8 מואדה ‏וכ]בֹוֹד הרבה להם הרבה מואדה. Most likely, the verb ‏הרבה, a Hifil *qatal* of ‏רבה, "to increase, to make great", has God as a subject, while the pronoun ‏להם stands for the nation of Israel (cf. Dan 11:39).[582]

‏גֹ.[ד]וֹל אדוני. This phrase may begin a section of praise. Psalms 48:2 and 145:3 employ the formula ‏גדול ה'. The scroll seems to replace the Tetragrammaton with ‏אדוני.

7.4 Discussion

The extant text of the scroll Mas 1039-211 alludes several times to the Book of Joshua.[583] However, unlike the scrolls 4Q378, 4Q379, and 4Q522, which offer an extensive reworking of several sections of this book, it seems to present a 3rd person summary of the events (*contra* Talmon).[584] Highlighting God's role as a deliverer of Israel, this brief account appears to serve as the background for the author's praise of God (line 8). If this interpretation is correct, Mas 1039-211 should not be associated with the RJ scrolls.[585]

Given the fragmentary nature of the scroll it is difficult to determine its thrust and purpose. Perhaps it also dealt with other periods in Israel's history, that similarly highlighted God's delivering acts.

The scroll's full orthography (‏מואדה [a 8], ‏ולוֹאֹ [a 5, 7]), its avoidance of the Tetragrammaton (frg. a 4, 6, 8), and its presumed affinity to 4Q378-4Q379 led Talmon to conclude that this work was composed at Qumran and written by a

---

582 HALOT, p. 1177.
583 Y. Yadin, "The Excavations of Masada 1963/64: Preliminary Report", *IEJ* 15 (1965), pp. 79-83, initially assumed that this scroll contains an apocryphal work concerned with the Book of Samuel.
584 Tov, "Rewritten Joshua", p. 254, notes that the scroll may echo a summary of contests in Josh 21:43-45. Tov's another suggestion (ibid.) that the scroll may rework Joshua's final speech (Josh 23-24) seems less likely, for, unlike Josh 23-24, it refers to the Israelites in the 3rd person.
585 For a similar conclusion, see Davies et al., *The Complete World*, p. 122; Qimron, *The Dead Sea Scrolls: The Hebrew Writings: Volume Two*.

Qumran scribe.[585] He argues that a refugee member of the Qumran community brought it to Masada. Yardeni proposes that Mas 1039-211 was penned by a scribe who was responsible for dozens of scrolls, of both sectarian and non-sectarian provenance, discovered in the caves of Qumran.[587] Still, neither the orthographic and scribal features of this scroll nor the identity of the scribe may serve as decisive criteria for classifying it as a sectarian work.[588] Since the extant text of Mas 1039-211 does not contain any sectarian ideas or terminology, there is no ground for classifying it as a sectarian composition.

---

586 Thus also Tov, "Rewritten Joshua", p. 252.

587 A. Yardeni, "A Note on a Qumran Scribe", in M. Lubetski (ed.), *New Seals and Inscriptions, Hebrew, Idumean, and Cuneiform* (Hebrew Bible Monographs 8; Sheffield: Sheffield Phoenix Press, 2007), pp. 287-290.

588 See Dimant, "Taxonomy", pp. 7-18.

8 The Rewritten Joshua Scrolls: One Composition or Several Literary Works?

The foregoing analysis of each of the Qumran scrolls reworking the Book of Joshua provides the pertinent data for exploring the relationships between these manuscripts. Scholarly publications frequently treat the RJ scrolls as copies of one composition, the Apocryphon of Joshua. The tendency to highlight the affinities between these texts was apparent already in the earliest publications dealing with the RJ scrolls (see Introduction). Tov made the most detailed case advancing the proposition that 4Q123, 4Q378, 4Q379, 4Q522, 5Q9, and Mas 1039-211 represent the same literary work.[589] He assumed with Strugnell and Newsom that 4Q378 and 4Q379 represent one composition. Tov then argued for their close affinities in style, contents, and orthography with 4Q522.[590] Next, he pointed out the similarity between the lists of geographical localities in 4Q522 9 i and 5Q9. Once the link between 4Q378, 4Q379, 4Q522, and 5Q9 was established, Tov suggested, with some hesitation, that Mas 1039-211, combining an allusion to Joshua's discourse from Josh 23 (line 7) with a liturgical passage, recalled 4Q379 17 and 22 i-ii. Finally, he linked these five scrolls with 4Q123, positing that 4Q379 1 contains a list of the tribal allocations to Levites (Josh 21), akin to that of 4Q123.[591]

Although widely accepted, Tov's analysis has been criticized by several scholars.[592] Thus, Puech envisions two separate groups of scrolls: one consisting of the scrolls 4Q378-379 and another including 4Q522 and 5Q9. He further suggests that 4Q123 and Mas 1039-211 should not be associated with these four scrolls.[593] Following his lead, Bethelot observes that 4Q522 and 4Q378-379 may contain two different compositions.[594] In a similar fashion, García Martínez notes that 4Q378-379 on the one hand and 4Q522 and 5Q9 on the other hand may preserve

---

589 Tov, "Rewritten Joshua", pp. 233-256.
590 Tov, ibid., p. 248.
591 W. van Peursen, "Who Was Standing on the Mountain? The Portrait of Moses in 4Q377", in A. Graupner & M. Wolter (eds.), *Moses in Biblical and Extra-Biblical Traditions* (BZAW 372; Berlin: de Gruyter, 2007), pp. 99-100, suggests that 4Q377 contains another work where Joshua is speaking. Yet the extant text of this scroll does not support this proposition. See further A. Feldman, "Revelation", pp. 155-172.
592 See the cautious remarks by Wise in Wise et al., *Dead Sea Scrolls*, p. 428
593 Puech, "4Q522", p. 71. The only argument he adduces (p. 72) is that Mas 1039-211 employs עליון and אל, instead of the Tetragrammaton.
594 Berthelot, "Joshua", p. 100 note 15.

two separate literary works.[595] Finally, Qimron, while allowing for the possibility that 4Q378, 4Q379, 4Q522, and 5Q9 belong with the same composition, observes that Mas 1039-211 is not concerned with the Book of Joshua.[596]

Affirming the tentative conclusion reached by other scholars, the foregoing study demonstrated that Mas 1039-211 does not rewrite the Book of Joshua. Hence, it is excluded from this discussion. The evidence regarding the relations between the remaining five RJ scrolls (4Q123, 4Q378, 4Q379, 4Q522, and 5Q9) appears to be more complex. In addition to highlighting the fact that these scrolls are concerned with the Book of Joshua, scholars observe that they share certain exegetical features. The following discussion will explore three questions: 1. Is there a textual overlap between the RJ scrolls? 2. Do they utilize common exegetical techniques? 3. Do the RJ scrolls witness to shared exegetical traditions and motifs? At the end, it will be argued that the five scrolls should be viewed as separate compositions.

8.1   Do the RJ Scrolls Overlap?

It is often stated that the RJ scrolls do not overlap. Those who view them as copies of the Apocryphon of Joshua explain the lack of the overlapping text as an accident. Preserving different sections of this putative work, these scrolls are taken as complementing each other.[597] Indeed, as the following synopsis demonstrates, the identifiable fragments of the RJ scrolls rarely address the same biblical passages, and when they do (as in the case of 4Q379 12 and 4Q522 1 2, as well as 4Q379 26 and 4Q522 4), they do not rework the same verses:[598]

---

595 However, he also does not discard a possibility that they represent different parts of a single work. García Martínez, "Book of Joshua", p. 105; ibid., "Light", p. 153.

596 Qimron, *The Dead Sea Scrolls: The Hebrew Writings: Volume Two.*

597 Tov, "Rewritten Joshua", p. 253; Newsom, "4Q378-379", p. 237. Dimant, "Two Discourses", pp. 59-60, observes that the treatment of different episodes from the Book of Joshua in 4Q378 and 4Q379 tallies well with Stegemann's proposal that 4Q378 comes from the beginning of the scroll, while 4Q379 represents a middle of the scroll. One caveat regarding this comment is that the paucity of the material evidence renders Stegemann's judgment highly tentative. It is not unlikely that his conclusion is, at least in part, based on the contents of the fragments, rather than on their physical features.

598 The RJ scrolls allude also to other biblical episodes, e.g., the appointment of Joshua (4Q378 22 i), Achan' sin (4Q378 6 i), the ruse of the Gibeonites, David's capture of Zion, his preparations for the construction of the Temple, Solomon's building of the Temple, and Zadok's officiating in the Temple (4Q522 9 ii). Yet, the references to these events are incorporated in prayers and a discourse, and not dealt with directly. Compare the list of the episodes addressed by RJ scrolls in Tov, "Rewritten Joshua", pp. 253-254.

	4Q123	4Q378	4Q379	4Q522	5Q9
Deut 34		Mourning for Moses (frg. 14)			
Josh 1		Joshua's address to Israel and their reply (frg. 3)			
Josh 2				The return of the two spies (frg. 1 1)	
Josh 3			The crossing of the Jordan (frgs. 12, 15-17[?])	Joshua gets ready for the crossing (frg. 1 2)	
Josh 6			Instructions pertaining to Jericho (frg. 3 i) The expanded curse on the builder of Jericho (frg. 22 ii)		
Josh 8			The conquest of Ai (frg. 26)	The ceremony at Mts. Ebal and Gerizim (frg. 4)	
				Israelites' conquests (frg. 9 i)	Israelites' conquests (frgs. 1,3-6)
Josh 18:1				Events leading to the setting of the Tent of Meeting in Shiloh (frg. 9 ii)	
Josh 21	Levitical cities (frgm. 1-4)				
Judg 1				List of the unconquered cities (frg. 8)	Unconquered cities (frg. 2)?

The only instance of a possible textual overlap between the RJ scrolls is found in 4Q522 8 4 and 5Q9 2 1. Both fragments mention the city of Sidon:[599]

<table>
<tr><td align="center">**4Q522 8 4**</td><td align="center">**5Q9 2 1**</td></tr>
<tr><td align="center" dir="rtl">צ[ידון וֹאֹת אֹחֹל]ב</td><td align="center" dir="rtl">[אֹת צידוֹן]</td></tr>
</table>

However, it is far from clear whether 4Q522 8 4 employs the same construction, 'nota accusativi + a toponym', as does 5Q9 2 1. In fact, there is some support for restoring 4Q522 8 4 (with Judg 1:31) as ואת יושבי צ[ידון (see Comment ad loc.). Yet, even if both texts read את צידון, their identity would not be established with certainty. The presumed overlapping text is very short and involves formulaic language.

8.2 Do the RJ Scrolls Utilize Common Exegetical Techniques?

It has been suggested that the scrolls 4Q378, 4Q379, and 4Q522 treat the underlying biblical texts in a similar way (Newsom; Tov).[600] The extant fragments of these manuscripts contain a limited amount of narrative (4Q378 14 1-3; 4Q379 12 1-3; 4Q522 1[?], 4, 8 8). These narrative sections are constructed using quotation (e.g., 4Q378 14 1-3; 4Q522 8) and paraphrase employing lexica from related biblical passages (e.g., 4Q522 4). Into this narrative framework various expansions, such as exegetical additions, speeches, praises, and prayers, are incorporated. These embellishments are fashioned by using parallel verses featuring complementary data (4Q379 12) and literary models (4Q379 1-2 following Deut 32), as well as by drawing lexica from various biblical passages.

The extant fragments of the remaining two RJ texts, 4Q123 and 5Q9, seem to lack the amplificatons of the biblical account that 4Q378, 4Q379, and 4Q522 abound with. Thus, 4Q123 appears to be a close paraphrase of Josh 21. The few words preserved in 5Q9 suggest that this is some kind of rewriting of Joshua's conquests (or unconquered territories) presented in a form of a list of toponyms occasionally interspersed with narrative (cf. frgs. 1c 1, 6 3). While it appears that all the five texts, diverse as they are, can be placed within the broad category of

---

599 The overlap suggested by Tov, "Rewritten Joshua", p. 251, i.e. that [ון]קטר in 4Q522 9 i 14 and]תֹֹנֹקט in 5Q9 6 1 stand for the same locality, is hardly convincing.
600 Newsom, "Psalms of Joshua", p. 56 (regarding 4Q378 and 4Q379); Tov, "Rewritten Joshua", p. 248 (regarding 4Q378, 4Q379, and 4Q522).

Rewritten Bible literature,[601] it is difficult to assume that a similarity in the strategy of rewriting in 4Q378, 4Q379, and 4Q522 would suffice to establish their identity. After all, expansion of the biblical text with exegetical, oratorical, and liturgical additions is common in this literature.

8.3 Do the RJ Scrolls Witness to Shared Exegetical Traditions and Motifs?

It has been also observed that the RJ scrolls, particularly, 4Q378, 4Q379, and 4Q522, share several exegetical traditions, tendencies, and motifs:

1. The amplification of the paraenetic/hortatory aspect of Joshua's biblical portrayal (Tov).[602] This observation applies primarily to 4Q378, constructing Joshua's speeches (frgs. 3 i, 11?) using Mosaic admonitory discourses from the Book of Deuteronomy. 4Q379 13 may also contain an admonitory discourse by Joshua. Joshua's speech in 4Q522 9 ii may hardly be described as paraenetic.

2. The depiction of Joshua as a prophetic figure (Tov).[603] As discussed in Chapters 1 and 9, this feature, present already in the biblical portrayal of Joshua, is not unique to the scrolls 4Q378, 4Q379, and 4Q522, but is amply attested in other Second Temple sources.[604]

3. The motif of guilt occurs in 4Q378 6 i 4, 6 ii 4-5, 22 i 1 (cf. also frgs. 1 1, 24 3), and 4Q522 9 ii 10-11 (Tov).[605] One may note that the passage in 4Q522 9 ii 10-11 records Joshua's personal confession of a sin in the case of the treaty with the Gibeonites, reflecting an interpretation of the Gibeonites' ruse which is unique to this scroll.

---

601 See, for instance, the recent study by A. Lange, "From Paratexts to Commentary", in A.D. Roitman et al. (eds.), *The Dead Sea Scrolls and Contemporary Culture* (STDJ 93; Leiden, Boston: Brill, 2011), p. 207. He suggests that the term "Rewritten Bible/Scripture" has to be replaced with a more neutral designation, "paratexts", and includes the RJ scrolls (with an exception of 4Q123; see above, note 555) among the paratexts that "rewrite a main base text but include secondary base texts into their re-narration as well".

602 Tov, "Rewritten Joshua", p. 248. He also observes that Joshua speaks in the first person in 4Q378-379 and 4Q522.

603 Tov, ibid.

604 One could add here that Joshua's prophetic utterances in 4Q379 22 ii and 4Q522 9 ii seem to share two features: 1. Both of them are concerned with three individuals, 2. The two passages employ an introductory formula 'הנה(כי/ו)+ participle'.

605 Tov, "Rewritten Joshua", pp. 248-249.

4. 4Q379 1 2 and 4Q522 9 ii 6-9 seem to apply the wording of the Mosaic blessing of Benjamin (Deut 33:12) to a Levitical/priestly figure: Levi and Zadok respectively (Dimant). A similar interpretation of this passage occurs in the Aramaic Levi Document.

In addition to these shared exegetical traditions and motifs,[606] the foregoing study pointed out to an exegetical tendency shared by two of the RJ scrolls, 4Q379 and 4Q522. Both scrolls appear to read events recorded in the Book of Joshua through the lens of the biblical law (or its interpretation):[607]

-   The account of the crossing of the Jordan is interpreted with an eye towards the Deuteronomic jubilean laws (4Q379 12 4-6).
-   Possible inclusion of a liturgy in the description of the crossing may reflect a reading influenced by the Mosaic injunctions in Deut 27 (4Q379 13, 15-17).
-   The story of the fall of Jericho seems to be read in light of the Deuteronomic legislation pertaining to an idolatrous city (4Q379 3 i 6).
-   Josh 8:33 is harmonized with the injunctions from Deut 11:29 and 27:12-13 (4Q522 4 2).
-   The account of the treaty with the Gibeonites is read with the regulations from Num 27:21 in view (4Q522 9 ii 10-11).
-   The setting of the Tent of Meeting in Shiloh is given a halakhic explanation (4Q522 9 ii).

As with the other shared exegetical features, a nomistic exegesis of the Book of Joshua is not unique to these two scrolls.[608] Instances of such exegesis are found in 4QJosh[a] I (see Chapter 3) and in the Greek translation of this book.[609]

---

606 One may note here, that Tov, "Rewritten Joshua", pp. 248, 252, also lists several similarities of a more general nature, e.g., the spelling of Joshua's name as יושע (4Q378 22 i 1; 4Q379 22 ii 7; 4Q522 9 ii 14; found also in Neh 8:17; CD V, 4; 1Q22 I, 12; 4Q175 21), the metion of Eleazar (4Q379 17 5 and 4Q522 9 ii 13), and an interest in geography, be it the Israelites' conquests (in 4Q522 and 5Q9, including the reference to Bethel in 4Q379 26 2; 4Q522 9 ii 13) or Levitical cities (4Q123).
607 One may add to this list the interpretation of David's conquest of Jerusalem in light of the Torah commands regarding the Canaanites in 4Q522 9 ii 4.
608 On the nomistic inner-biblical interpretation, see Tov, *Textual Criticism*, pp. 252-253, 261-262 (and the bibliography cited there).
609 See L. Mazor, "A Nomistic Re-Working of the Jericho Conquest Narrative Reflected in the LXX to Joshua 6:1-20", *Textus* 18 (1995), pp. 47-62.

8.4 Conclusions

Of all the types of data analysed above, i.e., a possible textual overlap, common exegetical techniques, and shared interpretational traditions, tendencies, and motifs, none seems to offer a conclusive proof in favor of the hypothesis ascribing all the RJ scrolls to a single composition. Neither does the cumulative weight of these shared features warrant such a conclusion. While there seems to be a place for some doubt in the case of 4Q522 and 5Q9, mainly because of the otherwise unattested tendency to list toponyms, it seems that in their present state of preservation the five RJ scrolls are better served if treated as five separate compositions.[610] If this conclusion is correct, it implies that the Book of Joshua was a subject of an intense literary/exegetical activity in the last two centuries BCE. In fact, it may well be the most frequently rewritten book of the Former Prophets among the Dead Sea scrolls.[611]

---

610 In light of the foregoing analysis the titles of some of the RJ scrolls have to be reconsidered. Both the term "apocryphon" (see Zahn, "Talking about Rewritten Texts", pp. 105-106) and the superscript a-c fail to convey the nature of these texts and the relationships between them. In his forthcoming edition of the RJ scrolls Qimron uses capital letters A-E (instead of the superscript a-e) to signal both the affinities and the distinctive nature of these texts. See meanwhile his remarks in Qimron, *Dead Sea Scrolls*, p. xix. Yet, with the possible exception of 4Q522 and 5Q9, even this may be unwarranted, as the similarities are of a general nature.
611 The Dead Sea scrolls rewriting the Former Prophets include 4Q160 (Samuel Apocryphon), 6Q9 (6Qpap apocrSam-Kings), 4Q382 (4Qpap paraKings), 4Q470 (4QText Mentioning Zedekiah), and 4Q481a (4QapocElisha). This evaluation may apply to both Former and Latter Prophets, although the precise count of works found at Qumran that recast the Books of Jeremiah and Ezekiel is somewhat uncertain. As in the case of the RJ texts, some scrolls associated with the Apocryphon of Jeremiah C and Apocryphon of Ezekiel may contain separate compositions. On the Apocryphon of Jeremiah A (4Q383), Apocryphon of Jeremiah C (4Q385a, 4Q387, 4Q388a, 4Q389, 4Q387a?, 4Q390?), and Apocryphon of Ezekiel (4Q385, 4Q386, 4Q388, 4Q385b?, 4Q385c?, 4Q391?) see D. Dimant, *Qumran Cave 4 XXI: Parabiblical Texts, Part 4: Pseudo-Prophetic Texts* (DJD 30; Oxford: Clarendon Press, 2001); idem, "Pseudo-Ezekiel and the Apocryphon of Jeremiah C in Perspective", *RevQ* 25 (2011), pp. 17-39.

9 The Rewritten Joshua Scrolls in Their Exegetical Context

One of the aims of this study is to place the RJ scrolls within their exegetical context. To achieve this goal, the analyses of each of the five scrolls focused particularly on the ways they treat the biblical text. While each of these scrolls may have its own distinctive exegetical "voice", this concluding chapter evaluates their collective contribution to the study of the transmission of the biblical text in Second Temple times and to the contemporary interpretation of the Book of Joshua.

9.1 The *Vorlagen* of the RJ Scrolls

A reconstruction of a *Vorlage* of a Rewritten Bible composition is famously complicated by the difficulty in distinguishing between genuine and exegetical variant readings. The former reflect the author's base text, while the latter represent his manipulation of it.[612] Despite this inherent obstacle, the scholarly consensus is that presumed variant readings found in such texts deserve to be studied. The RJ scrolls contain several passages that preserve readings diverging from the MT, mostly from the Book of Deuteronomy, but also from Exodus, Numbers, Joshua, and Judges. These readings often reflect minor variations in prepositions and morphology. Frequently, these are paralleled by other textual witnesses. There are also several extensive pluses and minuses. Thus, the scroll 4Q378, providing most of the textual evidence regarding the Book of Deuteronomy, seems to attest to both a shorter text of Deut 8:8-9 (frg. 11 5-7) and to a harmonistic expansion of Deut 8:7-9 and 34:8 with parallel formulations from Exodus and Numbers (frgs. 11 4-6, 14 1-2). Similar harmonizations are found in the Qumran copies of Deuteronomy, as well as in the ancient versions.

As for the Book of Joshua, the presumed variant readings occur mostly in 4Q379 and include one instance of a shorter text (Josh 6:26 [frg. 22 ii 7-9]) and one case of a longer text, introducing a clarifying addition (Josh 3:15 [frg. 12 7]). Both are supported by the LXX, while the latter is paralleled also by 4QJosh[b]. Harmonistic expansions of Joshua passages are found in 4Q123 (Josh 21:2 [frg. 2 1]) and Mas 1039-211 (Josh 23:14 [line 7]).

---

612 Tov, *Textual Criticism*, pp. 114, 189-190.

Of the RJ's quotations from and allusions to other biblical books, mention should be made of a harmonistic expansion of Exod 34:16 with Deut 7:3 in 4Q378 3 i 2. A longer reading of Judg 1:31 in 4Q522 8 3-4 may also reflect harmonization.

In the past, scholars tended to link the presumed *Vorlagen* of 4Q378 and 4Q379 with the Hebrew *Vorlagen* of the LXX Deuteronomy and Joshua. While their affinities with the LXX should not be disregarded, the unique variant readings preserved in these, as well as in other RJ scrolls, may rather place their *Vorlagen* within those numerous scrolls that Tov designates as "non-aligned" Qumran biblical manuscripts.[613] If one were to single out a common feature of the presumed variant readings listed above, it would be the tendency to harmonization, amply attested to in numerous Qumran biblical scrolls, as well as in the LXX and Smr.

9.2 Biblical Exegesis in the RJ Scrolls

As noted above, each of the RJ scrolls may have its own distinctive exegetical "voice". Yet, the absence of the parallel materials in RJ manuscripts renders a comparison between their exegetical approaches difficult. Still, much can be learned from a comparison between the interpretation of the Book of Joshua in the RJ texts as a group and in other Second Temple sources surveyed in Chapter 1. The following table provides a list of the exegetical traditions reflected in the RJ scrolls and notes parallels in contemporary and later literature:[614]

Scroll	Exegetical Tradition/Motif	Parallels
4Q378 22 i 3	Joshua is given a share of God's splendor.	
4Q378 3 i	Assuming the role of leader after Moses' demise, Joshua addresses people foretelling their apostasy, punishment, and repentance.	LAB; SamJosh
4Q378 3 ii	All of Israel responds to Joshua, affirming their obedience to him.	LAB; SamJosh
4Q379 12 3-6	The year of the crossing of the Jordan is the first year of the jubilean computation.	SamJosh

---

613 Tov, *Textual Criticism*, pp. 109-110. On the need to re-think this category, see M. Segal, "The Text of the Hebrew Bible in Light of the Dead Sea Scrolls", *Materia Giudaica* 12 (2007), pp. 5-20.
614 Rab. stands here for Rabbinic literature, while SamJosh refers to the Samaritan Joshua traditions.

4Q379 13, 15-17	The crossing is accompanied by praises and blessings(?).	SamJosh
4Q379 12 6-7	The Jordan overflows with water at the time of the crossing. The overflowing lasts until the wheat harvest in Sivan.	Josephus
4Q379 22 i-ii 7	Joshua (?) praises God following the fall of Jericho.	
4Q379 22 ii 7-15	Joshua's curse from Josh 6:26 is applied to contemporary events. Within the exposition of the curse, the preposition -ב in בבכרו ... ובצעירו is interpreted as *bet instrumentalis*.	
4Q378 6 i-ii	Joshua (?) admonishes Israel and prays following Achan's sin.	
4Q522 9 i and 5Q9	Additions to the biblical records of the sites subdued by the Israelites.	
4Q522 8 3	Inability to dispossess Beth-Shean is attributed to Issachar.	
4Q522 9 ii	The setting of the Tent in Shiloh is explained as the result of the presence of the Canaanite population in Jerusalem (Jebusites) and its vicinities (Gibeonites). Joshua foretells the events leading to the construction of the Temple in Jerusalem.	
4Q522 9 ii 2, 4	The accounts regarding the conquest of Jerusalem are harmonized by assuming a partial conquest by Joshua and the future capture of the "rock of Zion" by David.	Josephus
4Q522 9 ii 4	David expels all the Amorites from Jerusalem.	Josephus
4Q522 9 ii 10	Joshua sins by failing to inquire God's will by means of Urim and Thummim in the case of the Gibeonites.	

The RJ scrolls' collective portrayal of Joshua may also be compared with that of the contemporaneous sources:

Feature	Scroll	Parallels
Pun on Joshua's name	4Q378 13 i 4	Sir; Philo
Minister of Moses	4Q378 22 i 2	Sir; Philo
Entrusted with the oversight over Israel	4Q378 22 i 2	As.Mos.; Philo; Josephus; LAB
Given a share of God's splendor	4Q378 22 i 3	
Military commander	4Q522 9 ii 14	Sir; Philo; Josephus
Faithfully fulfills Moses' commands	4Q379 13, 15-17(?); 4Q522 4 2	4QJoshª; Josephus
Praises God	4Q379 14, 17, 22 i-ii 1-6	SamJosh
Prophesies	4Q378 3 i; 4Q379 22 ii 6-15; 4Q522 9 ii 1-9	Sir; Eupolemus; Josephus; LAB; Rab.; SamJosh
Prays	4Q378 frg. 6 ii (numerous other prayers could be his: 4Q378 19 ii [communal], 4Q379 1-2, 18 [personal])	Sir; LAB
Confesses a sin	4Q522 9 ii 9-11	

Some of the aspects of Joshua's portrayal in the RJ texts (e.g., being Moses' minister entrusted with the oversight of Israel) are explicit in the biblical account. Others constitute a modification of the characteristics of the scriptural Joshua. Thus, while the Bible depicts Joshua as praying on behalf of Israel (7:7-9, 10:12-13), the RJ scrolls introduce additional prayers, not only communal, but also personal. Also, while the Book of Joshua depicts Joshua as admonishing Israel at the end of his life (Josh 23-24), 4Q378 envisions him offering a paraenetic address upon assuming the leadership after Moses' death. Moreover, like other Second Temple sources,[615] the RJ scrolls develop and amplify the scriptural representation of Joshua as a prophetic figure.[616] Yet, unlike the majority of the contemporary texts,

---

615 The depiction of Joshua as endowed with a prophetic gift is attested also in the Aramaic Targumim (T[O,Ps.-J.] to Num 27:18) and Midrash (e.g., Num. Rab. 12:9).

616 Multiple features of the biblical portrayal of Joshua may be interpreted as prophetic. He is a minister of Moses, as Elisha was to Elijah (1 Kgs 19:21). Joshua has a spirit (Num 27:15-20; Deut 34:9). His commission shares features of prophetic commissions (cf. Jer 1:8, 17, 19; Ezek 2:6, 3:9).

they also provide actual prophetic statements by Joshua, as does also LAB. The amplification of Joshua's prophetic gift may reflect an attempt to present him as a worthy successor of Moses.[617] One example would be 4Q378 3 i, where he delivers a Moses-like admonitory prophetic speech.[618] Yet, it may also mirror the placement of the Book of Joshua within the "Prophets", implying that the chief protagonist and, presumably, the author of this book was a prophet.[619]

Two aspects of the RJ's portrayal of Joshua seem to be absent (or, at least, not explicit) from the Hebrew Bible and Second Temple Jewish literature. These are the depiction of Joshua as praising God and confessing a sin. The latter feature is closely related to 4Q522's peculiar view of the treaty with the Gibeonites, whose preservation by Joshua is taken to be one of the factors precluding the setting of the Tent of Meeting in Zion.

As the previous tables demonstrate, many of the exegetical traditions and motifs embedded in the RJ scrolls are shared by other Second Temple sources. Thus, these new texts are very much at home within the Second Temple Jewish literature dealing with the Book of Joshua. To be more specific, the way the RJ scrolls, especially, 4Q378, 4Q379, and 4Q522, treat the biblical text places them along two other Rewritten Bible texts concerned with the Book of Joshua, namely, Jewish Antiquities and LAB. These works and the RJ scrolls share various exegetical techniques, including the use of speeches and prayers as the dominant "cre-

---

God speaks to Joshua (e.g., 1:1-9, 3:7-8, 4:1-3, 4:15, 5:2, 9, 6:1-5, 7:10-15, 8:1-3, 18, 10:8, 22, 11:6, 20:1-9). He transmits the divine words to the people (3:9, 6:6-10, 24:2). Joshua warns the nation of the consequences of transgressing the covenant (23:5-16, 24:19-20). He pronounces a prophetic curse on the rebuilder of Jericho (6:26; 1 Kgs 16:34). Joshua performs miracles (3:7-4:18, 10:12-13). Finally, he intercedes with God on Israel's behalf (7:7-9). See further Rofé, "Joshua", pp. 338-339, 343, 347; Chapman, "Joshua son of Nun", pp. 21-23; Hall, *Conquering Character*.

617 Second Temple Jewish literature offers other instances of elevating biblical figures to the status of prophets, such as Enoch (Jude 1:14), David (11QPs[a] XXVII, 11; Acts 2:25-30 [cf. also Mk 12:36-37 and parallels]; Acts 1:16, 4:25; J. Ant 6.166, 8.109-110), Job (Sir 49:9[Ms B]). See further J.L. Kugel, "David the Prophet", in idem (ed.), *Poetry and Prophecy: The Beginnings of a Literary Tradition* (Ithaca, NY: Cornell University Press, 1990), pp. 45-55; P.W. Flint, "The Prophet David at Qumran", in M. Henze (ed.), *Biblical Interpretation at Qumran* (Grand Rapids: Eerdmans, 2005), pp. 158-167; Jassen, *Mediating the Divine*, pp. 250-255.

618 On Joshua as a prophet like Moses (Deut 18:15) in the Hebrew Bible see Chapman, "Joshua son of Nun", pp. 20-21. On the representation of Joshua as a prophet like Moses in Ben Sira see Corley, "Canonical Assimilation", pp. 63-64, 71-72.

619 For a similar conclusion regarding Ben Sira's depiction of Joshua as a prophet see Beentjes, "Prophets", pp. 139-140; Goshen-Gottstein, "Praise", p. 242. On the references to "the Prophets" in Second Temple sources see the essays included in M. McDonald & J.A. Sanders (eds.), *The Canon Debate* (Peabody, MA: Hendrickson, 2002), as well as G.J. Brooke, "'Canon' in the Light of the Qumran Scrolls", in P.S. Alexander & J.-D. Kaestli (eds.), *The Canon of Scripture in Jewish and Christian Tradition* (Belfort: Éditions du Zèbre, 2007), pp. 81-98.

ative narrative technique".[620] Sometimes the RJ texts expand on those sections of Joshua that are amplified also in Josephus and Pseudo-Philo. Thus, both 4Q378 and LAB greatly elaborate the transition from Moses to Joshua, employing similar exegetical and compositional techniques (with the RJ elaborating more on the speeches and LAB expanding more Joshua's transformation into a prophet). Yet, in other cases, the RJ scrolls focus on passages that seem to be of lesser interest for the other two works. For instance, neither J. Ant. nor LAB show interest in the calendrical significance of the crossing of the Jordan, its possible ceremonial aspects, the contemporary fulfillment of Joshua's curse, the geographical aspect of the Israelites' conquests, and the halakhic implications of the peace treaty with the Gibeonites.

These expansions highlight the particular interests of some of the RJ scrolls: the sanctity of the Promised Land, the proper observance of the Law, and the fulfillment of the divine oracles. Moreover, some of these exegetical amplifications suggest Levitical/priestly concerns. In fact, these concerns seem to be reflected in the majority of the RJ scrolls.[621] Thus, the extant fragments of 4Q123 rework the list of the Levitical cities from Josh 21. Several passages in 4Q379 highlight the elevated status of Levi and Aaron and his sons (frgs. 1 2-4, 17 3-4). The expansion clarifying the starting point of the jubilean count in 4Q379 12 4-6 suggests an interest in Levitical matters. 4Q522's concern with selecting an appropriate location for the Tent of Meeting and the justification offered for setting it in Shiloh, rather than in Jerusalem, may reflect a Levitical/priestly milieu. A similar conclusion can be drawn from its apparent application of Deut 33:12 to Zadok and his priestly line (frg. 9 ii 8-9).

In the past, several scholars suggested that some of the RJ scrolls were composed by the Qumran sectarians (Milik [4Q378-379]; Talmon [4Q378-379; Mas 1039-211]; Puech [4Q522]; Tov [4Q378-379; 4Q522; Mas 1039-211]). Yet, given the absence of the sectarian nomenclature and worldview from these texts, such a classification seems to be unwarranted (Newsom [4Q378-379]; Eshel [4Q378-379; 4Q522]). There also seems to be no basis for placing the RJ scrolls within an intermediary category posited by Dimant, as neither 4Q379's use of the *pesher*-type interpretation (its presumed use of solar calendar lacks textual support) nor 4Q522's emphasis on the ascendancy of the priestly leadership over the political, necessitates such a classification.[622] At the most, one can argue for a Levitical/priestly

---

620 Jacobson, "Interpretation", p. 181.
621 As observed by Newsom, "Psalms of Joshua", p. 59-60 (with reference to 4Q378 and 4Q379); Tov, "Rewritten Joshua", p. 256 (with reference to 4Q522 9 ii).
622 It remains to be seen whether the creation of such an intermediate category is justified. See its critique in F. García Martínez, "Aramaica Qumranica Apocalyptica", in K. Berthelot & D. Stökl

milieu of the majority of the RJ scrolls. Given the fact that two of them seem also to reflect a critique of the contemporary Hasmonean ruler(s) (4Q379 22 ii 7-15; 4Q522 9 ii 9-12), it is possible that at least these two works (paleographically dated to Hasmonean times) originated within those Levitical/priestly circles that became dissatisfied with the Hasmoneans.

If some of the RJ scrolls were indeed composed in the Hasmonean period, this would help explain, at least partially, the presence of five works rewriting the Book of Joshua among the Dead Sea scrolls. Although both Josephus and, to a lesser extent, *LAB* rework large segments of the Book of Joshua, they are doing so as a part of a larger literary enterprise. In contrast, the RJ scrolls appear to focus on Joshua.[623] Perhaps, the parallels between the events narrated in the Book of Joshua and the events of the Hasmonean rule prompted the rewriting of the Book of Joshua.

9.3 Topics for Further Study

This analysis suggests several topics for future study. As the scholarly conversation on the adequacy of the term "Rewritten Bible", as well as the criteria for determining which works belong to it, continues, it may become possible to define more precisely the relationship between the RJ scrolls and other compositions reflecting similar exegetical techniques. One of the problems that the scholarship on the Rewritten Bible encounters is the great diversity of the texts that have been placed within this category by various scholars. Two of the RJ scrolls present examples of such diversity. In addition to the usual array of the Rewritten Bible techniques, such as paraphrase, expansion, and omission, the scroll 4Q379 includes an actualizing, *pesher*-type, interpretation (22 ii 7-15),[624] while the scroll 4Q522 cites Psalm 122 in its entirety.[625]

Another important topic in the current scholarly debate is the issue of the authority enjoyed by certain Second Temple writings. 4QTestimonia's quotation

---

Ben Ezra (eds.), *Aramaica Qumranica* (STDJ 94; Leiden: Brill, 2010), p. 442; idem, "The Groningen Hypothesis Revisited", in A.D. Roitman et al. (eds.), *The Dead Sea Scrolls and Contemporary Culture* (STDJ 93; Leiden, Boston: Brill, 2011), pp. 27-28.

623 Still, the passages paraphrasing Deut 34 (4Q378) and Judg 1 (4Q522) indicate that some of the RJ scrolls are also interested in the events that immediately precede or follow the Book of Joshua.

624 The use of actualizing interpretation along with Rewritten Bible techniques is not unique to 4Q379. One example is 4Q252, where the rewritten Flood story and the Abrahamic cycle are followed by the *pesher* interpretation of Jacob's blessings. Another text, 4Q464, employs the construction פשר על in a work that appears to be a rewriting of the patriarchal stories.

625 García Martínez, "The Book of Joshua", pp. 107-108; idem, "Lights", pp. 155-156.

from the composition preserved in 4Q379, placed alongside the quotations from Exodus, Numbers, and Deuteronomy, suggests that this text was viewed as having a degree of authority. As scholars develop more nuanced terminology and criteria for defining textual authority in Second Temple times, it may become possible to describe this composition's status with more precision.

Finally, some of the RJ's exegetical traditions that find no parallel in other contemporary texts on Joshua surface in the Samaritan Joshua lore. These include typologically similar expansions of the biblical account (e.g., the extensive verbal exchange between Joshua and the people as he assumes leadership over Israel and the liturgy accompanying the crossing of the Jordan) and halakhic views (the beginning of the jubilean count in the year of the crossing). Further study of the Samaritan traditions pertaining to Joshua is needed in order to ascertain whether these similarities point to their antiquity or represent similar developments within the Samaritan exegetical lore.[626]

---

[626] Nodet, *Search*, p. 200, suggests in passing that Psalms of Joshua may have "some connection with a Samaritan tradition".

Bibliography

Aharoni, Y. *The Land of the Bible: A Historical Geography*. Philadelphia: The Westminster Press, 1979².

Ahituv, S. *Canaanite Toponyms in Ancient Egyptian Documents*. Jerusalem: Magnes Press, 1984.

—, *Joshua: Introduction and Commentary*. A Bible Commentary for Israel. Tel Aviv: Am Oved Publishers, Jerusalem: The Magnes Press, 1995.

Alexander, P.S. "Notes on the Imago Mundi in the Book of Jubilees", *JJS* 33 (1982), pp. 197-213.

—, "Jerusalem as the Omphalos of the World: On the History of a Geographical Concept". In L.I. Levine, ed. *Jerusalem: Its Sanctity and Centrality to Judaism, Christianity, and Islam*. New York: Continuum, 1999, pp. 104-119.

Allegro, M. "Further Messianic References in Qumran Literature", *JBL* 75 (1956), pp. 174-187.

Anderson, G.A. "Intentional and Unintentional Sin in the Dead Sea Scrolls". In D.P. Wright et al., eds. *Pomegranates and Golden Bells*. Winona Lake, Ind.: Eisenbrauns, 1995, pp. 49-64.

Assis, E. "Divine versus Human Leadership: An Examination of Joshua's Succession". In M. Poorthuis & J. Schwartz, eds. *Saints and Role Models in Judaism and Christianity*. Jewish and Chrsitian Perspectives Series 7. Leiden, Boston: Brill, 2004, pp. 26-42.

Auld, A.G. *Joshua: Jesus Son of Nauē in Codex Vaticanus*. Septuagint Commentary Series. Leiden, Boston: Brill, 2005.

Avi-Yonah, M. "Ashkelon". *Encyclopaedia Judaica*. Detroit: Macmillan, 2007², vol. 2, p. 568.

Bar-Asher, M. "Two Phenomena in Qumran Hebrew. Synchronic and Diachronic Aspects", *Meghillot* 1 (2003), pp. 167-183 (Hebrew).

Bar-Kochva, B. *Judas Maccabeus: The Jewish Struggle against the Seleucids*. Cambridge: Cambridge University Press, 1989.

Barr, J. "Migraš in the Old Testament", *JSS* 29 (1984), pp. 15-31.

Bartlett, J.R. *Jews in the Hellenistic World: Josephus, Aristeas, the Sibylline Oracles, Eupolemus*. Cambridge: Cambridge University Press, 1985.

Baumgarten, J.M. "The Exclusion of Nethinim and Proselytes in 4QFlorilegium". In idem, *Studies in Qumran Law*. Leiden: Brill, 1977, pp. 75-87.

—, "Exclusions from the Temple: Proselytes and Agrippa I", *JJS* 33 (1982), pp. 215-225.

—, "The Qumran-Essene Restraints on Marriage". In L.H. Schiffman, ed. *Archaeology and History in the Dead Sea Scrolls*. Sheffield: Sheffield Academic Press, 1990, pp. 13-24.

— & Schwartz, D.R. "Damascus Document". In J.H. Charlesworth et al., eds. *The Dead Sea Scrolls: Hebrew, Aramaic, and Greek Texts with English Translations: Damascus Document, War Scroll, and Related Documents*. PTSDSSP. Tübingen: Mohr (Siebeck), Louisville: Westminster John Knox, 1995, pp. 4-57.

—, "Damascus Document", *EDSS*, vol. 1, pp. 166-170.

Beentjes, P.C. "Prophets and Prophecy in the Book of Ben Sira". In M.H. Floyd & R.D. Haak, eds. *Prophets, Prophecy, and Prophetic Texts in Second Temple Judaism*. New York: T&T Clark, 2006, pp. 135-150.

Begg, C.T. "Israel's Treaty with Gibeon according to Josephus", *OLP* 28 (1997), pp. 123-145.

—, "The Transjordanian Altar (Josh 22:10-34) according to Josephus (*Ant.* 5.100-114) and Pseudo-Philo (*LAB* 22.1-8)", *AUSS* 35 (1997), pp. 5-12.

—, "The Ceremonies at Gilgal/Ebal according to Pseudo-Philo", *ETL* 73 (1997), pp. 72-83.

—, "David's Capture of Jebus and its Sequels according to Josephus", *ETL* 74 (1998), pp. 93-108.

—, "The Ai-Achan Story (Joshua 7-8) according to Josephus", *Jian Dao* 16 (2001), pp. 1-20.

—, "The Fall of Jericho according to Josephus", *Estudios Bíblicos* 63 (2005), pp. 323-340.

—, "The Rahab Story in Josephus", *Liber Annuus* 55 (2005), pp. 113-130.

—, *Flavius Josephus: Judean Antiquities 5–7*. Flavius Josephus: Translation and Commentary 4. Leiden: Brill, 2005.

—, "The Crossing of the Jordan according to Josephus", *Acta Theologica* 26 (2006), pp. 1-16.

—, "The Demise of Joshua according to Josephus", *HTS* 63 (2007), pp. 129-145.

—, "Joshua's Southern and Northern Campaigns according to Josephus", *BZ* 51 (2007), pp. 84-97.

Ben-Dov, J. "Jubilean Chronology and the 364-Day Year", *Meghillot* 5-6 (2007), pp. 49-60 (Hebrew).

Ben-Dov, M. "נפה—A Geographical Term of Possible 'Sea People' Origin", *Tel-Aviv* 3 (1976), pp. 70-73.

Ben-Hayyim, Z. "The Samaritan Tradition and Its Relation to the Language of the Dead Sea Scrolls and to the Rabbinic Hebrew", *Leshonenu* 22 (1958), pp. 223-245 (Hebrew).

Benoit, P. et al., "Le travail d'édition des fragments manuscripts de Qumrân", *RB* 63 (1956), pp. 49-67. 65(="Editing the Manuscript Fragments from Qumran", *BA* 19 [1956], pp. 75-96).

Berthelot, K. "La notion de גר dans les textes de Qumrân", *RevQ* 19 (1999), pp. 171-216.

—, "Philo of Alexandria and the Conquest of Canaan", *JSJ* 38 (2007), pp. 39-56.

—, "The Biblical Conquest of the Promised Land and the Hasmonaean Wars according to 1 and 2 Maccabees". In G. Xeravits & J. Zsengellér (eds.), *The Books of the Maccabees: History, Theology, Ideology*. JSJS 118. Leiden: Brill, 2007, pp. 45-60.

—, "4QTestimonia as a Polemic against the Prophetic Claims of John Hyrcanus". In K. De Troyer & A. Lange, eds., *Prophecy after the Prophets?* Leuven-Paris-Walpole, MA: Peeters, 2009, pp. 99-116.

—, "The Canaanites Who 'Trusted in God': An Original Interpretation of the Fate of the Canaanites in Rabbinic Literature", *JJS* 62 (2011), pp. 233-261.

Betz, O. "Donnersöhne, Menschenfischer und der Davidische Messias", *RevQ* 3 (1961-62), pp. 41-70.

Bickerman, E. "The Warning Inscriptions of Herod's Temple", *JQR* 37 (1946-47), pp. 387-45.

Blidstein, G. "4Q Florilegium and Rabbinic Sources on Bastard and Proselyte", *RevQ* 8 (1974), pp. 431-435.

Bloch, R. "Juda engendra Pharès et Zara, de Thamar". In *Mélanges bibliques, rédigés en l'honneur de André Robert*. Travaux de l'institut catholique de Paris 4. Paris: Bloud & Gay, 1957, pp. 381-389.

Bóid, I.R.M.M. "The Transmission of the Samaritan Joshua-Judges", *Dutch Studies* 6 (2004), pp. 1-30.

Borowski, O. *Agriculture in Iron Age Israel*. Winona Lake, Indiana: Eisenbrauns, 1987.

Brawer, A.Y. "The Sharon on the Coast", *BJES* 7 (1940), pp. 34-38 (Hebrew).

Brewer, D.I. "Nomological Exegesis in Qumran 'Divorce' Texts", *RevQ* 18 (1998), pp. 568-569.

Brin, G. "The Bible as Reflected in the Temple Scroll", *Shnaton* 4 (1979-80), pp. 182-225 (Hebrew).

Brooke, G.J. *Exegesis at Qumran: 4QFlorilegium in its Jewish Context*. JSOTSS 29. Sheffield: JSOT Press, 1985.

—, "Psalms 105 and 106 at Qumran", *RevQ* 14 (1989), pp. 285-290.

—, "Testimonia", *ABD*, vol. 6, pp. 391-392.

—, "Levi and the Levites in the Dead Sea Scrolls and the New Testament". In Z.J. Kapera, ed. *Papers on the Dead Sea Scrolls Offered in Memory of Jean Carmignac*. Kraków: Enigma, 1993, pp. 105-129.

—, "Some Remarks on 4Q252 and the Text of Genesis", *Textus* 19 (1998), pp. 1-25.

—, "Deuteronomy 5-6 in the Phylacteries from Qumran Cave 4". In S.M. Paul et al., eds. *Emanuel.* VTSup 94. Leiden: Brill, 2003, pp. 59-68.

—, "'Canon' in the Light of the Qumran Scrolls". In P.S. Alexander & J.-D. Kaestli, eds. *The Canon of Scripture in Jewish and Christian Tradition.* Belfort: Éditions du Zèbre, 2007, pp. 81-98.

—, "Pesher and Midrash in Qumran Literature: Issues for Lexicography", *RevQ* 24 (2009), pp. 81-87.

—, "Some Remarks on the Reconstruction of 4QJudges[b]". In D. Minutoli & R. Pintaudi, eds. *Papyri Grecae Schøyen: Essays and Texts in Honour of Martin Schøyen.* Papyrologica Florentina XL. Firenze: Edizioni Gonneli, 2010, pp. 107-115.

—, "Testimonia (4Q175)", *EDEJ*, pp. 1297-1298.

—, "Aspects of the Physical and Scribal Features of Some Cave 4 "Contunuous" Pesharim". In S. Metso et al., eds. *The Dead Sea Scrolls: Transmission of Traditions and Production of Texts.* STDJ 92. Leiden, Boston: Brill, 2010, pp. 134-150.

Broshi, M. & Yardeni, A. "On Netinim and False Prophets". In Z. Zevit, ed. *Solving Riddles and Untying Knots.* Winona Lake, Indiana: Eisenbrauns, 1995, pp. 32-33.

Brown, R.E. et al. *Preliminary Concordance to the Hebrew and Aramaic Fragments from Qumran II-X.* Published privately, Göttingen, 1988.

Burgman, H. *Der Sitz im Leben in den Joshuafluch-texten in 4Q379 22ii und 4QTestimonia.* Qumranica Mogilanensia 1. Kraków: "Secesja" Press, 1990.

Campbell, J.G. *The Exegetical Texts.* Companion to the Qumran Scrolls. London, New York: T&T Clark International, 2004.

Carmignac, J. et al., eds. *Les Textes de Qumran.* Paris: Éditions Letouzey et Ané: 1963, 2 vols.

Chapman, S.B. "Joshua son of Nun: Presentation of a Prophet". In J.J. Ahn & S.L. Cook, eds. *Thus Says the Lord: Essays on the Former and Latter Prophets in Honor of Robert R. Wilson.* New York: T & T Clark, 2009, pp. 13-26.

Charlesworth, J. "XJoshua". In J. Charlesworth et al., eds. *Miscellaneous Texts from the Judaean Desert.* DJD 38. Oxford: Clarendon Press, 2000, pp. 231-239.

Chesnutt, R.D. "Solomon, Wisdom of", *EDEJ*, pp. 1242-44,

Chester, A. "Citing the Old Testament". In D.A. Carson et al., eds. *It is Written: Scripture Citing Scripture.* Cambridge: Cambridge University Press, 1988, pp. 141-169.

Cohen, G.M. *The Hellenistic Settlements in Syria, the Red Sea Basin, and North Africa.* Berkeley: University of California Press, 2006.

Cohen, S. *The Beginning of Jewishness: Boundaries, Varieties, Uncertainties.*
Berkeley: University of California Press, 1999.

Collins, J.J. "Canon, Canonization", *EDEJ*, pp. 460-463.

Colson, F.H. & Whitaker, G.H. *Philo.* LCL. Cambridge: Harvard University Press,
1966, vols. 1-10.

Corley, J. "Joshua as a Warrior in Hebrew Ben Sira", *Deuterocanonical and Cognate Literature Yearbook* (2010), pp. 207-248.

—, "Canonical Assimilation in Ben Sira's Portrayal of Joshua and Samuel". In J.
Corley & H. van Grol, eds. *Rewriting Biblical History.* Berlin: de Gruyter, 2011,
pp. 57-77.

Cross, F.M. "The Evolution of a Theory of Local Texts". In F.M. Cross & Sh. Talmon,
eds. *Qumran and the History of the Biblical Text.* Cambridge, MA: Harvard
University Press, 1975, pp. 306-320.

—, *The Ancient Library of Qumran.* Sheffield: Sheffield Academic Press, 1994[3].

—, "Testimonia". In J.H. Charlesworth et al., eds. *Pesharim, Other Commentaries, and Related Documents.* The Dead Sea Scrolls: Hebrew, Aramaic, and
Greek Texts with English Translations 6B. Tübingen: Mohr Siebeck, Louisville:
Westminster John Knox Press, 2002, pp. 308-327.

Crown, A.D. "The Date and Authority of the Samaritan Hebrew Book of Joshua as
Seen in Its Territorial Allotments", *PEQ* 96 (1964), pp. 79-100.

—, "Was There a Samaritan Book of Joshua?" In T.W. Hillard et al., eds. *Ancient
History in a Modern University.* Grand Rapids, Michigan, Cambridge, UK:
Eerdmans, 1998, pp. 15-22.

Curtis, A.H.W. *Joshua.* Old Testament Guides. Sheffield: Sheffield Academic Press,
1998.

Davies, P.R. *Behind the Essenes.* Brown Judaic Studies 94. Atlanta: Scholars Press,
1987.

Davies, P.R., Brooke, G.J., and Callaway, P.R., *The Complete World of the Dead
Sea Scrolls.* London: Thames and Hudson, 2002.

Day, J. "Gibeon and the Gibeonites in the Old Testament". In R. Rezetko et al.,
eds. *Reflection and Refraction.* Leiden: Brill, 2007, pp. 113-138.

Dihi, H. "The Morphological and Lexical Innovations in the Book of Ben Sira".
PhD diss., Ben-Gurion University of the Negev, Beer-Sheva 2004.

Dimant, D. "Between Sectarian and Non-Sectarian: The Case of the Apocryphon
of Joshua". In idem et al., eds. *Reworking the Bible: Apocryphal and Related
Texts at Qumran.* STDJ 58. Leiden: Brill, 2005, pp. 105-134.

—, *Qumran Cave 4 XXI: Parabiblical Texts, Part 4: Pseudo-Prophetic Texts.* DJD
30. Oxford: Clarendon Press, 2001.

—, "The Apocryphon of Joshua—4Q522 9 ii: A Reappraisal". In S.M. Paul et al.,
eds. *Emanuel.* SVT 94. Leiden: Brill, 2003, pp. 179-204.

—, "Two Discourses from the Apocryphon of Joshua and Their Context (4Q378 3 i-ii)", *RevQ* 23 (2007), pp. 43-61.

—, "Criteria for the Identification of Qumran Sectarian Texts". In M. Kister, ed. *The Qumran Scrolls and Their World*. Jerusalem: Yad Ben-Zvi, 2009, vol. 1, pp. 49-86 (Hebrew).

—, "Exegesis and Time in the Pesharim from Qumran", *REJ* 168 (2009), pp. 373-393.

—, "Sectarian and Non-Sectarian Texts from Qumran: The Pertinence and Usage of a Taxonomy", *RevQ* 24 (2009), pp. 7-18.

—, *Connected Vessels: The Dead Sea Scrolls and the Literature of the Second Temple Period*. Asuppot 3. Jerusalem: The Bialik Institute, 2010 (Hebrew).

—, "Pseudo-Ezekiel and the Apocryphon of Jeremiah C in Perspective", *RevQ* 25 (2011), pp. 17-39.

Downing, F.G. "Redaction Criticism: Josephus' Antiquities and the Synoptic Gospels", *JSNT* 8 (1980), pp. 46-65.

Duncan, A. "Deuteronomy, Book of", *EDSS*, vol. 1, pp. 198-202.

Dupont-Sommer, A. *The Essene Writings from Qumran*. Trans. G. Vermes. Oxford: Blackwell, 1961.

Dussaud, R. *Topographie historique de la Syrie antique et medieval*. Bibliothèque Archéologique et historique. Paris: Librarie orientaliste Paul Geuthner, 1927.

Ebeling, E. & Messier, B. *Reallexicon der Assyriologie*. Berlin: Walter de Gruyter, 1978, 2 vols.

Edgerton, W.F. & Wilson, J.A. *Historical Records of Ramses III: The Texts in Medinet Habu: Volumes 1 and II*. Chicago: University of Chicago, 1936.

Eisenman, R.H. & Wise, M. *The Dead Sea Scrolls Uncovered*. Shaftesbury, Dorset, Rockport, Massachusetts: Element, 1992.

Elitzur, Y. *Ancient Place Names in the Holy Land: Preservation and History*. Jerusalem: The Magnes Press: 2004.

Elssner, T.R. *Josue und seine Kriege in jüdischer und christlicher Rezeptionsgeschichte*. Stuttgart: Kohlhammer, 2008.

Eshel, E. "4QDeut^n—A Text That Has Undergone Harmonistic Edition", *HUCA* 62 (1991), pp. 117-154.

—, "Jubilees 32 and the Bethel Cult Traditions in Second Temple Literature". In E.G. Chazon et al., eds. *Things Revealed*. Leiden: Brill, 2004, pp. 21-36.

—, "The Imago Mundi of the Genesis Apocryphon". In L. LiDonnici & A. Lieber, eds. *Heavenly Tablets: Interpretation, Identity and Tradition in Ancient Judaism*. Leiden: Brill, 2007, pp. 111-131.

Eshel, H. "The Historical Background of the Pesher Interpreting Joshua's Curse on the Rebuilder of Jericho", *RevQ* 15 (1991-92), pp. 409-420.

—, *The Dead Sea Scrolls and the Hasmonean State*. Grand Rapids, Michigan: Eerdmans, Jerusalem: Yad Ben-Zvi, 2008.

Evans, C. "Joshua, Apocryphon of", *EDEJ*, p. 841.

Feldman, A. "The Sinai Revelation according to 4Q377 (Apocryphal Pentateuch B)", *DSD* 18 (2011), pp. 155-172.

—, "Reading Exodus with Deuteronomy in 4QApocryphal Pentateuch A (4Q368 2)", *JAJ* 3 (2012), pp. 329-338.

—, "Moses' Farewell Address according to 1QWords of Moses", *JSP* (forthcoming).

Feldman, L.H. "Josephus' Portrait of Joshua", *HTR* 82 (1989), pp. 351-376.

—, *Josephus's Interpretation* of the Bible. Hellenistic Culture and Society 27. Berkeley: University of California Press, 1998.

—, "Philo's Interpretation of Joshua", *JSP* 12 (2001), pp. 165-178.

—, *"Remember Amalek!"* MHUC 31. Hebrew Union College, 2004.

—, "The Portrayal of Sihon and Og in Philo, Pseudo-Philo, and Josephus", *JJS* 53 (2002), pp. 264-272.

—, "The Command, According to Philo, Pseudo-Phio, and Josephus, to Annihilate the Seven Nations of Canaan", *AUSS* 41 (2003), pp. 13-29.

—, "The Rehabilitation of Non-Jewish Leaders in Josephus' Antiquities", in idem, *Judaism and Hellenism Reconsidered*. SJSJ 107. Leiden: Brill, 2006, pp. 579-606.

Fields, W.W. *The Dead Sea Scrolls: A Full History*. Leiden: Brill, 2009.

Fishbane, M. *Biblical Interpretation in Ancient Israel*. Oxford: Clarendon Press, 1985.

Fisk, B.N. *Do You Not Remember? Scripture, Story and Exegesis in the Rewritten Bible of Pseudo-Philo*. JSPSS 37. Sheffield: Sheffield Academic Press, 2001.

Flint, P.W. "The Prophet David at Qumran". In M. Henze, ed. *Biblical Interpretation at Qumran*. Grand Rapids: Eerdmans, 2005, pp. 158-167.

Florentin, M. *The Tulida: A Samaritan Chronicle*. Jerusalem: Yad Izhak ben Zvi, 1999.

Franke, J.R., ed. *Ancient Christian Commentary on Scripture: Old Testament IV: Joshua, Judges, Ruth, 1-2 Samuel*. Downers Grove, Illinois: InterVarsity Press, 2005.

Fuks, G. "Antagonistic Neighbours: Ashkelon, Judaea, and the Jews", *JJS* 51 (2000), pp. 42-62.

—, "The Jews of Hellenistic and Roman Scythopolis", *JJS* 33 (1982), pp. 407-416.

García Martínez, F. & Tigchelaar, E. *The Dead Sea Scrolls: Study Edition*. Leiden: Brill, 1997-98, 2 vols.

García Martínez, F. "The Dead Sea Scrolls and the Book of Joshua". In N. Dávid & A. Lange, eds. *Qumran and the Bible: Studying the Jewish and Christian*

Scriptures in Light of the Dead Sea Scrolls. Leuven, Paris, Walpole, MA: Peeters, 2010, pp. 97-109.

—, "Aramaica Qumranica Apocalyptica". In K. Berthelot & D. Stökl Ben Ezra, eds. *Aramaica Qumranica*. STDJ 94. Leiden: Brill, 2010, pp. 435-449.

—, "The Groningen Hypothesis Revisited". In A.D. Roitman et al. eds. *The Dead Sea Scrolls and Contemporary Culture*. STDJ 93. Leiden, Boston: Brill, 2011, pp. 17-29.

—, "Light on the Joshua Books from the Dead Sea Scrolls". In H. Ausloos et al., eds. *After Qumran: Old and Modern Editions of the Biblical Texts—The Historical Books*. BETL. Leuven-Paris-Walpole, Peeters, 2012, pp. 145-159.

Gaster, M. "Das Buch Josua in hebräisch-samaritanischer Rezension. Entdeckt und zum ersten Male hereausgegeben", *ZDMG* 62 (1908), pp. 209-279, 494-549.

Gilat, Y. "A Comment to 'The Acceptance of Sacrifices from Gentiles'", *Tarbiẕ* 49 (1980), pp. 422-423 (Hebrew).

Ginzberg, L. *An Unknown Jewish Sect*. New York: Jewish Theological Seminary, 1976.

Ginzberg, L. *Legends of the Jews*. Philadelphia: The Jewish Publication Society, 2003, 2 vols.

Goldman, L. "The Rules Regarding Fighting a Permitted War in 4Q376", *Meghillot* 8-9 (2010), pp. 319-342 (Hebrew).

Goldstein, J.A. *1 Maccabees*. AB. Garden City, N.Y.: Doubleday, 1974.

—, *2 Maccabees*. AB. Garden City, N.Y.: Doubleday, 1983.

Goshen-Gottstein, A. "Ben Sira's Praise of the Fathers: A Canon-Conscious Reading". In R. Egger-Wenzel, ed. *Ben Sira's God*. Berlin: de Gruyter, 2002, pp. 235-267.

Greenspoon, L. "The Qumran Fragments of Joshua: Which Puzzle are They Part of and Where Do They Fit?" In G.J. Brooke & B. Lindars, eds. *Septuagint, Scrolls and Cognate Writings*. Atlanta: Scholars Press, 1992, pp. 159-194.

Gruen, E.S. *Heritage and Hellenism*. Berkeley: University of California Press, 1988.

Halpern-Amaru, B. "Judith, Book of", *EDEJ*, pp. 855-857.

Haran, M. "The Gibeonites, the Nethinim and the Sons of Solomon's Servants", *VT* 11 (1961), pp. 159-69.

Harrington, H. "Keeping Outsiders Out: Impurity at Qumran". In F. García Martínez & M. Popović, eds. *Defining Identities: We, You, and the Other in the Dead Sea Scrolls*. STDJ 70. Leiden: Brill, 2008, pp. 187-203.

—, "How Does Intermarriage Defile the Sanctuary". In G.J. Brooke et al., eds. *The Scrolls and Biblical Traditions*. STDJ 103. Leiden: Brill, 2012, pp. 177-195.

Hayes, C.E. "Intermarriage and Impurity in Ancient Jewish Sources", *HTR* 92 (1999), pp. 3-36.

—, *Gentile Impurities and Jewish Identities: Intermarriage and Conversion from the Bible to the Talmud*. New York: Oxord University Press, 2002.

Heller, B. & Rippin, A. "Yusha'". In P.J. Bearman et al., eds. *The Encyclopedia of Islam*. Leiden: Brill, 2002, vol. 11, p. 351.

Hieke, T. "The Role of the 'Scripture' in the Last Words of Mattathias (1 Macc 2:49-70)". In G. Xeravits & J. Zsengellér, eds. *The Books of the Maccabees: History, Theology, Ideology*. JSJS 118. Leiden: Brill, 2007, pp. 61-74.

Hjelm, I. "What Do Samaritans and Jews Have in Common? Recent Trends in Samaritan Studies", *Currents in Biblical Research* 3 (2004), pp. 42-44.

Hofmann, N.J. *Die Assumptio Mosis: Studien zur Rezeption massgültiger Überlieferung*. SJSJ 67. Leiden, Boston, Köln: Brill, 2000.

Hogan, K.M. "Ezra, Fourth Book of", *EDEJ*, pp. 621-623.

Holladay, C.B. *Fragments from Hellenistic Jewish Authors: Volume 1: Historians*. SBL Texts and Translations 20. Pseudepigrapha 10. Chico, California: Scholars Press, 1983.

Hooker, P.K. "The Location of the Brook of Egypt". In M.P. Graham et al., eds. *History and Interpretation*. JSOTSS 173. Sheffield: JSOT Press, 1993, pp. 203-214.

Horbury, W. "Monarchy and Messianism in the Greek Pentateuch". In M.A. Knibb, ed. *The Septuagint and Messianism*. BETL 195. Leuven, 2006, pp. 79-128.

Howard, D.M. "All Israel's Response to Joshua: A Note on the Narrative Framework of Joshua 1". In A.B. Beck et al., eds. *Fortunate the Eyes that See*. Grand Rapids, Michigan, Cambridge, U.K.: Eerdmans, 1995, pp. 81-91.

Hultgren, S. *From the Damascus Covenant to the Covenant of the Community*. STDJ 66. Leiden: Brill, 2007.

Hurvitz, A. "Continuity and Innovation in Biblical Hebrew—the Case of "Semantic Change" in Post-Exilic Writings". In T. Muraoka, ed. *Studies in Ancient Hebrew Semantics*. Louvain: Peeters Press, 1995, pp. 1-10.

—, "The Linguistic Status of Ben Sira as a Link between the Biblical and the Mishnaic Hebrew: Lexicographical Aspects". In T. Muraoka & J.F. Elwolde, *The Hebrew of the Dead Sea Scrolls and Ben Sira*. STDJ 26. Leiden: Brill, 1997, pp. 78-85.

Ishay, R. "Qumran Literature Related to the Eschatological War; Manuscripts 4Q491-496: Editions, Commentaries, and Comparisons with the War Scroll (1QM)". Ph.D. diss., University of Haifa 2006.

Jacobson, H. *A Commentary on Pseudo-Philo's Liber Antiquitatum Biblicarum*. AGJU 31. Leiden: Brill, 1996.

—, "Biblical Interpretation in Pseudo-Philo's Liber Antiquitatum Biblicarum". In M. Henze, ed. *A Companion to Biblical Interpretation in Early Judaism*. Grand Rapids, MI, Cambridge, UK: Eerdmans, 2012, pp. 180-199.

Jassen, A.P. *Mediating the Divine: Prophecy and Revelation in the Dead Sea Scrolls and Second Temple Literature.* STDJ 68. Leiden: Brill, 2007.

Jastram, N. "A Comparison of Two "Proto-Samaritan" Texts from Qumran: 4QpaleoExod^m and 4QNum^b", *DSD* 5 (1998), pp. 264-289.

Jastrow, M. *Dictionary of the Targumim, the Talmud Bavli and Yerushalmi, and the Midrashic Literature.* New York: Judaica Press, 1982.

Juynboll, T.W.J. *Chronicon Samaritanum, Arabice Conscriptum, cui titulus est Liber Josuae.* Lugduni Batavorum: S&J. Luchtmans, 1848.

Kugel, J. "Levi's Elevation to the Priesthood in Second Temple Writings", *HTR* 86 (1993), pp. 1-64.

—, "David the Prophet". In idem, ed. *Poetry and Prophecy: The Beginnings of a Literary Tradition.* Ithaca, NY: Cornell University Press, 1990, pp. 45-55.

—, "Biblical Interpretation at Qumran". In M. Kister, ed. *The Qumran Scrolls and Their World.* Between Bible and Mishnah. Jerusalem: Yad Ben Zvi Press, 2009, pp. 387–408 (Hebrew).

Kallai, Z. "Biblical Geography in Josephus", *Eretz Israel* 8 (1967), pp. 269-272 (Hebrew).

—, "The Boundaries of Canaan and the Land of Israel in the Bible", *Eretz Israel* 12 (1975), pp. 27-34 (Hebrew).

—, *Historical Geography of the Bible: The Tribal Territories of Israel.* Jerusalem-Leiden: The Magnes Press, 1986.

Kartveit, M. *The Origins of the Samaritans.* Leiden, Boston: Brill, 2009.

Kasher, A. *Jews and Hellenistic Cities in Eretz Israel.* TSAJ 21. Tübingen: J.C.B. Mohr Paul Siebeck, 1990.

Kempinsky, A. "'When History Sleeps, Theology Arises': A Note on Joshua 8:30-35 and the Archaeology of the 'Settlement Period'", *Eretz Israel* 24 (1993), pp. 175-183 (Hebrew).

Kister, M. & Qimron, E. "Observations on 4QSecond Ezekiel (4Q385 2-3)", *RevQ* 15 (1992), pp. 595-602.

—, "5Q13 and the "*Avodah*": A Historical Survey and its Significance", *DSD* 8 (2001), pp. 136-148.

—, "Some Further Thoughts on Identifying Sectarian Writings at Qumran". In idem, ed. *The Qumran Scrolls and Their World.* Jerusalem: Yad Ben-Zvi, 2009, vol. 1, pp. 87-90.

Klawans, J. "Notions of Gentile Impurity in Ancient Judaism", *AJSReview* 20 (1995), pp. 285-312

Knohl, I. "The Acceptance of Sacrifices from Gentiles", *Tarbiz* 48 (1979), pp. 341-347 (Hebrew).

Koskenniemi, V. *The Old Testament Miracle-Workers in Early Judaism.* WUNT 2. Reihe, 206. Tübingen: Mohr Siebeck, 2005.

Kotter, W.R. "Timnah", *ABD*, vol. 6, pp. 556-557.

Kratz, R.G. "Friend of God, Brother of Sarah, and Father of Isaac: Abraham in the Hebrew Bible and in Qumran". In D. Dimant & R.G. Kratz, eds. *The Dynamics of Language and Exegesis at Qumran*. Tübingen: Mohr Siebeck, 2009, pp. 79-105.

—, "'Blessed be the Lord and Blessed Be His Name Forever': Psalm 145 in the Hebrew Bible and in the Psalms Scroll 11Q5". In J. Penner et al., eds. *Prayer and Poetry in the Dead Sea Scrolls and Related Literature*. Leiden: Brill, 2012, pp. 229-244.

Kutscher, E.Y. *The Language and Linguistic Background of The Isaiah Scroll (1QIsa ᵃ)*. Leiden: Brill, 1974.

Lange, A. & Mittmann-Richert, U. "Annotated List of the Texts from the Judaean Desert Classified". In E. Tov, ed. *The Texts from the Judaean Desert: Indices and an Introduction to the Discoveries in the Judaean Desert Series*. DJD 39. Oxford: Clarendon Press, 2002, pp. 115-164.

Lange, A. *Handbuch der Textfunde vom Toten Meer: band 1: Die Handschriften biblischer Bücher von Qumran und den anderen Fundorten*. Tübingen: Mohr Siebeck, 2009.

—, "From Paratexts to Commentary". In A.D. Roitman et al., eds. *The Dead Sea Scrolls and Contemporary Culture*. STDJ 93. Leiden, Boston: Brill, 2011, pp. 195-216.

Lange, A. & Weigold, M. *Biblical Quotations and Allusions in Second Temple Jewish Literature*. Göttingen: Vandenhoeck & Ruprecht, 2011.

Lebhar Hall, S. *Conquering Character: The Characterization of Joshua in Joshua 1-11*. New York, London: T&T Clark, 2010.

Levine, B.A. "The Netinim", *JBL* 82 (1963), pp. 207-212.

—, "Later Sources on the Nethinîm". In H.A Hoffner, ed. *Orient and Occident*. Neukirchen-Vluyn: Neukirchener Verlag, 1973, pp. 101-107.

Levison, J.R. "Prophetic Inspiration in Pseudo-Philo's 'Liber Antiquitatum Biblicarum'", *JQR* 85 (1995), pp. 297-329.

Lim, T.H. "The 'Psalms of Joshua' (4Q379 22 ii): A Reconsideration of Its Text", *JJS* 44 (1993), pp. 309-312.

Lipínski, E. *Itineraria Phoenicia*. Orientalia Lovaniensia Analecta. Leuven: Peters, 2004.

Livneh, A. "The Composition Pseudo-Jubilees from Qumran (4Q225; 4Q226; 4Q227): A New Edition, Introduction, and Commentary". Ph.D. diss., University of Haifa, 2010 (Hebrew).

Lübbe, J. "A Reinterpretation of 4QTestimonia", *RevQ* 12 (1985-86), pp. 187-197.

Lucassen, B. "Josua, Richter und CD", *RevQ* 18 (1997-98), pp. 373-396.

Luckenbill, D.D. *Ancient Records of Assyria and Babylonia*. New York: Greenwood Press Publishers, 1968.

Macdonald, J. *The Samaritan Chronicle No. II (or: Sepher Ha-Yamim): From Joshua to Nebuchanezzar*. Berlin: Walter de Gruyter & Co, 1969.

Machiela, D. *The Dead Sea Genesis Apocryphon*. STDJ 79. Leiden: Brill, 2009.

—, "Once More, with Feeling: Rewritten Scripture in Ancient Judaism - A Review of Recent Developments", *JJS* 61 (2010), pp. 308-320.

Mack, B.L. *Wisdom and the Hebrew Epic*: *Ben Sira's Hymn in Praise of the Fathers*. Chicago: University of Chicago Press, 1985.

Mason, S. *Flavius Josephus: Judean War 2*. Flavius Josephus Translation and Commentary 1B. Leiden, Boston: Brill, 2008.

—, "Josephus, Jewish Antiquities", *EDEJ*, pp. 834-838.

Mazor, L. "The Origin and Evolution of the Curse upon the Rebuilder of Jericho: A Contribution of Textual Criticism to Biblical Historiography", *Textus* 14 (1988), pp. 1-26.

—, "The Septuagint Translation of the Book of Joshua—Its Contribition to the Understanding of the Textual Transmission of the Book and Its Literary and Ideological Development". Ph.D. diss., Hebrew University, Jerusalem 1994.

—, "A Nomistic Re-Working of the Jericho Conquest Narrative Reflected in the LXX to Joshua 6:1-20", *Textus* 18 (1995), pp. 47-62.

McCarter, P.K., Jr. "Geography in the Documents", *EDSS*, vol. 1, pp. 306-308.

McDonald, M. & Sanders, J.A., eds. *The Canon Debate*. Peabody, MA: Hendrickson, 2002.

McLean, M.D. "The Use and Development of Palaeo-Hebrew in the Hellenistic and Roman Periods". Ph.D. diss., Harvard University, 1982.

Mendels, D. *The Land of Israel as a Political Concept in Hasmonean Literature*. TSAJ 15; Tübingen: Mohr Siebeck, 1987.

—, *The Rise and Fall of Jewish Nationalism*. New York: Doubleday, 1992.

Milik, J.T. "Dires de Moïse". In O.P. Barthélemy & J.T. Milik, *Qumran Cave I*. DJD 1. Oxford: Clarendon Press, 1955, pp. 91-97.

—, *Dix ans de découvertes dans le désert de Juda*. Paris: Editions du Cerf, 1957 (=*Ten Years of Discovery in the Wilderness of Judaea*. Transl. by J. Strugnell. Studies in Biblical Theology 26. London: SCM Press, 1959).

—, "5Q9. Ouvrage avec Toponymes". In M. Baillet et al., eds. *Les 'Petites Grottes' de Qumran*. DJD 3. Oxford: Clarendon Press, 1962, pp. 179-180.

Moatti-Fine, J. *La Bible d'Alexandrie: Jésus (Josué): Traduction du texte grec, introduction et notes*. Paris: Cerf, 1996.

Moynihan Gillihan, Y. "The גר Who Wasn't There: Fictional Aliens in the Damascus Rule", *RevQ* 25 (2011), pp. 282-295.

Murphy, F.J. *Pseudo-Philo*: *Rewriting the Bible*. New York: Oxford University Press, 1993.

Na'aman, N. "The Brook of Egypt and Assyrian Policy on the Border of Egypt", *Tel Aviv* 6,1-2 (1979), pp. 74-90.

Netzer, E. "The Hasmonean and Herodian Palaces at Jericho", *IEJ* (1975), pp. 89-100.

—, *Hasmonean and Herodian Palaces at Jericho*. Jerusalem: Israel Exploration Society, Institute of Archaeology, The Hebrew University of Jerusalem, 2001.

Neubauer, A. *La géographie du Talmud*. Hildesheim: G. Olms, 1967.

Neusner, J. *The Mishnah: A New Translation*. Yale: Yale University Press, 1991.

Newsom, C.A. "'The Psalms of Joshua' from Qumran Cave 4", *JJS* 39 (1988), pp. 56-73.

—, "4Q378 and 4Q379: An Apocryphon of Joshua". In H.-J. Fabry & A. Lange, eds. *Qumranstudien*. SIJD 4. Göttingen: Vandenhoeck & Ruprecht, 1996, pp. 35-85

—, "4Q378-379. Apocryphon of Joshua[a-b]". In G.J. Brooke et al., eds. *Qumran Cave 4.XVII: Parabiblical Texts, Part 3*. DJD 22. Oxford: Clarendon Press, 1996, pp. 237-288.

Niessen, F. *Eine Samaritanische Version des Buches Yehošua' und die Šobak-Erzählung*. TSO 12. Hildesheim: Georg OlmsVerlag, 2000.

Nitzan, B. *Pesher Habakkuk: A Scroll from the Wilderness of Judaea*. Jerusalem: Bialik Institute, 1986.

Noam, V. *From Qumran to the Rabbinic Revolution: Conceptions of Impurity*. Jerusalem: Yad Ben Zvi Press, 2010 (Hebrew).

Nodet, E. *A Search for the Origins of Judaism*. Transl. E. Crowley. JSOTSS 248. Sheffield: Sheffield Academic Press, 1997.

Noort, E. "The Traditions of Ebal and Gerizim: Theological Positions in the Book of Joshua". In M. Vervenne & J. Lust, eds. *Deuteronomy and Deuteronomic Literature*. BETL 133. Leuven: University Press, 1997, pp. 161-180.

—, "4QJosh[a] and the History of Tradition", *JNSL* 24 (1998), pp. 127-144.

—, *Das Buch Josua: Forschungsgeschichte und Problemfelder*. Erträge der Forschung 292. Darmstadt: Wissenschaftliche Buchgesellschaft, 1998.

Notley, R.S. & Safrai, Z. *Eusebius, Onomasticon: A Triglot Edition with Notes and Commentary*. Leiden, Boston: Brill, 2005.

Pérez Fernández, M. *An Introductory Grammar of Rabbinic Hebrew*. Leiden: Brill, 1997.

Polzin, R. *Moses and the Deuteronomist: A Literary Study of the Deuteronomic History: Part One: Deuteronomy, Joshua, Judges*. New York: The Seabury Press, 1980.

Powels, S. "The Samaritan Calendar". In A.D. Crown, ed. *The Samaritans*. Tübingen: J.C.B. Mohr, 1989, pp. 691-742.

Pressler, C.J. "Achor", *ABD*, vol. 1, p. 56.

Puech, É. "Fragment du Psaume 122 dans un manuscript hébreu de la grotte IV", *RevQ* 19 (1978), pp. 547-554.

—, "The Tell el-Fûl Jar Inscription and the 'Nĕtînîm'", *BASOR* 261 (1986), pp. 69-72.

—, "La Pierre de Sion et l'autel des holocaustes d'après un manuscript hébreu de la grotte 4 (4Q522)", *RB* 99 (1992), pp. 676-696.

—, "4Q522. 4QProphétie de Josué (4QapocrJosué^c?)". In idem, *Qumrân Grotte 4.XVIII: Textes Hébreux (4Q521-4Q528, 4Q576-4Q579)*. DJD 25. Oxford: Clarendon Press, 1998, pp. 39-74.

—, "Un autre fragment du Psaume 122", *RevQ* 20 (2001), pp. 129–32.

—, "559. 4QpapChronologie biblique ar". In idem, *Qumran Cave 4.XXVII: Textes araméens, deuxième partie: 4Q550-575, 580-582*. DJD 37. Oxford: Clarendon Press, 2009, pp. 263-302.

Qimron, E. "A Grammar of the Hebrew Language of the Dead Sea Scrolls". Ph.D. diss., The Hebrew University, Jerusalem, 1976 (Hebrew).

—, *The Hebrew of the Dead Sea Scrolls*. HSS 29; Atlanta: Scholars Press, 1986.

—, "Concerning 'Joshua Cycles' from Qumran", *Tarbiz* 63 (1993-94), pp. 503-508 (Hebrew).

—, *The Dead Sea Scrolls: The Hebrew Writings: Volume One*. Between Bible and Mishnah. Jerusalem: Yad Ben-Zvi Press, 2010 (Hebrew).

—, *The Dead Sea Scrolls: The Hebrew Writings: Volume Two*. Between Bible and Mishnah. Jerusalem: Yad Ben-Zvi Press, forthcoming.

Qimron, E. & Strugnell, J. *Qumran Cave 4. V: Miqṣat Ma'ase Ha-Torah*. DJD 10. Oxford: Clarendon Press, 1994.

Rainey, A. "Toponymic Problems", *Tel Aviv* 9 (1982), pp. 131-132.

Rappaport, U. "Maccabees, First Book of", *EDEJ*, pp. 903-905.

Reinmuth, E. "Zwischen Investitur und Testament: Beobachtungen zur Rezeption des Josuabuches im Liber Antiquitatum Biblicarum", *SJOT* 16 (2002), pp. 24-43.

Rodgers, Z. "Josephus's Biblical Interpretation". In M. Henze, ed. *A Companion to Biblical Interpretation in Early Judaism*. Grand Rapids, MI, Cambridge, UK: Eerdmans, 2012, pp. 436-463.

Rofé, A. "The End of the Book of Joshua according to the Septuagint", *Shnaton* 2 (1977), pp. 217-228 (Hebrew ="The End of the Book of Joshua according to the Septuagint", *Henoch* 4 [1982], pp. 17-35).

—, "Joshua Son of Nun in the History of Biblical Tradition", *Tarbiz* 73 (2004), pp. 333-364 (Hebrew).

Rosenfeld, B.-Z. "Flavius Josephus and His Portrayal of the Cost (Paralia) of Contemporary Roman Palestine: Geography and Ideology", *JQR* 91 (2000), p. 143-183.

Safrai, Z. *Boundaries and Administration in Eretz-Israel in the Mishnah-Talmud Period*. Tel-Aviv: Ha-Kibutz Ha-Meuhad, 1980 (Hebrew).

—, "The Gentile Cities of Judea: Between the Hasmonean Occupation and the Roman Liberation". In G. Galil & M. Weinfeld, eds. *Studies in Historical Geography and Biblical Historiography*. SVT 81. Leiden: Brill, 2000, pp. 63-90.

Sanderson, J.E. *An Exodus Scroll from Qumran: 4QpaleoExodᵐ and the Samaritan Tradition*. Harvard Semitic Studies. Atlanta, Georgia: Scholars Press, 1986.

Schiffman, L.H. "Laws Pertaining to Women in the Temple Scroll". In D. Dimant & U. Rappaport, eds. *The Dead Sea Scrolls: Forty Years of Research*. STDJ 10. Leiden: Brill, 1992, pp. 216-217.

Schiffman, L.H. *The Halakhah at Qumran*. Leiden: Brill, 1975.

—, "Exclusion from the Sanctuary and the City of the Sanctuary in the Temple Scroll". In idem, *The Courtyards of the House of the Lord*. STDJ 75. Leiden: Brill, 2008), pp. 384-386.

—, "Non-Jews in the Dead Sea Scrolls". In idem, *Qumran and Jerusalem*. Grand Rapids, Michigan, Cambridge, UK, Eerdmans, 2010, pp. 365-382.

—, "Political Leadership and Organization in the Dead Sea Scrolls Community". Ibid., pp. 98-111.

Schwartz, D.R. "On Two Aspects of a Priestly View of Descent at Qumran". In L.H. Schiffman, ed. *Archaeology and History in the Dead Sea Scrolls*. JSOT/ASOR Monographs 2. Sheffield: JSOT Press, 1990, pp. 157-179.

—, "Maccabees, Second Book of", *EDEJ*, pp. 905-907.

Schwartz, S. *Imperialism and Jewish Society, 200 BCE to 640 CE*. Princeton: Princeton University Press, 2001.

Segal, M. *The Book of Jubilees: Rewritten Bible, Redaction, Ideology and Theology*. JSJSup 117. Leiden: Brill, 2007.

Segal, M.Z. *The Complete Book of Ben Sira*. Jerusalem: The Bialik Institute, 1997.

Skehan, P.W. "Two Books on Qumran Studies", *CBQ* 21 (1959), pp. 71-78.

Skehan, P.W. & DiLella, A.A. *The Wisdom of Ben Sira*. AB 39; New York: Doubleday, 1987.

Skehan, P.W., Ulrich, E., & Sanderson. "4Q123. 4QpaleoParaJoshua". In P. Skehan et al. *Qumran Cave 4.IV: Paleo-Hebrew and Greek Manuscripts*. DJD 9. Oxford: Clarendon Press, 1992, pp. 201-203.

Sokoloff, M. *A Dictionary of Jewish Palestinian Aramaic of the Byzantine Period*. Ramat Gan: Bar Ilan University Press, Baltimore and London: The Johns Hopkins University Press, 2002.

Spijkerman, P.A. "Chronique du Musée de la Flagellation", *Liber annus* 12 (1961-62), pp. 324-325.

Spilsbury, P. *The Image of the Jew in Flavius Josephus' Paraphrase of the Bible*. TSAJ 69. Tübingen: Mohr Siebeck, 1998.

Starcky, J. "Les Maîtres de Justice et la chronologie de Qumrân". In M. Delcor, ed. *Qumrân: Sa piété, sa théologie et son milieu*. Paris-Gembloux: Duculot, 1978, pp. 249-256.

Stenhouse, P. *The Kitāb Al-Tarīkh of Abu 'L-Fatḥ*. Studies in Judaica 1. Sydney: The Mandelbaum Trust, 1985.

—, "Samaritan Chronicles". In A.D. Crown, ed. *The Samaritans*. Tübingen: J.C.B. Mohr, 1989, pp. 219-264.

Steudel, A. "Testimonia", *EDSS*, vol. 2, pp. 936-938.

Strugnell, J. "Notes en marge du Volume V des ,Discoveries in the Judaean Desert of Jordan'", *RevQ* 1 (1969-71), 163-276.

—, "Moses-Pseudepigrapha at Qumran: 4Q375, 4Q376, and Similar Works". In L.H. Schiffman, ed. *Archaeology and History in the Dead Sea Scrolls*. JSPSS 8. Sheffield: Sheffield Academic Press, 1990, pp. 221-256.

Sussmann, Y. "A Halakhic Inscription from the Beth-Shean Valley", *Tarbiẓ* 43 (1974), pp. 88-158 (Hebrew).

Talmon, Sh. "A Fragment of the Apocryphal Joshua Scroll from Masada". In M. Goshen-Gottstein et al., eds. *Shai Le-Hayyim Rabin*. Jerusalem: Academon, 1991, pp. 147-157 (Hebrew).

—, "Fragments of a Joshua Apocryphon—Masada 1039-211 (final photo 5254)", *JJS* 47 (1996), pp. 128-139.

—, "A Papyrus Fragment Inscribed in Palaeo-Hebrew Script". In idem et al., eds. *Masada VI: Yigael Yadin Excavations 1963-65 Final Reports*. Jerusalem: Israel Exploration Society, The Hebrew University of Jerusalem, 1999, pp. 138-147.

—, "Hebrew Fragments from Masada: (b) Mas 1039-211". In idem et al., eds. *Masada VI: Yigael Yadin Excavations 1963-65 Final Reports*. Jerusalem: Israel Exploration Society, The Hebrew University of Jerusalem, 1999, pp. 105-116.

Thackeray, H.St.J. *Josephus: Jewish Antiquities, Books I-IV*. LCL. London: Heinemann, 1930.

Thoma, C. "The High Priesthood in the Judgment of Josephus". In L.H. Feldman & G. Hata, eds. *Josephus, the Bible and History*. Leiden: Brill, 1988, pp. 197-215.

Tigay, J.H. *Deuteronomy*. JPS Torah Commentary. Philadelphia: Jewish Publication Society, 1996.

Tigchelaar, E. "In Search of the Scribe of 1QS". In S.M. Paul et al., eds. *Emanuel*. SVT 94. Leiden: Brill, 2003, pp. 439-452.

—, "A Cave 4 Fragment of Divre Mosheh (4QDM) and the Text of 1Q22 1:7-10 and Jubilees 1: 9, 14", *DSD* 12 (2005), pp. 303-312.

—, "The Dead Sea Scrolls", *EDEJ*, pp. 163-180.

—, "Assessing Emanuel Tov's 'Qumran Scribal Practice'". In S. Metso et al., eds. *The Dead Sea Scrolls: Transmission of Traditions and Production of Texts*. STDJ 92. Leiden, Boston: Brill, 2010, pp. 173-207.

Tov, E. "The Temple Scroll and Old Testament Textual Criticism", *Eretz-Israel* 16 (1982), pp. 100-111 (Hebrew).

—, "The Nature and Background of the Harmonizations in Biblical Manuscripts", *JSOT* 10 (1985), pp. 3-29.

—, "4Q48. 4QJosh[b]". In E. Ulrich et al., eds. *Qumran Cave 4.IX: Deuteronomy, Joshua, Judges, Kings.* DJD 14. Oxford: Clarendon Press, 1995, pp. 153-160.

—, "The Growth of the Book of Joshua in Light of the Evidence of the Septuagint". In idem, *The Greek and Hebrew Bible.* SVT 72. Leiden, Boston, Köln: Brill, 1999, pp. 385-396

—, "The Rewritten Book of Joshua as Found at Qumran and Masada". In M.E. Stone & E.G. Chazon, eds. *Biblical Perspectives: Early Use and Interpretation of the Bible in Light of the Dead Sea Scrolls.* STDJ 28. Leiden: Brill, 1998, pp. 233-256(=*Hebrew Bible, Greek Bible and Qumran: Collected Essays.* TSAJ 121. Tübingen: Mohr Siebeck, 2008, pp. 72-91).

—, *Scribal Practices and Approaches Reflected in the Texts Found in the Judean Desert.* STDJ 54. Leiden, Boston: Brill, 2004.

—, "Some *Sequence Differences* between the MT and LXX and Their Ramifications for the Literary Criticism of the Bible". In idem, *The Greek and Hebrew Bible: Collected Essays on the Septuagint.* Leiden: Brill, 1999, pp. 411-418.

—, "Textual Harmonizations in the Ancient Texts of Deuteronomy". In N.S. Fox et al., eds. *Mishneh Todah.* Winona Lake, Indiana: Eisenbrauns, 2009, pp. 15-28.

—, "Joshua, Book of", *EDSS*, pp. 431-434.

—, "Some Reflections on Consistency in the Activity of Scribes and Translators". In U. Dahmen & J. Schnocks, eds. *Juda und Jerusalem in der Seleukidenzeit: Herrschaft—Widerstand—Identität: Festschrift für Heinz-Josef Fabry.* Bonner Biblische Beiträge 159. Göttingen: V&R Unipress, 2010, pp. 325-337.

—, *Textual Criticism of the Hebrew Bible.* Minneapolis: Fortress, 2012[3].

—, "Literary Development of the Book of Joshua as Reflected in the Masoretic Text, the LXX, and 4QJosh[a]". In E. Noort, ed. *The Book of Joshua and the Land of Israel* (forthcoming).

Tov, E. & Pfann, S.J. "List of the Texts from the Judaean Desert". In E. Tov et al., eds. *The Texts from the Judaean Desert: Indices and Introduction to the Discoveries in the Judaean Desert.* DJD 39. Oxford: Clarendon Press, 2002, pp. 27-113.

Treves, M. "On the Meaning of the Qumran Testimonia", *RevQ* 2 (1959-60), pp. 569-571.

Tromp, J. *The Assumption of Moses: A Critical Edition with Commentary.* Leiden: Brill, 1993.

Ulrich, E. "The Palaeo-Biblical Biblical Texts from Qumran Cave 4". In D. Dimant & L.H. Schiffman, eds. *Time to Prepare the Way in the Wilderness.* STDJ 16. Leiden: Brill, 1994, pp. 103-129.

—, "4Q47. 4QJosh^a". In E. Ulrich et al., eds. *Qumran Cave 4.IX: Deuteronomy, Joshua, Judges, Kings.* DJD 14. Oxford: Clarendon Press, 1995, pp. 143-152.

Ulrich, E. et al., eds. *Qumran Cave 4.XI: Psalms to Chronicles.* DJD 16. Oxford: Clarendon Press, 2000.

Van der Meer, M.N. *Formation and Reformulation.* SVT CII. Leiden, Boston: Brill, 2004.

—, "Provenance, Profile, and Purpose of the Greek Joshua". In M.K.H. Peters, ed. *XII Congress of the International Organization for Septuagint and Cognate Studies, Leiden 2004.* SBL Septuagint and Cognate Studies. Leiden, Boston: Brill, 2006, pp. 55-80.

Van Kooten, G.H. & van Ruiten, J. *The Prestige of the Pagan Prophet Balaam in Judaism, Early Christianity and Islam.* Leiden: Brill, 2008.

Van Peursen, W. "Who Was Standing on the Mountain? The Portrait of Moses in 4Q377". In A. Graupner & M. Wolter, eds. *Moses in Biblical and Extra-Biblical Traditions.* BZAW 372. Berlin: de Gruyter, 2007, pp. 99-113.

VanderKam, J.C. "Zadok and the Spr Htwrh Hhtwm", *RevQ* 11 (1984), pp. 561-570.

—, "Putting Them in Their Place: Geography as an Evaluative Tool". In J.C. Reeves & J. Kampen, eds. *Pursuing the Text.* JSOTSS 184. Sheffield: JSOT Press, 1994, pp. 46-69.

—, "Jubilees' Exegetical Creation of Levi the Priest", *RevQ* 17 (1996), pp. 359–373.

—, "The Wording of Biblical Citations in Some Rewritten Scriptural Works". In *The Bible as Book: the Hebrew Bible and the Judaean Desert Discoveries.* In E.D. Herbert & E. Tov, eds. London: British Library; New Castle, DE: Oak Knoll Press, 2002, pp. 41-56.

Vermes, G. "Sectarian Matrimonial Halakha in the Damascus Rule". In idem, *Post-Biblical Jewish Studies.* SJLA 8. Leiden: Brill, 1975, pp. 50-56.

—, *The Dead Sea Scrolls: Qumran in Perspective.* London: Collins, 1977.

Wacholder, B.-Z. "The 'Sealed' Torah versus the 'Revealed' Torah: An Exegesis of Damascus Covenant V, 1-6 and Jeremiah 32, 10-14", *RevQ* 12 (1986), pp. 351-367

—, *The New Damascus Document.* STDJ 56. Leiden: Brill, 2007.

Wacholder, B.Z. & Abegg, M.G. *A Preliminary Edition of the Unpublished Dead Sea Scrolls.* Washington, D.C.: Biblical Archaeology Society, 1995, 3 vols.

Waitz, Y. "Was the Sharon on the Sea Coast", *BJES* 6 (1940), pp. 132-141 (Hebrew).

Waltke, B.K. & O'Connor, M. *An Introduction to Biblical Hebrew Syntax.* Winnona Lake, Indiana: Eisenbrauns, 1990.

Weinfeld, M. *Deuteronomy 1-1.* AB; New York: Doubleday, 1991.

Werman, C. "Jubilees 30: Building a Paradigm for the Ban on Intermarriage", *HTR* 90 (1997), 1-22.

Wise, M. "To Know the Times and the Seasons: A Study of the Aramaic Chronograph 4Q559", *JSP* 8 (1997), pp. 3-51.

Wise, M.O., Abegg, M.G., and Cook, E.M. *The Dead Sea Scrolls: A New Transla-tion*. San Francisco: HarperCollins, 2005.

Witte, M. "Der „Kanon" heiliger Schriften des antiken Judentums im Spiegel des Buches Ben Sira/Jesus Sirach". In E.-M. Becker & S. Scholz, eds. *Kanon in Konstruktion und Dekonstruktion*. Berlin: de Gruyter, 2012, pp. 215-241.

Yadin, Y. *The Temple Scroll*. Jerusalem: The Israel Exploration Society: 1983, 3 vols.

Yalon, H. *Studies in the Dead Sea Scrolls*. Jerusalem: Shrine of the Book, America-Israel Cultural Foundation, Kiryat Sefer, 1967 (Hebrew).

Zahn, M.M. "Talking about Rewritten Texts: Some Reflections on Terminology". In H. von Weissenberg et al., eds. *Rewriting and Interpreting Authoritative Traditions in the Second Temple Period*. Berlin: de Gruyter, 2011, pp. 93-119.

—, "Genre and Rewritten Scripture: A Reassessment", *JBL* 131 (2012), pp. 271-288.

Zsengellér, J. *Gerizim as Israel: Northern Tradition of the Old Testament and the Early History of the Samaritans*. Utrecht: Universiteit Utrecht 1998.

Index

Names and Subjects